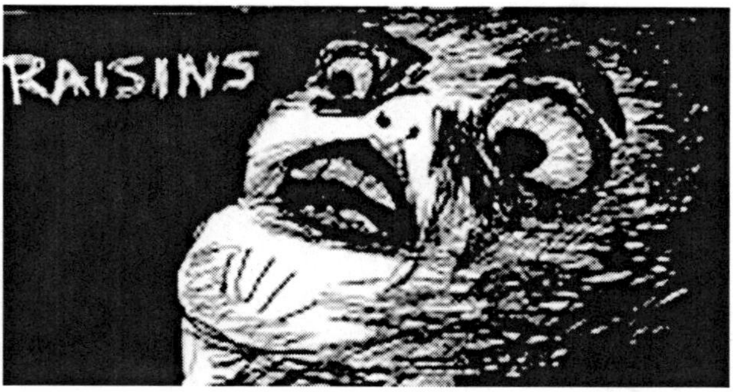
RAISINS

CONTENTS:

1. Dogfather 1. Dead Santa 2. Bed Monsters 3. Sparknotes 5. BLT 6. Fat lady under water 6. Smoking math 7. Fap memory 8. Baby jacket 8. Expensive blender 9. pokey 9. breastfeeding 10. Life vs. the internet 10. D answer sweet 11. 2007 fap 12. Cheat zap 13. Derper derperman 14. Dorito tacos 15. Chill dad 16. Not my mom 17. D prof answers 17. Not my GF 18. Close enough 18. Friday meat 19. ET IBM 20. Head eating 21. Time of my life 21. The daddy test 23. Sexy box 23. Lovin' it 24. Blacksmith 25. Prego 26. Aloe vera 27. Rap ist 28. Forever a cone 29. Pizza box 30. Eating alone 31. Impossible question 31. All my GFs 32. Printer lady love 33. I love my iphone 34. laptop umbrella 35. Fish people 36. Shower fap dinosaurs 37. The best BJ 38. Corridor dance 39. Dead Tony 40. Me Froderp 41. Kiss my wee wee mommy 42. Jogging action 43. Egg people 44. I need an abortion 44. Bitch you're in McDerps 45. Star trek BF 45. Trolldad camping 46. Red dot lying 47. Dumbyderp subtitles 48. Dumbyderp juice 48. Girl peeing standing up. 49. Cable clusterfuck 50. Cigarette guy. 50. Video past present 51. Dumbyderp never move 51. Not funny 53. Fieldtrip fap. 54. Flirt on your own time 54. Halloween past and present 55. Leaf monster 55. Stretch derp 56. Balloon pool nail idea 57. I just had sex 57. Breakfast robbery 58. Fat woman dieting 59. Fried grilled cheese 59. Pathetic fool 60. Mustached pedophile 62. Troll rock climbing partner 62. Lawn-mowing crap 63. College class attendance 63. Forever Alone – no friends 64. Skin colored crayon 64. Under Peach's skirt 65. I shouldn't be alive 65. Trolldad – car fart 66. Trolldad – horn 66. Big tit waitress 68. Cheez app 68. Ninja Turtle daughter 69. Credit card clusterfuck 70. WTF car leash 70. How come I'm dead 71. Meant for each other 71. High kids 72. College friends forever 73. Super salad 74. That's not candy 75. Candy store hack 76. Night time inspiration 77. Teeth loneliness 77. Pee sneeze 78. Baby why!? 78. Covered in mayo 79. Train station wizard 80. Good morning pee-wee 81. Dumbyderp job 82. Friends 83. How babies are born 85. Dead friends. 85. Dinner for two 86. Idiot customers 86. Female pigeon 87. Home alone 87. Bed alone 88. Honey 88. Talking computer command 89. Tangled legs 89. Facebook trolling 90. Jellybean doctor 91. I am the alpha wolf 92. Stick bug on head 93. Light switches everywhere 94. Almost hack 95. Link sucks 97. USPS hack 97. Causing HIV 98. Elevator jerk 99. Facebook you? 100. I make-a da pizza 101. Trolled by hot dogs 102. Genie troll 103. Reeces for breakfast 105. Back to the Future 3 sucks 106. High School vs Vietnam 107. Jogging mugger 108. Dropped number 108. TV show clusterfuck 109. Put girl in the trunk 110. Ironing trollface 111. Dumbyderp – jellybeans 111. Dumbyderp – eat 112. I am a toilet 113. Volume clusterfuck 114. The young molester 115. Tissues puberty 115. Fapping with vacuum 117. Chemicals! 117. Broomfu 118. Barfing eagle 119. Save the cat 119. Trolling GF 121. Trolled by pigeon 121. Marrying a depressed girl 122. Semen mom 123. Dumbyderp closed store 124. Crazy internet girl 125. Dancing men vs. women 126. The lost fifty 127. My childhood died 128. Crunchy dog treat 128. Dumbyderp – wireless 129. You're really hot 130. Evil mall Spiderman 131. Dumbyderp – hormones 131. Butt bread 132. Paused for you 132. Ancient computer girl 134. Album covers 137. Rank sneezing 138. Drunk conversations 139. Pool torpedo 139. Real life trolling 141. Mean cat 142. Earned my stripes 142. Apple juice 143. Dumbyderp littering 143. Barfing job interview 144. Brother skype spider

145. WTF fake eye 146. Poke 147. Drinking puke 148. TV advice 149. Glasses haters 149. My gun is bigger 151. Goldfish ingredients 151. Three times as many 152. The British invasion 153. Road stand-off 155. Private Ryan helmet clusterfuck 155. Sky spiders 156. Mattress comfort 157. Bottom half of woman 158. Wife witch 158. The past. 159. Condom coins 161. Ramen hidden language 161. Mustache 162. Dinner time troll 163. Father influence 164. Chex mix seasoning 165. Essay hack 166. Fools 166. Egg 167. The beautiful hag 168. Got real 168. Toasted ants 169. Nintendo 170. Dumb kid 172. Booze makers 172. Squishing the bees 173. Lego clusterfuck 174. Unused bag 175. Bathroom troll 175. Forever alone COD 176. Dumb professor 177. Impeach 178. Chips and salsa 180. Incestual sexytimes 181. Japanese – yummy 182. Wendys clusterfuck 183. Redtube troll 183. Japanese – I am being cooked 184. Justice is served 185. Forever alone plant 186. An angry life 188. Hack the spammers 189. Swim-off 190. Japanese – give me presents 190. I am Samus 191. Jihad IE 192. Dart Mission 193. Penis grandma 194. The mic was on 195. Girl on the spot 196. Trolling your GF 196. Expensive camera 197. Frozen pizzas 197. Trolldad soda 198. Freezer friends 199. How it looked 201. Color in the lines 202. Password ex 203. Hug your friend 203. Social anxiety 205. MS Gustav 205. Dumbyderp time machine 206. Killing an annoying child 207. Psychic girl 208. Breakfast all day 209. Class progression 210. Spying on girls 211. Forever a terrorist 212. Pizza hut phone number 212. Chocolate cake 213. Dumbyderp drive-thru 214. Heart attacks NBD 215. Angry mom vacation 216. Hot bath 217. I love taco bell 219. Sleeping with sound on 219. Rage comics are sexy 220. Cardboard box 220. Eat in car 221. Spaghetti public vs alone 221. Kindle in mailbox 222. Infirmary anal attack 223. Turkey in shower 224. Death by sweater 224. I am a rapist? 225. What desk 226. The last slice 227. Never having kids 227. Psychic movie 228. Useless class 228. Cucumber condom 229. Me gusta montage 230. Vampire waitress 230. Old toys space jam 231. Juice box compensation 232. Toilet paper wild 233. Useless professor 234. Diabeetus 234. Spock to the rescue 236. Internet explorer GTFO 237. The impossible milk 238. Skittles Jesus 239. Korean BF 240. Trolldad Dark Knight 241. Dumbyderp money 241. Unworthy 243. Preggie pill 243. Tentacle porn search 244. Funny grandma 245. The real Wendy 245. Fearless 246. Animal wars 247. Whale lady 247. Bread tango 248. Twist ending 249. Dumbyderp book 250. Car insurance sucks 251. Egg sick 252. Porn on disc confession 254. WTF cheese 255. no haircut ever again 255. Chocolate saves lives 256. Forever alone baby 257. The black market 258. Trolldad cereal 259. Gee bees 260. Security camera clusterfuck 261. Ffjx 261. Porn trolldad 262. Trolldad high exposure 263. Nail-cut oh no 264. Holy crap 265. Naked delivery 266. Impossible machine 267. Wiimote fap 267. Popsicle BJ 269. I saw everything 269. Nana my doodle 270. Cafeteria compensation 271. Light blocking 271. Lying rug stores 272. Butt identity 272. Funny troll teacher 274. Buzzing 274. Branding seatbelt 275. McDerps morons 275. Funny troll teacher II 276. New glasses 276. Mexican restaurant forever alone 277. Troll physics sun 277. Troll physics apple pie 278. Eat the pussy 278. Troll physics animal orgasms 279. Greece or grease 280. I am pizza 281. Sad girlfriend 281. Ignorant girlfriend 282. Spongebob rewind 283. Forever alone doctor 283. GTA hack parents 284. Obama new campaign 286. Tired relationship 286. A woman is a keyhole 288. Beer ID hack 289. The look 290. Never on time 291. Love this job

292. Pizza high 294. Affairs in order 294. Mike and Peter 295. Smelly man 296. Trollcat 297. Hacking death 297. Knife Confidence 298. Hacking the window 298. Hacking the coin machines 299. Idiot drive-thru humans 300. Spanish people 301. Rulers 301. Anal 302. Wrong move 303. Free gizmos 304. Dumbyderp corn water 305. condom watch 306. Hamster ball 307. I am Moses 307. Destroy it, peasant 307. Comfy pillow 308. Looking at ass 308. Asian mom 309. Massage mom's head 310. What I want 310. Trolling from the grave 311. Forever alone groups 312. Fork in vagina 313. How to babysit 314. Kids on lesbians 314. We? 315. Make me a sandwich, bitch 316. Where the magic happens 317. Ride my trusty steed 317. Bermuda triangle pen 318. Trolldad weed

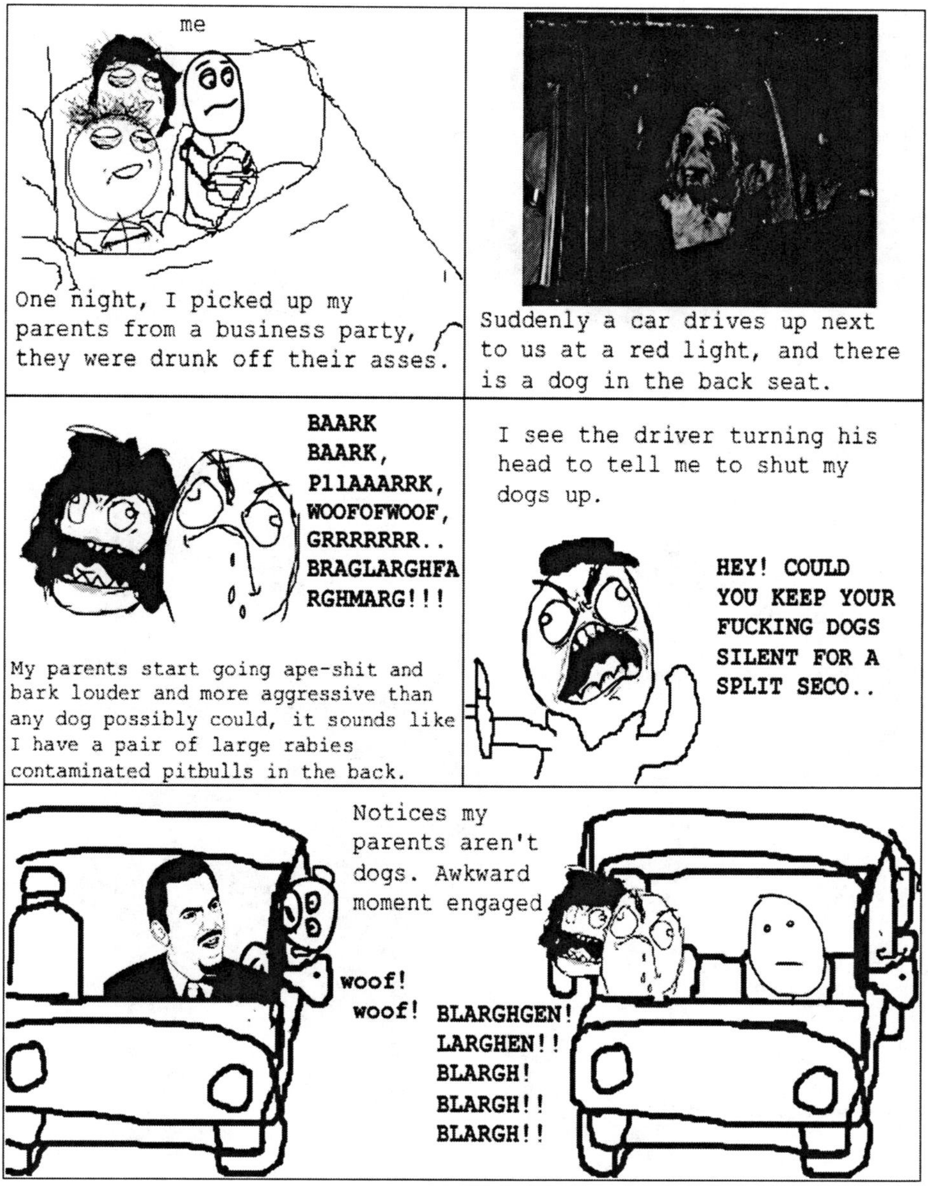
me
One night, I picked up my parents from a business party, they were drunk off their asses.
Suddenly a car drives up next to us at a red light, and there is a dog in the back seat.
BAARK BAARK, P11AAARRK, WOOFOFWOOF, GRRRRRRR.. BRAGLARGHFA RGHMARG!!!
My parents start going ape-shit and bark louder and more aggressive than any dog possibly could, it sounds like I have a pair of large rabies contaminated pitbulls in the back.
I see the driver turning his head to tell me to shut my dogs up.
HEY! COULD YOU KEEP YOUR FUCKING DOGS SILENT FOR A SPLIT SECO..
Notices my parents aren't dogs. Awkward moment engaged
woof! woof!
BLARGHGEN! LARGHEN!! BLARGH! BLARGH!! BLARGH!!

My my.. why are you crying son?
You LIED to me.. You told me santa was REAL!!

No no, he is real..
He's just dead.

DERP YOUR ROOM IS A MESS GO AND CLEAN IT UP!!!
Mom
6 year old me
ONE MINUTE THIRTY SEVEN SECONDS LATER...
Room Cleaned Mission Accomplished
LATER THAT NIGHT
See a TV show where there is a monster monster under kids bed.
2.
Suddenly realize something

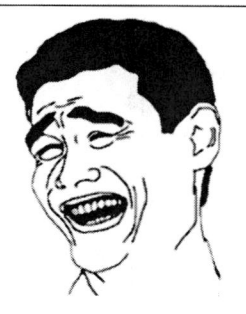

IVE GOT WAY TOO MUCH SHIT UNDER MY BED FOR THAT MONSTER TO EVEN MOVE..

You're dismissed. Next week, come to class prepared to discuss Book 1 of Spenser's "The Faerie Queene."

*me

No problem!

LATER...

Alrighty, let's see what this 'Faerie Queene' business is all about.

*opens book

THE FIRST
BOOKE OF THE
FAERIE QVEENE.

Conteyning
THE LEGENDE OF THE
KNIGHT OF THE RED CROSSE.
OR
OF HOLINESSE.

LO I the man, whose Muse whilome did maske,
As time her taught, in lowly Shepheards weeds,

3.

At that good knight so cunningly didst roue,
That glorious fire it kindled in his hart,
Lay now thy deadly Heben bow apart,
And with thy mother milde come to mine ayde:
Come both, and with you bring triumphant Mart,
In loues and gentle iollities arrayd,
After his murdrous spoiles and bloudy rage allayd.
And with them eke, O Goddesse heauenly bright,
Mirrour of grace and Maiestie diuine,
Great Lady of the greatest Isle, whose light
Like Phoebus lampe throughout the world doth shi
Holy nose hair of Zeus!
How long does this go on?
flip
flip
flip
Pg.172
*sparknotes
*scribble
*scribble
essay
A++
COMPLETELY
USELESS
ENGLISH DEGREE

le me and girlfriend watching tv
"make me a sandwich"
"okay!"
"BLT? okay. can you just put a flying pan on the stove and turn it on."
sure least i can do for a sandwich
*jamie oliver fry pan
"and grab the bacon and tomato and cheese and lettuce and egg"
"she's gonna put egg on it. win!"
"now just throw the bacon on, it takes the longest, and cut the tomato"
"don't forget to put the toast down""
"this shall be the best sandwich ever"
"now butter the toast and make the sandwich!"
"oh this sandwich is awesome, thanks babe!"
"wait a minute..."
"I'm dating the devil"

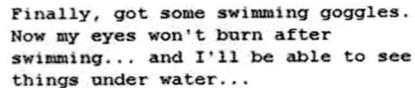

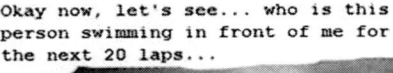

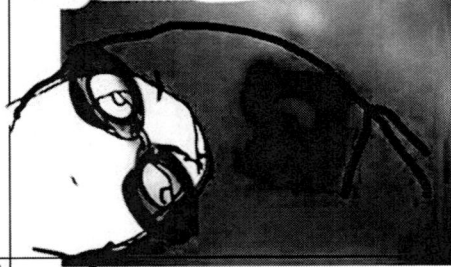

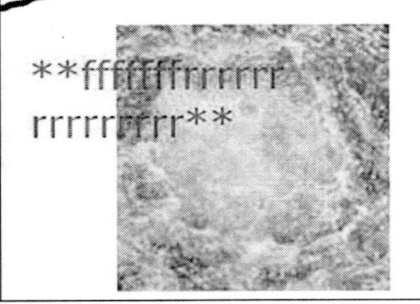

Panel 1: Finally, got some swimming goggles. Now my eyes won't burn after swimming... and I'll be able to see things under water...

Panel 2: Okay now, let's see... who is this person swimming in front of me for the next 20 laps...

Panel 3: **ffffffffrrrrrr rrrrrrrrr**

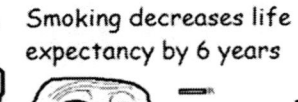

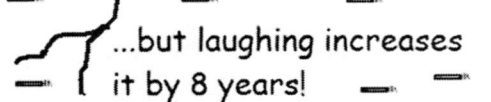

Is smoking making you die faster?
Ya Sucks

Smoking decreases life expectancy by 6 years ...but laughing increases it by 8 years!

Laugh furiously while you smoke!
Ha Ha Ha Ha Ha Ha Ha Ha Ha Ha Ha Ha Ha Ha Ha Ha Ha Ha Ha Ha Ha Ha Ha Ha
Brotip: magnetslol

-6+8=2   Live 2 years longer!
Problem, healthyfags?

6.

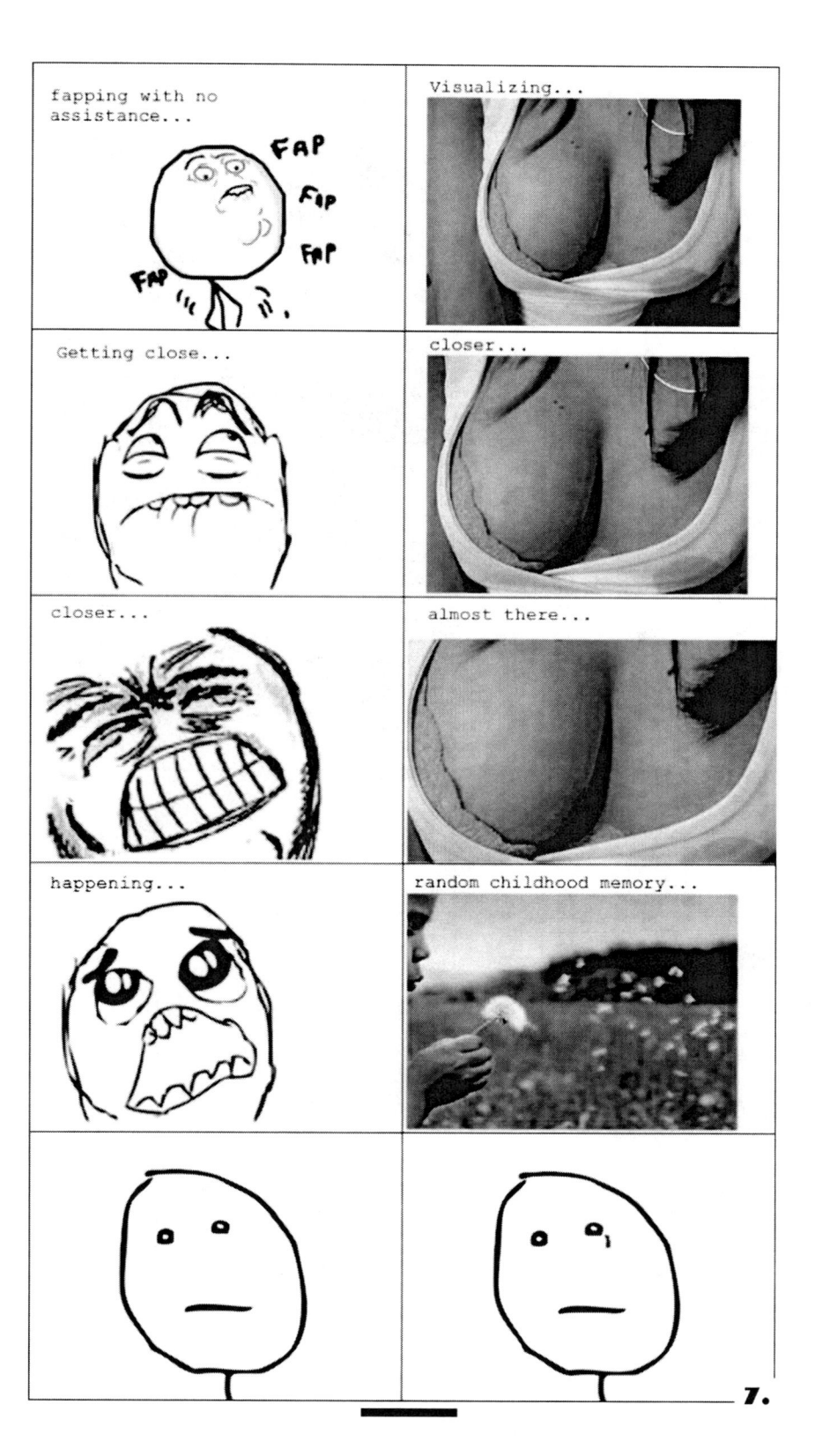

fapping with no assistance...	Visualizing...
Getting close...	closer...
closer...	almost there...
happening...	random childhood memory...

Ok amazon, lets se what cool stuff you have for me today...

Moi

Baby Carrying Jacket

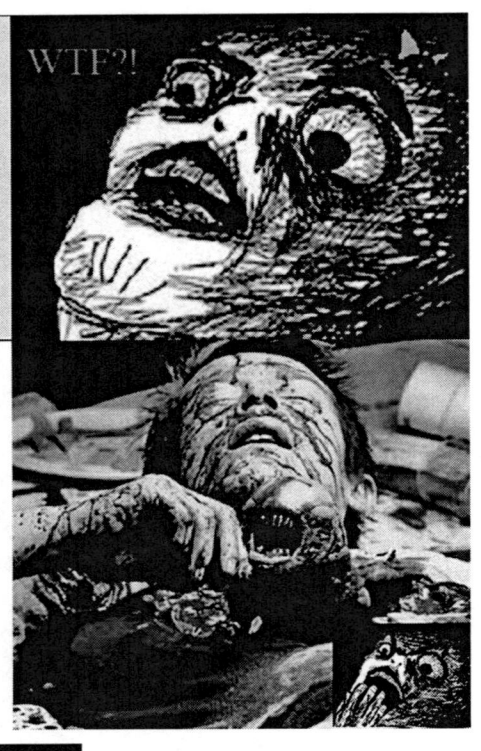

WTF?!

Kenwood KM070 Cooking Chef Major Mixer, Titanium
£996

Kenwood KM070
£995

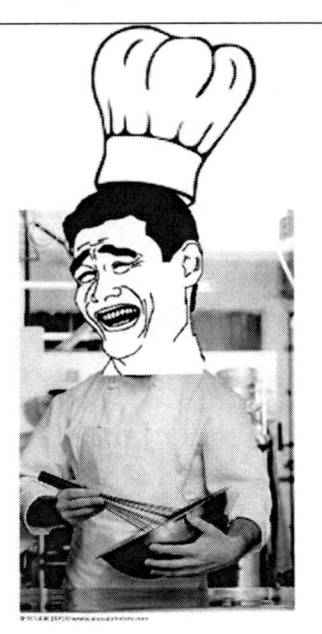

8.

Getting kinky with le gf
Hey babe
Yea?
I'll bet I can make you scream with just 1 finger
Ok, do it!

me
derping around at a high school party with some people i sort of know
i met this lady at my job at derpmart that had 7 kids!
shit thats a lot of kids!
I would never put my self through that. I don't even know if I want one!
Maybe she was really into breastfeeding!
why the fuck did I say that

	15 Years ago	Today
Listening to music		
Watching a movie		
Contacting people		
Reading the news		
Making Music		
Having sex		

me happily taking a test in class

My answer sheet

1. A
2. B
3. A
4. C
5. **D**
6. **D**
7. **D**
8. **D**

10.

ONE OF THOSE D's IS FUCKING WRONG

Creepin' Facebook

Decide to lurk a super hot co-worker's page...

... a co-worker that I have only ever said 2 words to.

Find her old vacation photo album for gratuitous bikini shots

FAP FAP FAP FAP

Accidently click 'Like' button.

Add a description
December 9, 2007 · Unlike · Comment
👍 You like this.

December 9, 2007
👍 You like this.

2007

CAUGHT FACE-STALKING 4 YEARS DEEP

11.

just got home from a two week vacation, time to speak to gf
hey hunny
hey babe
we need to talk..
What have i done?
im sorry babe but ive cheated on you..
NOTHING TO DO HERE
with a girl..
changed my mind
and she gave me a disease..
NOTHING TO DO HERE
but its gone now..
changed my mind
and i have her number..

i wonder what she looks like..
NOTHING TO DO HERE
le gf friend*

doing art
Me checking out Herpette Derper across the art room a few years ago
"man, she's pretty hot"
Realise I have her on msn some time later as 'Herpette'
Windows Live Messenger
In linea (3)
herp
derp
Herpette
Non in linea (104)
chatting for an hour. things going well
starting cybersexing (text. no webcam)
tell her I'm going off the computer and we should sms each other some more
feeling like a boss
lots more dirty texting follows
typing
"I can't believe we've never hung out or even spoken before!"
"yea me neither!"
dirty talk etc
"yeah and to think I was too shy to talk to you in the art room the other day"
"uhh...I wasn't in the art room the other day"
"no you definitely were..."

"pretty sure I wasn't"

"what...no you were..I don't...wait..."

Herpette Derper

Herpette Derperman

"Herpette"
(with no surname)

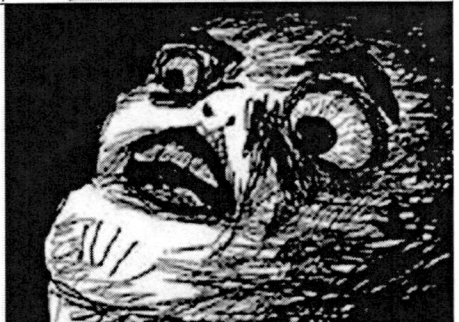

TACO ON THE INSIDE. Doritos ON THE OUTSIDE.
TACO BELL

14.

AAAAAAAYYYYYYY
SSSSSSSSSIIIIIIIII

Hey dad.	*Sigh*...What?
We're outta cereal.	
LET'S FUCKIN' ROLL	

15.

Ya know what dad? You're actually pretty cool.
Trix
Keep your pants on son.

At the grocery store with my mom
Get distracted by something awesome
FRUIT GUSHERS
omg where's mom
oh there she is, hey can I get some...
Uh, hello?
POKER FACE
NOT MY MOM.

I think I shall test my students tomorrow.	(Making the test like a teacher.)
A FEW MOMENTS LATER	DONE!
Answer Key 1. A 2. C 3. B 4. D 5. D 6. D 7. D 8. D	U nervous about those answers students?

Meeting le gf in mall at Victoria's Secret

I approach her from behind while she is apparently looking at underwear

17.

If you buy those I can't promise I wont be taking them off you later
POKER FACE
THAT WAS NOT MY GIRLFRIEND

*12 y/o cousin
You're on r/atheism?
Is atheism the religion of making fun of other religions?
CLOSE ENOUGH

Le eating lunch at catholic university
What are you doing? it's friday!

you can't eat meat!

Hey, you know what's funny? If you move each letter one to the right in the alphabet...

"HAL" becomes "IBM"!

snrk
snrk

I see. And what happens if you do the same with "EEEE TTTTT"?

FFFFFFF
FFFFFFF
FFFFFF
FFFUU
UUUU
UUUU
UUUU
UUUU
UUUU-

19.

*Me, coming home from banging my hot secretary

*le wife

Hey hon, did you get...

DID YOU CHEAT ON ME?

Err, no?

BAD POKER FACE

*le hot secretary

Hey derp, it is your Grandpa's birthday tomorrow, are you coming along?

*mom

sure mom

*22yo me

THE NEXT DAY

20.

all my uncles and aunts sitting with GP in the backyard I must say that I'm actually really worried with our leaders these days blahblahblah	I get into the house being the oldest of the grandchildren, all the kids
When Suddenly the little ones notice me hey guys... It's cousin derp! Jaay!	1st I play risk with them to make them cool down till dinner... So If you Conquer that country you will have the advantage Oh, I think I get it...
After dinner we play hide-and-seek for 3 hours straight... no one will find me LOL	we get back, and the little ones are tired as hell... Let's get home guys... That was fun...
when everybody's back home... wow derp you did a terrific job keeping the kids busy, thanks alot!	I had the time of my life

I was out walking with my 4 year old daughter.	*She picked up something off the ground and started to put it in her mouth*

21.

I took the item away from her and I asked her not to do that. GAH GAH	*my daughter asked* Why ?
Because it's been on the ground, you don't know where it's been, it's dirty, and probably has germs	Daddy how do you know all this stuff, you are so smart.
I was thinking quickly. All Fathers know this stuff It's on the daddy test, you have to know it	*We walked along in silence for 2 or 3 minutes, but she was evidently pondering this new information.*
OH...I get it! *she beamed* So if you don't pass the test you have to be the mommy	Clever Girl

22.

Ordering stuff for sexytimes online
EVENTUALLY...
NICK.com
Troll dad appears!
"Derplyn! You have something in the post..."
box arrives with giant sex shop labels all over it and description notice of whats inside
Lol! You ordered sex toys!
I will never be able to make eye contact with my Father ever again.

*Le boyfriend
for our one year anniversary let's rent a hotel and make sexy time all night
sounds perfect!
*c'est moi
get romance themed room with heart shaped jacuzzi tub and massive king sized bed
*he comes out of the hotel bathroom to find me like this
happy anniversary baby
i am going to fuck you all night, every which way i can

TWO HOURS LATER
i'm lovin' it

Me (Herp)
Friend (Derp)
Le talking about different jobs
Hey Herp, do you know any blacksmiths?
Indeed, good Derp, I do.
Oh yeah? Who?!?
Will Smith

Hey baby
We need to talk
What do we need to talk about?
I need to tell you something...
Oh god, what have I done now? Are you breaking up with me?
No, i'm not breaking up with you...
Then what is it?
It's just that i'm...
100% Natural
Prego
Tomato Basil Garlic
AWWWWWWWWW
YEEEAAAAAH

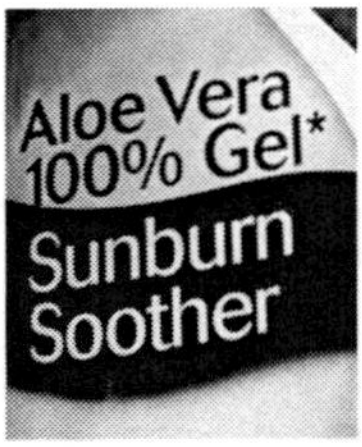
Aloe Vera
100% Gel*
Sunburn
Soother

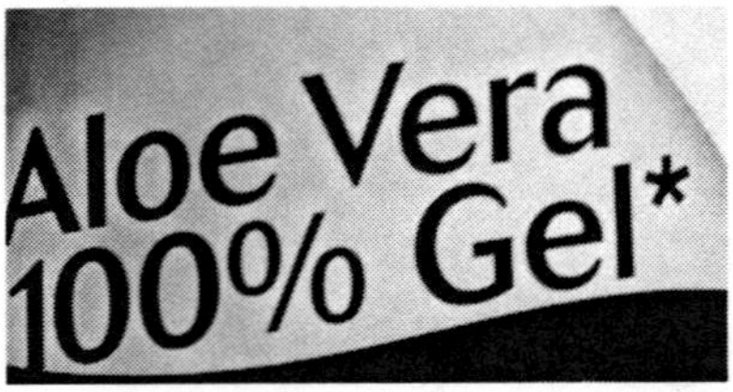
Aloe Vera
100% Gel*

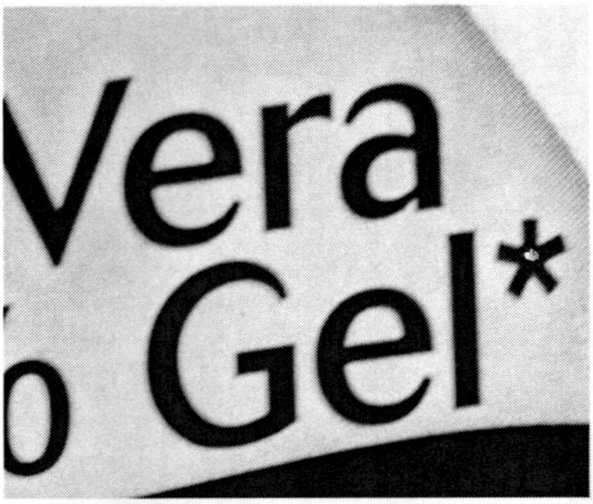
Vera
Gel*

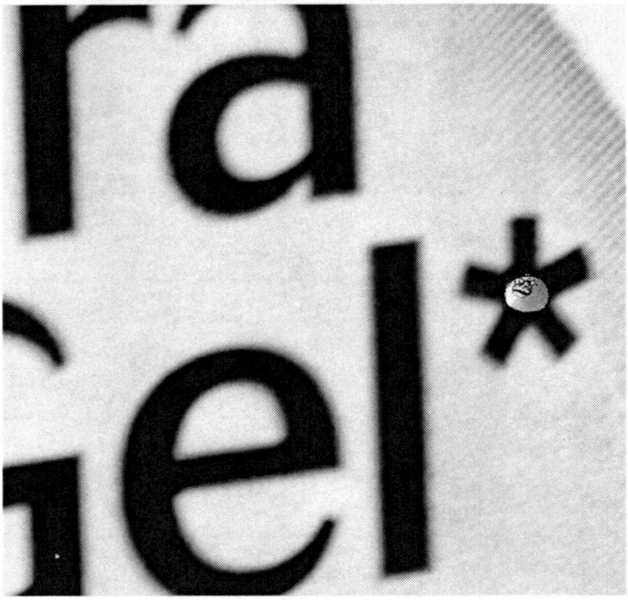

*Plus stabilizers and preservatives to insure potency and efficacy.

WE LIED!!!!

---

*me walking down the road passing some dude.

*I notice his shirt.

RAP

That's funny and non-specific.

Then...

IST

27.

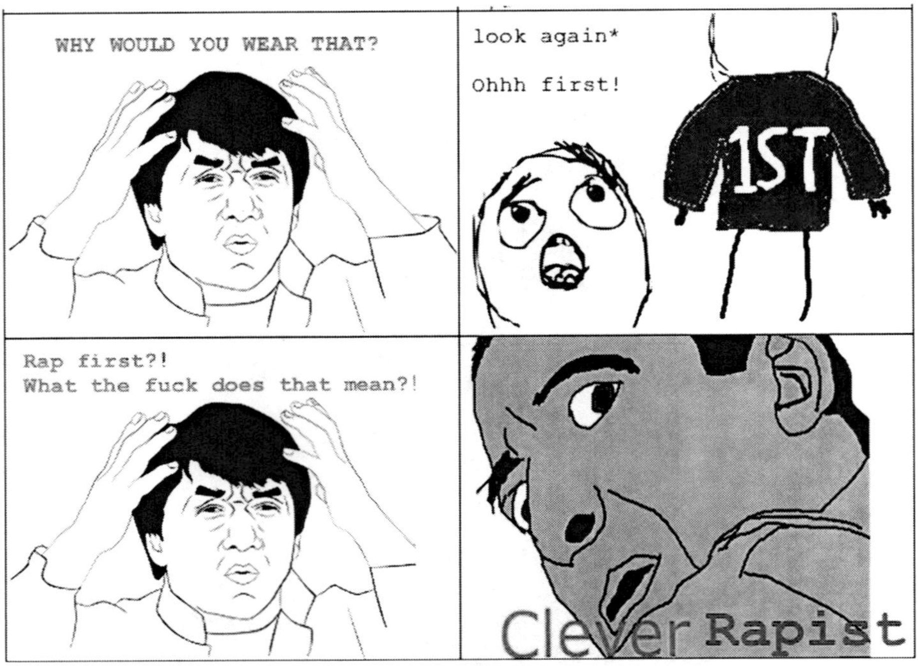
WHY WOULD YOU WEAR THAT?
look again*
Ohhh first!
1ST
Rap first?!
What the fuck does that mean?!
Clever Rapist

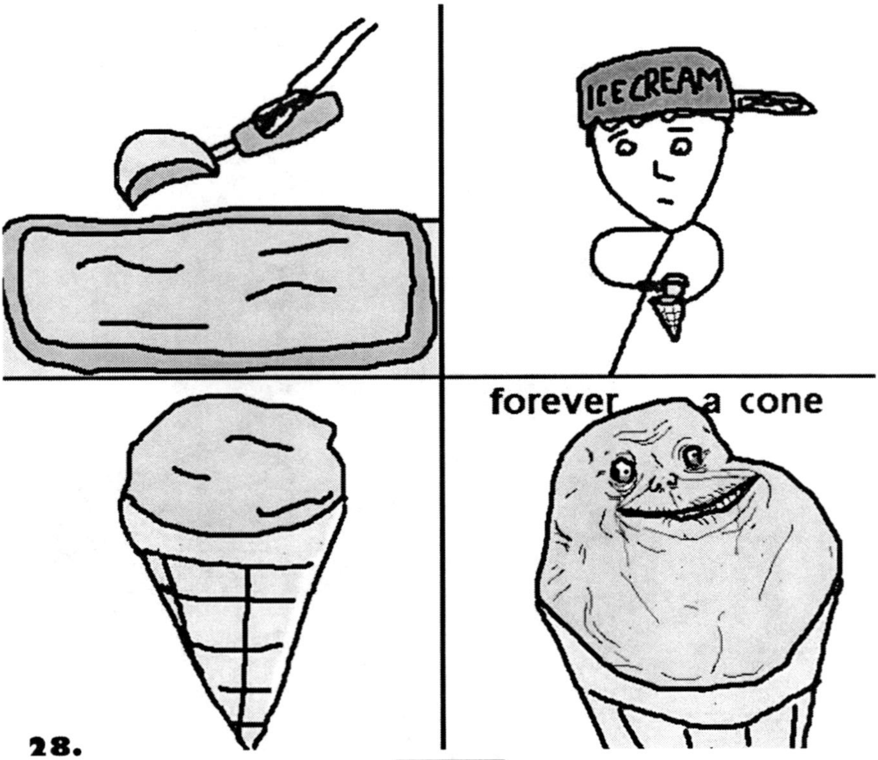
ICECREAM
forever a cone

Y U HAVE NO FOOD?
hello? i need the biggest pizza you sell!
FEAST.
suddenly, a wild sexy pizza guy shows up with my fifty pizzas.
you having a party or something?
yes.
guys! pizza's here!
* le me, yelling into the house as sexy pizza boy wanders off.
there is no party.

Me eating with other people (specially girls):

"Indeed, truly this is delicious and the quantity is quite enough. And this wine is an impressive combination"

Me eating alone:

---

le me, taking a 7th Grade math exam, when suddenly...

Find the sum of all the natural numbers from 1 to 100.

We never covered anything like this! I don't have enough time to work it out! I guess I'm just going to get it wrong!

ACTUALLY...

30.

IT'S NOT OKAY

If I pair the numbers from the ends, 1 + 100 = 101. 2 + 99 = 101, etc. So, 101 x 50 pairs is... 5050.

LIKE A GAUSS.

Grade 8-9: First girlfriend, the relationship lasts halfway through grade 9. Reason for breakup: We didn't like the whole bf gf thing. Still friends.	Grade 10: Second girlfriend, relationship lasts 3 months. Reason for dumping: I pointed out she was fawning over an exchange student and she dumped me.
Summer (Grade 10-11): Third girlfriend, relationship lasts for 5 months Reason for breakup: She moves away. We remain friends.	Grade 11: Fourth girlfriend, relationship lasts the whole year of grade 11. Reason for dumping: She cheated on me with both of her exes.
Summer - Grade 12: Fifth girlfriend, relationship was amazing and we were heading for marriage. Sadly she was killed by a hit and run drunk driver while she was walking to work.	3 years after her death I was convinced to date again by a bunch of friends. Me Blind Date

While on the date she asks about my previous relationships, When I get to my last one she had this to say.	Well at least I don't have to worry about you running back to her.
Listen bitch, I know it's been 3 years but I still miss her every single day.	

Been at job for about a year, desk is right by one of two printers on opposite sides of the office...	Once a day, good looking coworker from other side of office would come over and print something. We would make small talk but not much else...
LATER	Few weeks ago, Coworker quits to go to graduate school. I'm bummed I won't see her again as our short interactions were best parts of my day...

32.

New coworker starts yesterday. First interaction, asks me how to choose a printer. I tell her the computer is set to print on default to the one closest to my office instead of hers...
I look at her work computer and notice her default printer is not the one by my desk, it is already the closer one...
That means everyday, for over a year, my previous coworker was specifically choosing the printer by my office rather than the closer one...
I MISSED OVER 365 HINTS

yeeeey a new phone! I'll love it and cherish it forever!!!
I DO

4 TO 6 WEEKS LATER
oh look I dropped it

Le me walking in the rain, holding a newspaper over my head to stay dry
When suddenly I see a girl holding her laptop over her head to stay dry

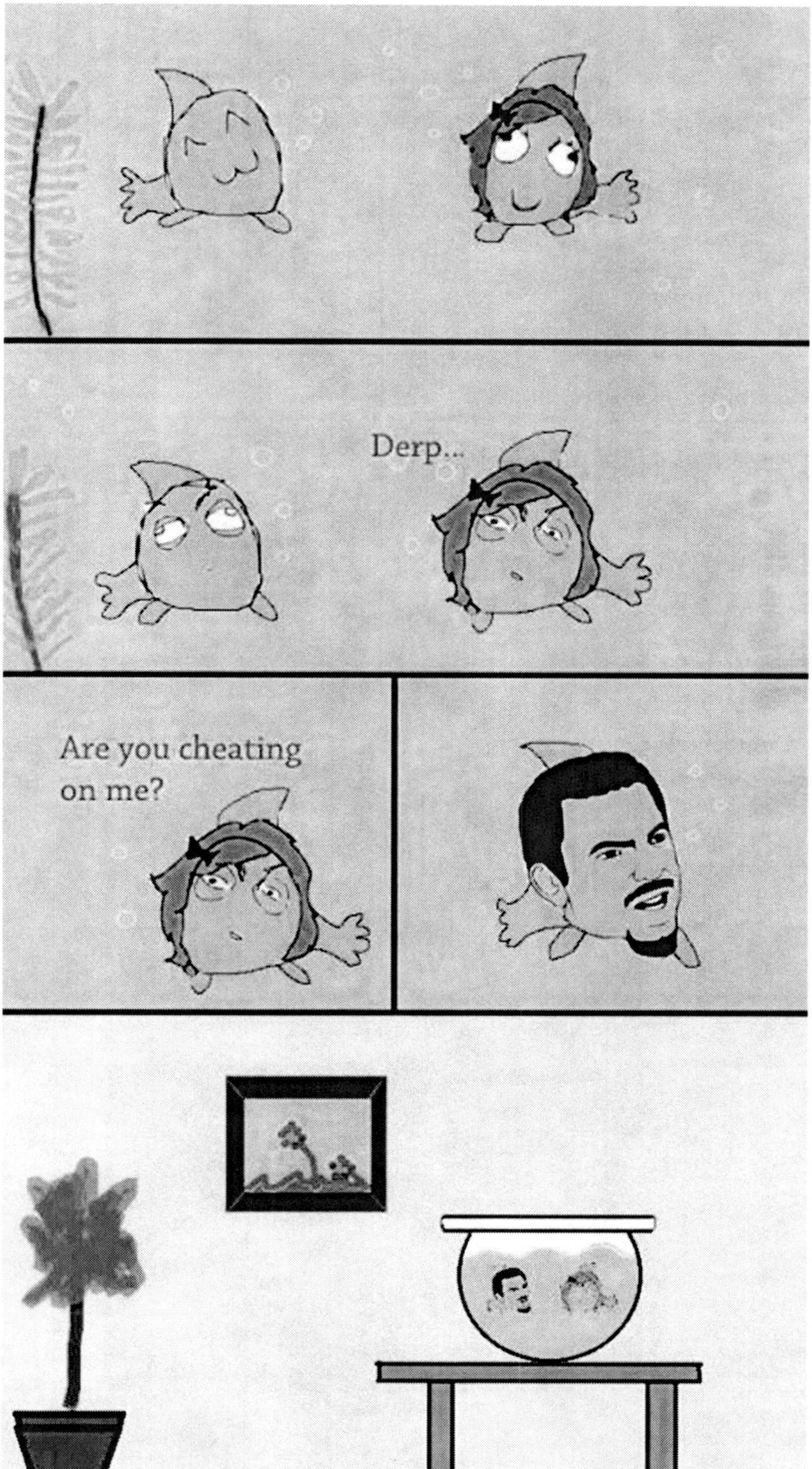
Derp...
Are you cheating on me?

what people THINK I do when i take long showers:

What I REALLY do when I take long showers:

36.

me giving new man a blowjob for the first time

20 Minutes Later
"If you're getting tired it's okay if you stop. No one's ever made me cum from a blowjob before."

I know what this sounds like...

CHALLENGE ACCEPTED

Continues. Like a boss

later...

I just imagined rage faces while giving someone a blowjob...

Walking down the corridor at work like a goddamn boss

wild colleague appears

le sidestep to move out her way

she goes the same way, then again, and again...

...Soon we start doing some strange leg shuffle dance to try and get past

TAKE MY HAND AND LET ME GUIDE YOU THROUGH THE NIGHT

*me, 9 am, working.

Derpo, the boss wants to see you. He's waiting in his office.

Ok, thnx. I'm going right now.

Later
AT HIS OFFICE

38.

Can I ask smth Derpo? Do you believe in God?
..hmmm...yes and no sir, sometimes yes sometimes No...but mostly I dont't believe.
Do you believe that there is Life after Death?
Certainly not, I don't believe that, there's no proof of it.
Well son, there is now some proof. After you left early yesterday to go to your cousin's funeral, he came here looking for you. I dont' believe you got two cousins named Tony?
POKER FACE
TONY

My dad has ADD, so I was used to the occasional impulse buy growing up...

Honey, we're home! Look at this lovely gold-plated spatula with port and starboard attachments that Derp picked out for you!

(Sometimes it gets a bit silly...)

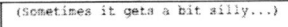

I thought this wacky waving inflatable arm flailing tube man would really brighten up our yard...great deal!

Getting ready to go back to college...

Hey Derp, I saw this great lithium-ion battery book light with mounting claw and adjustable brightness at the store, so I got one for each of us!

Thanks, Dad! That's actually pretty cool.

Next week, Irene coming to fuck everyone's shit up.

Guess I'll just stay in and finish reading LOTR...

That night, reading The Two Towers when the power goes out...

"Problem, Derp?"

(It's rain against a night sky, okay?)

I know! I'll use Trolldad's book light!

Now I can finish reading about the fate of Frodo and Sam!

Wait a minute...

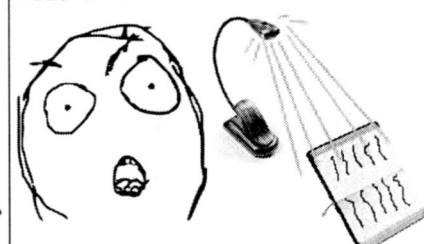

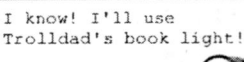

For you, Ring-Bearer, I have prepared this...

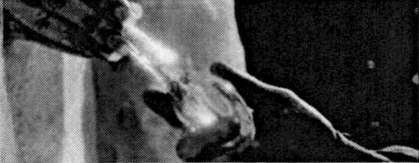

In this phial...is caught the light of Eärendil's star. It will shine still brighter when night is about you. May it be a light to you in dark places...

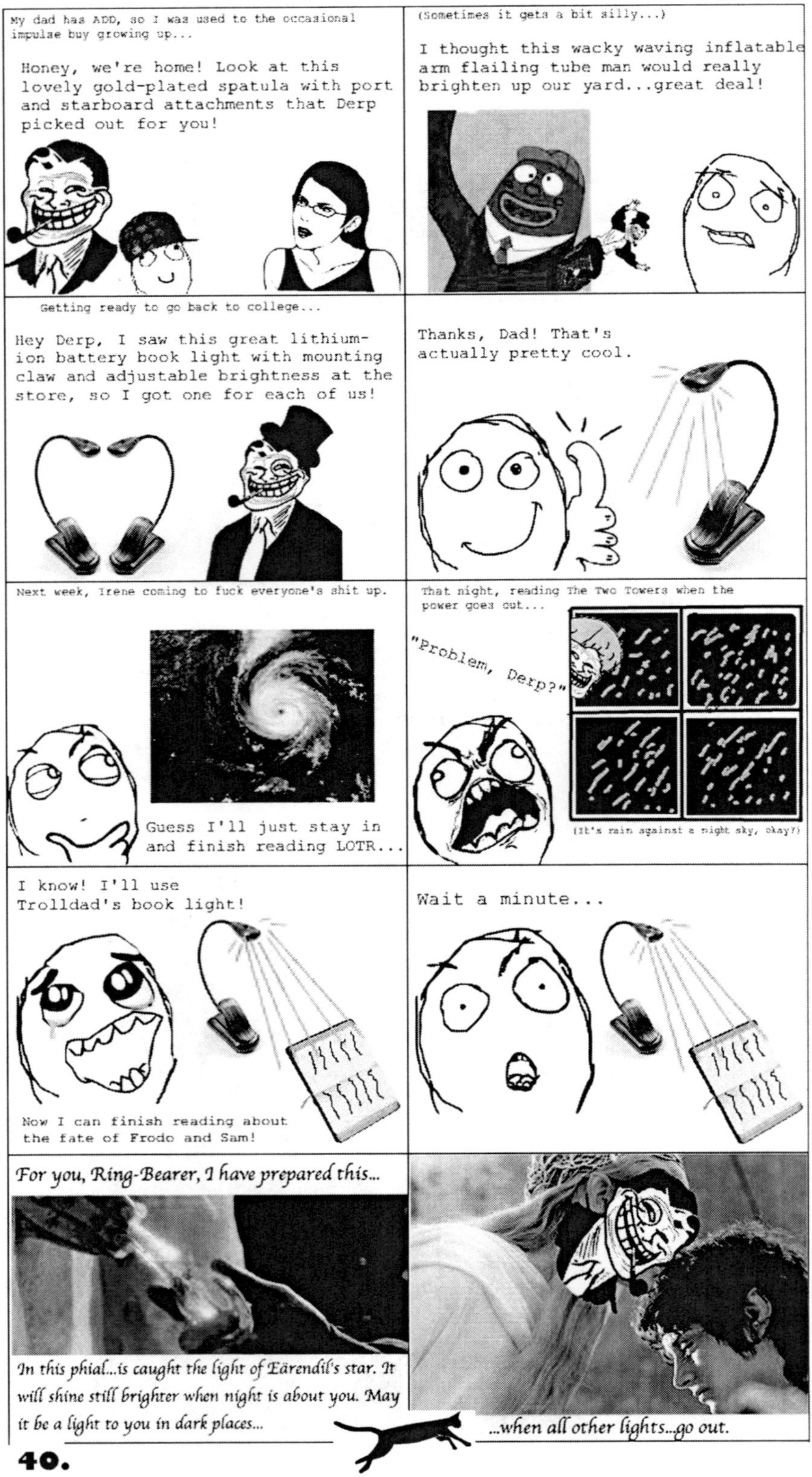

...when all other lights...go out.

40.

I am... **Froderp!**

For the Shire

*Just little me doin' the deed

When all of a sudden...

slam

"OWWW, MOMMY HELP!!!"

"What's the matter?!?"

"I HURT MY PEEPEE KISS IT AND MAKE IT FEEL BETTER!!"

"I'm sorry sweetie I can't..."

DO IT!

41.

"Thanks, mommy it feels better now!"
OH GOD
WHY

Me, running in arboretum like a bose
Up ahead!
Two people walking on the trail!
No prob, I'll just run up on the side

Incoming message from the right foot!

Captain, traction has failed, going into emergency flail mode!

Incoming message from the right hand!

Assuming command. Belay that, right foot, strong, smooth strides. I have a plan.

Baby, you make the BEST breakfast! One of the many reasons I love you so much!

The key is timing. You want everything to be done at the same time so it's nice and hot...like you tee hee

t e e   h   e

forever alone

43.

Panel 1: Me, cashier, just finished scanning someone's items.

Panel 2: Uhh I forgot my wallet at home, can you abort this transaction?
*customer

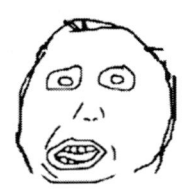

Panel 3: Sure, I just need a manager override...oh wait I see him a few aisles down.
Manager derp

Panel 4: I shout out to him..
Hey derp, I need an abortion!

Panel 5: POKER FACE

Panel 6: (penguin image)

Panel 7: *Me waiting in line at Mcdonalds
woman with baby "Fries with LIGHT salt, a milkshake LIGHT on the chocolate...."

Panel 8: "And don't make the chicken nuggets too crispy. The baby can't chew them. And is your water filtered

Panel 9: BECAUSE I ONLY WANT THE BEST FOR MY LITTLE DERPINA

Panel 10: Bitch you're in fucking MCDONALDS

44.

2 years ago when my bf and i started dating

Star Trek? Sounds stupid...

I'm not sure this relationship is going to work

after the new star trek movie

wow! that was pretty cool! i wanna watch the tv shows now!

yay!! spock is my favorite.. you should start with the original series!

yesterday

Why hasn't bf called yet? its getting late ...

bf: hi .. im going to bed

me:but you haven't even called me yet!!

bf: sorry... i forgot...

me: how could you forget? i was waiting... what were you doing??

bf: watchign star trek

I've created a monster...

hey son do you want to go camping

ive always wanted to

go outback and pick up the sticks on the ground so we can make a fire

great idea

45.

*huge trees and lots of twigs

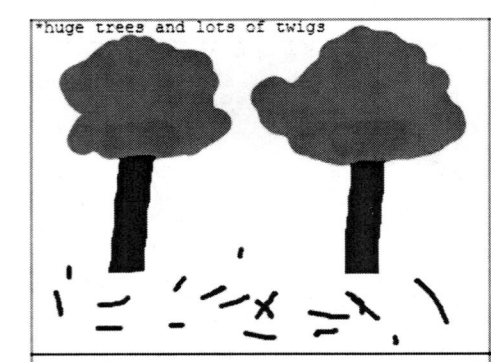

look at all the firewood dad

thanks for cleaning up the yard son

how dare you

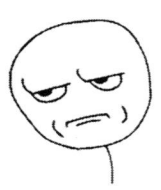

There's a 13 year difference between my lil bro and me. I love him to bits.

However, around age 4, he started lying; he was bad at it, so I always caught him.

BAD POKER FACE

Finally, one day he asks:

"Hey sis, how come you always know when I don't tell the truth?"

"Well, people older than you can see a red dot on your forehead when you lie."

46.

Much, Much, Much Later
"Sis, I'm sure this kid lied to me, but I didn't see the dot! You need to teach me how!"
POKER FACE
"Wait a second... there's no such thing... is there?!"
"Nope!"
And that's how I kept my brother honest for several years!
FFFFFFF FFFFFFF FFFFFF FFFUU UUUU UUUU UUUU UUUU UUUU-

*Le moi, just about to watch an awesome foreign film
I'm a TV
*Bro walks in
Hey, wanna watch this with me?
Nah.
It's a known fact the you can't read subtitles and watch a film at the same time
Well...How come I watch and enjoy them?
So that you can say you do and sound smart

Me, shopping for groceries with new roommate About to get some juice when roommate says...	Hey, watch out, they try to trick you with that juice!
It says "No Sugar Added" but that's a lie because if you look on the back it clearly says 28g of sugar	That's because there is already sugar in apples
No, what they do is pour sugar in the bottle BEFORE they put the juice in, that way they didn't technically add the sugar, they added the juice	
Me at about age 5. I wanted to go to the bathroom by myself like a big kid. I accidently go into the men's room	I walk in and see some guy taking a piss

48.

I bet I can pee standing up too
I straddled the child size urinal, so I too could piss standing up
OH GOD WHY

Well thats my cables neat and tidy
5 MiNUTES LATER...
FFFFFFF
FFFFFFF
Problem?

How I see myself when I'm having a cigarette

How people see me when I'm having a cigarette

How people think I see myself when I'm having a cigarette

1996

Waiting for a video to load

TWO HOURS LATER

Alright! Now I can watch

2011

Waiting for a video to load

TWELVE SECONDS LATER

50.

*le disabled me walking with my cane

Yo dawg why you walk with a cane and shit?

Oh because I have a disability that makes it hurt to move!

So then like....why don't you like never move dawg?

AWESOME VIDEO DERPETTE...

MY TURN! OMG THIS IS SO FUNNY. HAVE YOU GUYS SEEN THE DERPLE VID?

No. No. No.

Le Click

POKER FACE
POKER FACE
POKER FACE
POKER FACE
OKER FACE
POKER FACE
POKER FACE
OKER FACE
POKER FACE
POKER FACE
6 minutes remaining...
cough

On a fieldtrip (6th grade) with the school we get to a "pisstop."

I see the weird kid from my class runs behind the nearest bush.

Since there actually were toilets, I was curious why he would rather piss in a bush.

So I investigate.

FAP FAP FAP

I HAVE TO SIT NEXT TO THAT FREAK THE NEXT 3 HOURS

in class

so anyways, i was like..and sh~~e was like~~ and w~~as like~~ and s~~he was~~ and s~~he was like~~ w~~as like~~ one and i~~m like~~ omg and sh~~e is like~~

hey i am about to start class. You guys can flirt on your own time.

Oh no Mrs. Derpston! we were just talking. we were not flirting at all!

...i was

Halloween as a kid:

Le awesome wizard hat.

CANDY!!!

Halloween as a college student:

54.

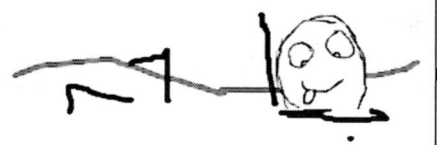

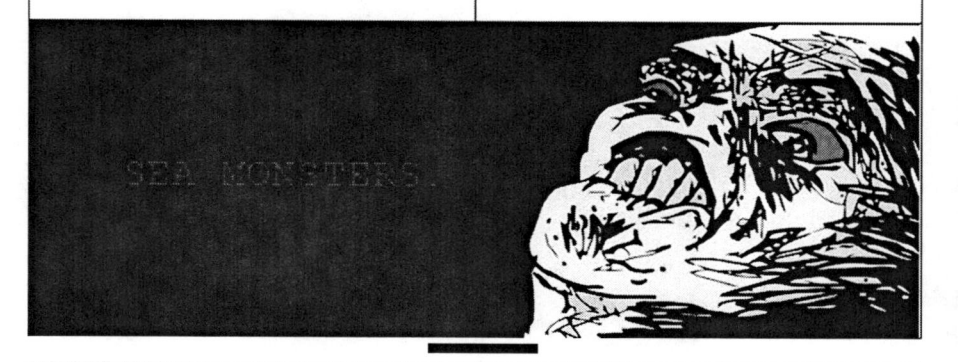

Me, swimming in a beautifully drawn lake	Suddenly, a leaf brushes my leg!

SEA MONSTERS.

Le highschool me in class* Damn i need to stretch.	
Yes derp?	

i just had a great idea
an empty swimming pool...
filled with party balloons
two pieces of wood..
with nails in them
strapped
to the
bottom
of your
feet..
and then you try to run all the
way across the top of the pool!!
NOT BAD

Me age 7 In Primary school

Today class we will be learning about road safety, everybody get a partner. *Teacher*

Hey Derpina do you want to be my partner?

Ok Derp.

OK now everyone hold hands and cross the road.

I JUST HAD SEX!

Waking up, ready for breakfast.

6:00 AM

57.

*le looking at the calendar
Hmmm, Florida in 2 months....
Bikini Season

*le eating salad

*le running

TWO HOURS LATER

CLOSE ENOUGH

58.

Some friends and I, going to Denny's. Haven't been there in a while.
WHAT.
IS.
THIS.
On the menu: fucking grilled cheese with mozzarella sticks in it
"What a fucking heart attack"
"I'd gain 500 pounds"
"Shit's for fucking crazy people"
le nibble
SWEET HOLY JESUS I WILL DIE YOUNG JUST GIVE IT TO ME

i luv u!!!!
omg ily2!!!
u r 2 qt!
lol lets kiss!
mwah
HEHEHEHEHEHE
forever alone

Warming up for a soccer game

me   *player on my team*

"Hey, look at that guy with the creepy mustache. He's a pedophile for sure."

"Dude... that's my dad."

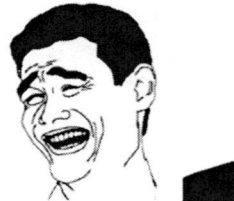

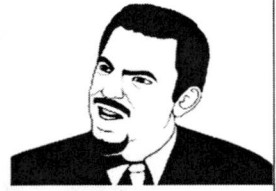

POKER FACE

60.

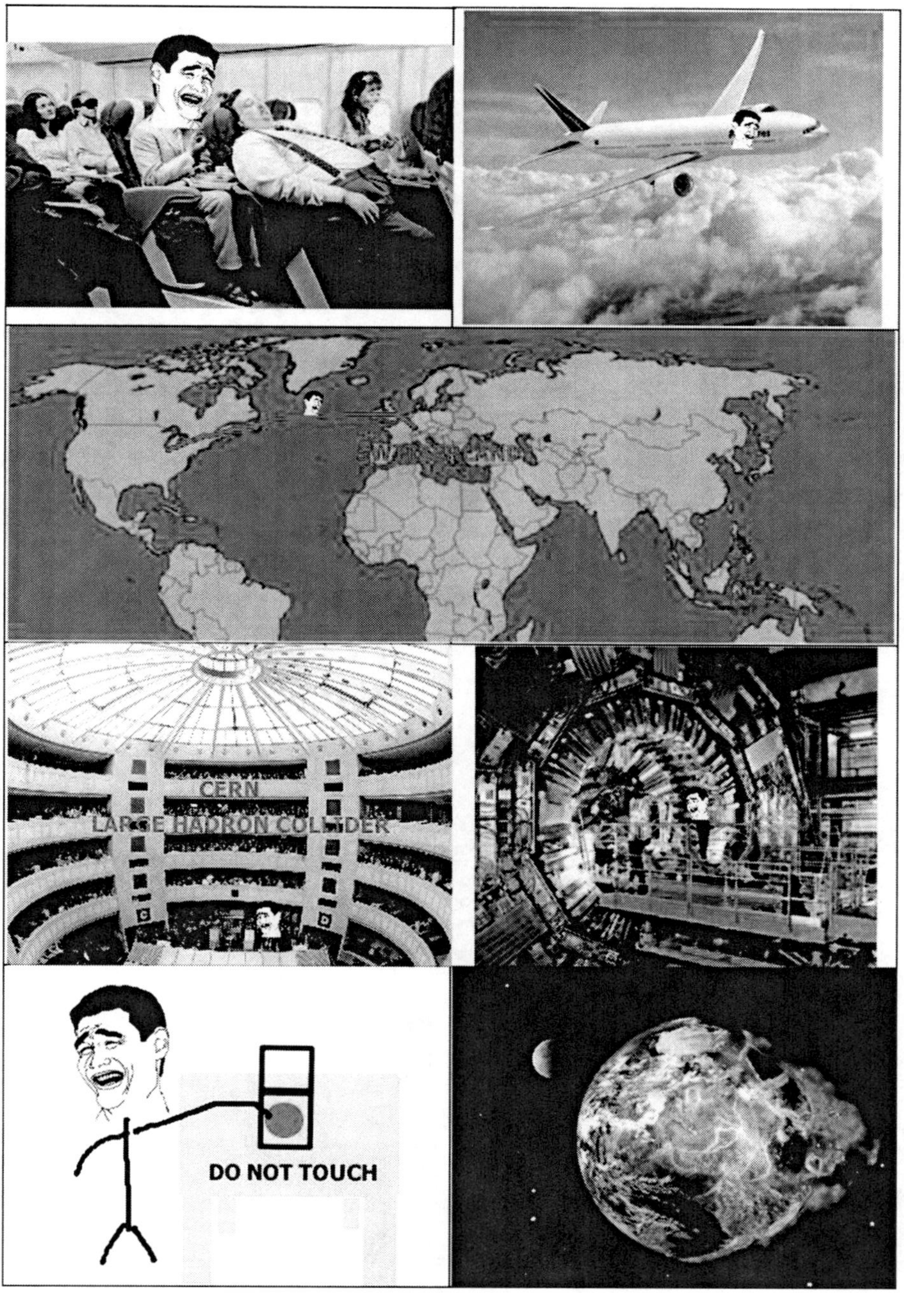
CERN
DO NOT TOUCH

* me securing a friend who is climbing

I made it! Let me down, slowly

Ok!

*Le drop

*Le jump

A swing rope!

Fuck .... you

Make sure you pick up the dog poop before you mow the lawn, Herpington.

Kay Mom!

LOL

* poorly drawn lawnmower *

62.

WEEK BEFORE EXAM

me

EXAM DAY

WHO ARE YOU PEOPLE?!

I finally finished my paper!

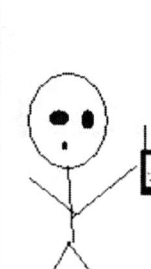

Who should I call to hang out with me???

All Contacts
Dad
Mom
Pizza Hut

forever alone

63.

in art class with black friend

will you pass me the skin color crayon?

Pauses le game

Playing Super smash bros. brawl

Wait a minute.... i can rotate the camera?

64.

Tipping back in le chair when suddenly...
I'M GONNA DIE, I'M GONNA DIE, I'M GONNA...
*le arms flail wildly
I SHOULDNT BE ALIVE

I don't always fart in the car...
but when I do
I always lock the windows

*me, hyperfocusing on the computer

*Dad

Hm?

inhale

BZZZZZZZZZZZZZZ

eating at resturant ...

gf   me

girl with big tits walks by in a slutty dress

in the resturant

66.

later watching a movie
gf
me
getting ice cream
gf
me
cuddling in bed ...thinking im going to get lucky
gf
me
i make a move and reach in...
DONT FUCKING TOUCH ME I KNOW YOU WANTED THAT SLUT AT THE RESTURANT *@&%^ I SAW YOU STARE AT HER TITS YOU FUCKING WHORE
but she walked by for one second and i didnt even stare
CAUGHT YOU... SO YOU DO ADMIT YOU STARED AT HER TITS... YOU EVEN REMEMBER WHO I WAS TALKING ABOUT... YOU FUCKING WHORE

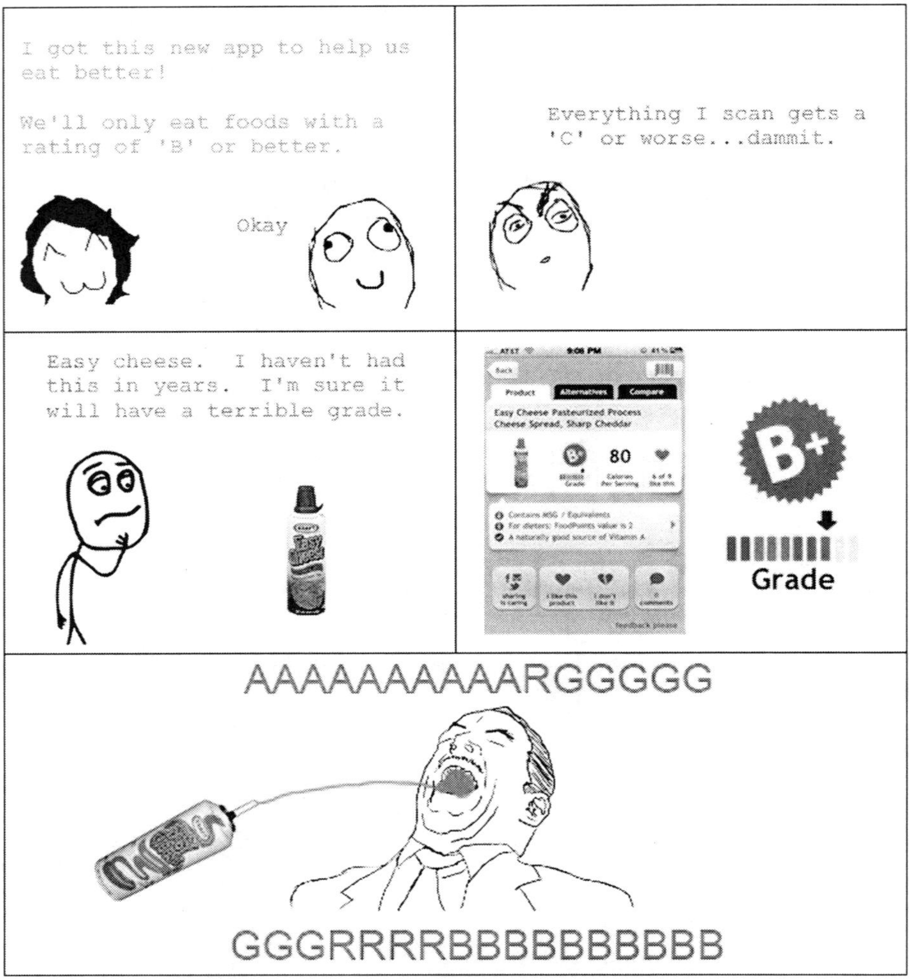
I got this new app to help us eat better!
We'll only eat foods with a rating of 'B' or better.
Okay
Everything I scan gets a 'C' or worse...dammit.
Easy cheese. I haven't had this in years. I'm sure it will have a terrible grade.
Product
Alternatives
Compare
Easy Cheese Pasteurized Process Cheese Spread, Sharp Cheddar
80
B+
Grade
AAAAAAAAAARGGGGG
GGGRRRRBBBBBBBBBB

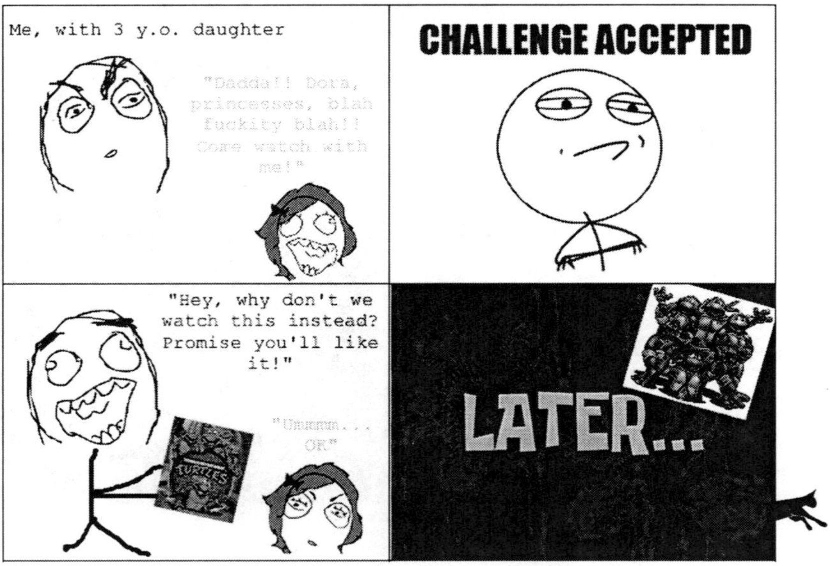
Me, with 3 y.o. daughter
"Dadda!! Dora, princesses, blah fuckity blah!! Come watch with me!"
CHALLENGE ACCEPTED
"Hey, why don't we watch this instead? Promise you'll like it!"
"Ummmm... OK"
LATER...

"DADDA I WANNA BE A NINJA!! I WANT PIZZA NOWWWWW!!"
"SURE!"
"Chocolate sprinkles and clams...NOW"
NO.
IT WAS ACTUALLY PRETTY DAMN TASTY

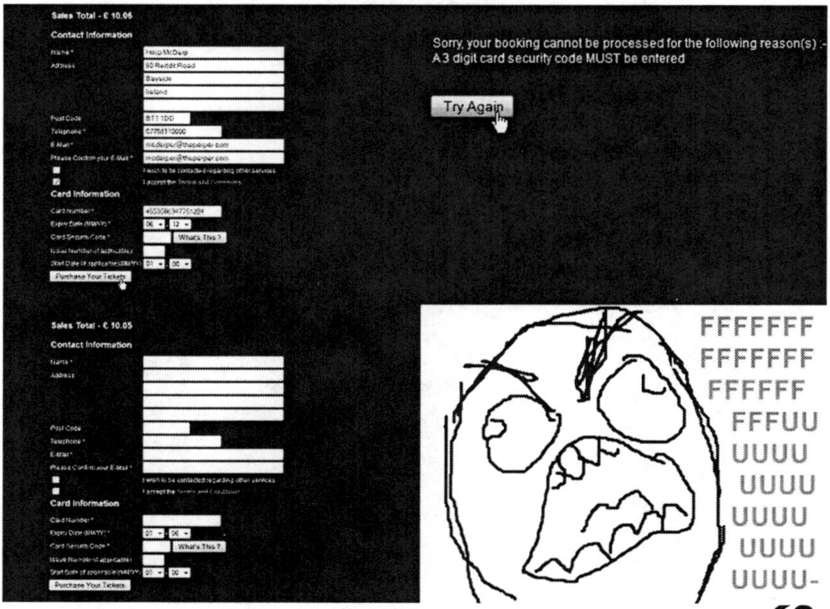
Contact Information
Card Information
What's This ?
Purchase Your Tickets
Sorry, your booking cannot be processed for the following reason(s) :-
A3 digit card security code MUST be entered
Try Again
Sales Total - € 10.05
Contact Information
Card Information
What's This ?
Purchase Your Tickets
FFFFFFF
FFFFFFF
FFFFFF
FFFUU
UUUU
UUUU
UUUU
UUUU
UUUU-

Me, doing my morning run like a bauss	When suddenly a very slow wild car appears!
As he got closer I noticed he was holding something out his window... Le poorly drawn dog leash	

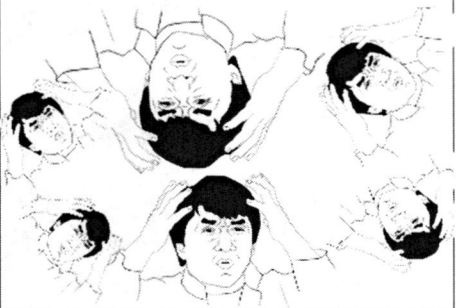

Google Canada

how come i
- how come i **have no friends**
- how come i **can't get a boyfriend**
- how come i **don't dream**
- how come i **can't lose weight**
- how come i **can't get wet**
- how come i **sweat so much**
- how come i **cant get abs**
- how come i **cant sleep**
- how come i **cant cry**
- how come i**'m dead**

GHOSTS ARE REAL AND THEY USE GOOGLE

le grocery shopping

Vaguely notice Phil Collins's "In The Air Tonight" is playing through the speakers

Suddenly realize that the drum solo is quickly approaching

"I know what I must do!"

dash into a deserted aisle and commence air drum solo

a wild male appears

begins his own air drum solo

"You know, this will be a funny story to tell our children when they ask us how we met."

POKER FACE   POKER FACE

Le' Me. Watching my two kids play in our living room.

Kids get the idea to start spinning in circles.

A minute or so of spinning.

Kids fall onto floor, filled with pleasure

"Like omg that felt SO good. lets keep doing this."

71.

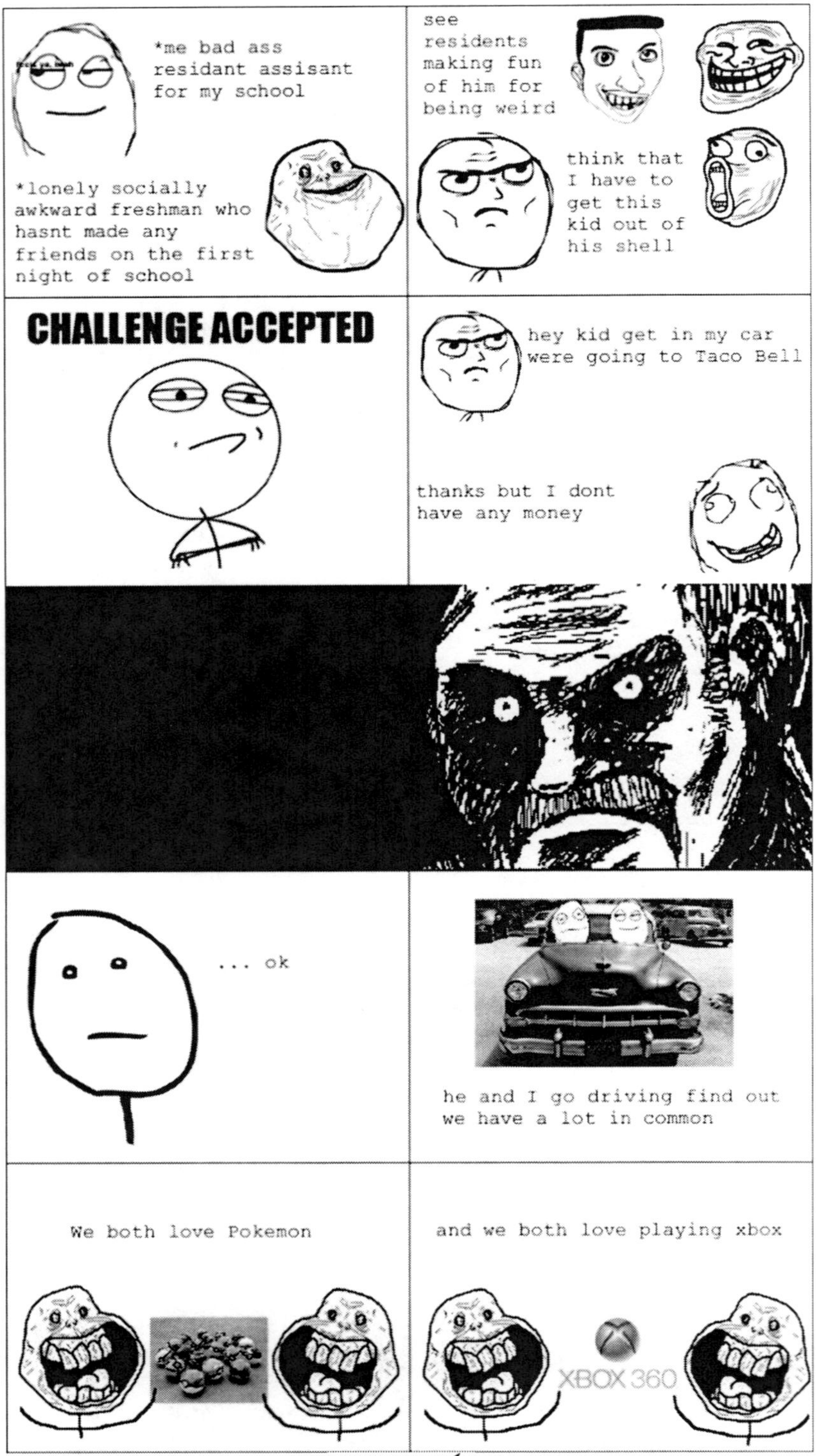
*me bad ass residant assisant for my school
*lonely socially awkward freshman who hasnt made any friends on the first night of school
see residents making fun of him for being weird
think that I have to get this kid out of his shell
CHALLENGE ACCEPTED
hey kid get in my car were going to Taco Bell
thanks but I dont have any money
... ok
he and I go driving find out we have a lot in common
We both love Pokemon
and we both love playing xbox
XBOX 360

then we gorged ourselfs on Taco Bell deliciousness

We quickly decided that we would become best friends

THE NEXT DAY

the next day I awake with a text message from the my newly best friend who I took to Taco Bell

*le crudely drawn phone

Hey thanks for taking me to Taco Bell last night I heard the kids making fun of me in the hall and it really made me upset I have been dealing with depression recently and I have been thinking about suicide and the kids last night almost made me want to do it.

But then you taking me to Taco Bell and becoming my friend made me forget about all of that I want to say thanks for being there you kind of saved my life last night

Derp

*8 year old me

and what would you like, sweetheart?

uuuuuum... spaghetti, please?

73.

alright, super salad?

Sure!

*dad *mom

LOL! LOL! LOL!

No sweetie...
Soup. or. salad?

Oh...

*working at a factory for the summer

do you want a candy?
no.

*old man   *me

how about you?
no.

he's gong to ask me next. i feel bad. this old man is trying to be nice.

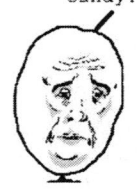

do you want a candy?
sure.

BAD POKER FACE

*he hands me a red candy

BAD POKER FACE

*i eat the candy.

74.

THAT WASN'T CANDY.

---

*me walking around at the mall

*A wild candy stand appears

I really want some candy, but I am completely broke. What can I do?

Excuse me, Miss, is there a minimum weight one is supposed to buy?

Not really, no.

*le put one candy in the bag

Here ya go, Miss.

Thank you, sir.

75.

0.00 LBS
$ 0.00
Okay
FREE CANDY
FUCK YEAH

me Having an awesome dream
wakes up
Better write that down. I could write a book and make Millions
creating memo
le handy
Seems legit. This will totally remind me of what i was dreaming
LATER...
remembers memo
memo: fskkipi edf hprrpie
FFFFFFF
FFFFFFF
FFFFFF
FFFUU
UUUU
UUUU
UUUU
UUUU
True Story

Le just got my braces off after 5 years
Notice anything different?
Nope!
No...
What?
Nobody knows anything about me
forever alone
Hey derp, you got your braces off!"
Who the hell are you?

Peein' like a boss
When suddenly, A wild sneeze appears
LE SNEEZE
FFFFFFF
FFFFFFF
FFFFFF
FFFUU
UUUU
UUUU
UUUU
UUUU
UUUU-

At the park, runs into bushes with bees, constantly runs out of the grass into the concrete sidewalk.

Near the river, lets go of hand and runs directly into water.

During bath, tries to drink soap and shampoo and stand up even though he'll slip and fall.

At lunch, ignores food, tries to leap from high chair or eat anything that isn't edible.

BABY, Y U TRYING TO KILL YOURSELF!!

---

*Drunk, getting my flirt on.

Hey girl, how do you like your men?

I like my men how I like my food.

Covered in mayonnaise.

*me at the train station, waiting for train to arive.

*An old man appears

*The old man sudenly points at something.

*I begin looking at what he is pointing, don't see anything.

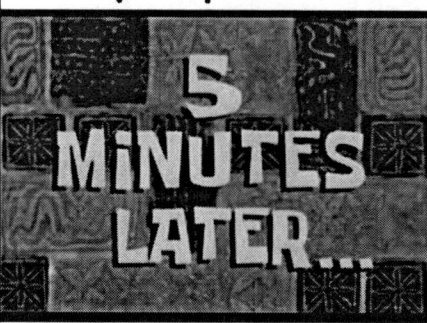

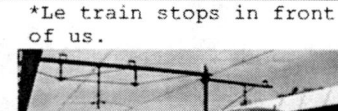

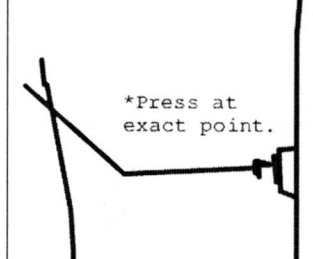

5 MINUTES LATER...

*Stil pointing.

*Le train arives

*Le train stops in front of us.

*Press at exact point.

*Doors open

79.

Are you a wizard?

Good morning, Pee-wee.

Good morning, Mr. Breakfast.

80.

How my resume portrays me, with a degree from a respected university and plenty of experience in my field.
Applying for laboratory jobs in my field like an unemployed person
LATER...
No Interviews. Well, money's getting kind of tight. I Should start looking for ANY job...
TWELVE SECONDS LATER
Applying for minimum wage retail, food service and labor jobs like an unemployed person
MUCH, MUCH LATER...
No interviews or phone calls? What's wrong with me?
I bet my degree and good jobs are keeping from getting these jobs.
How my new resume portrays me. No degree, only work experience is minimum wage

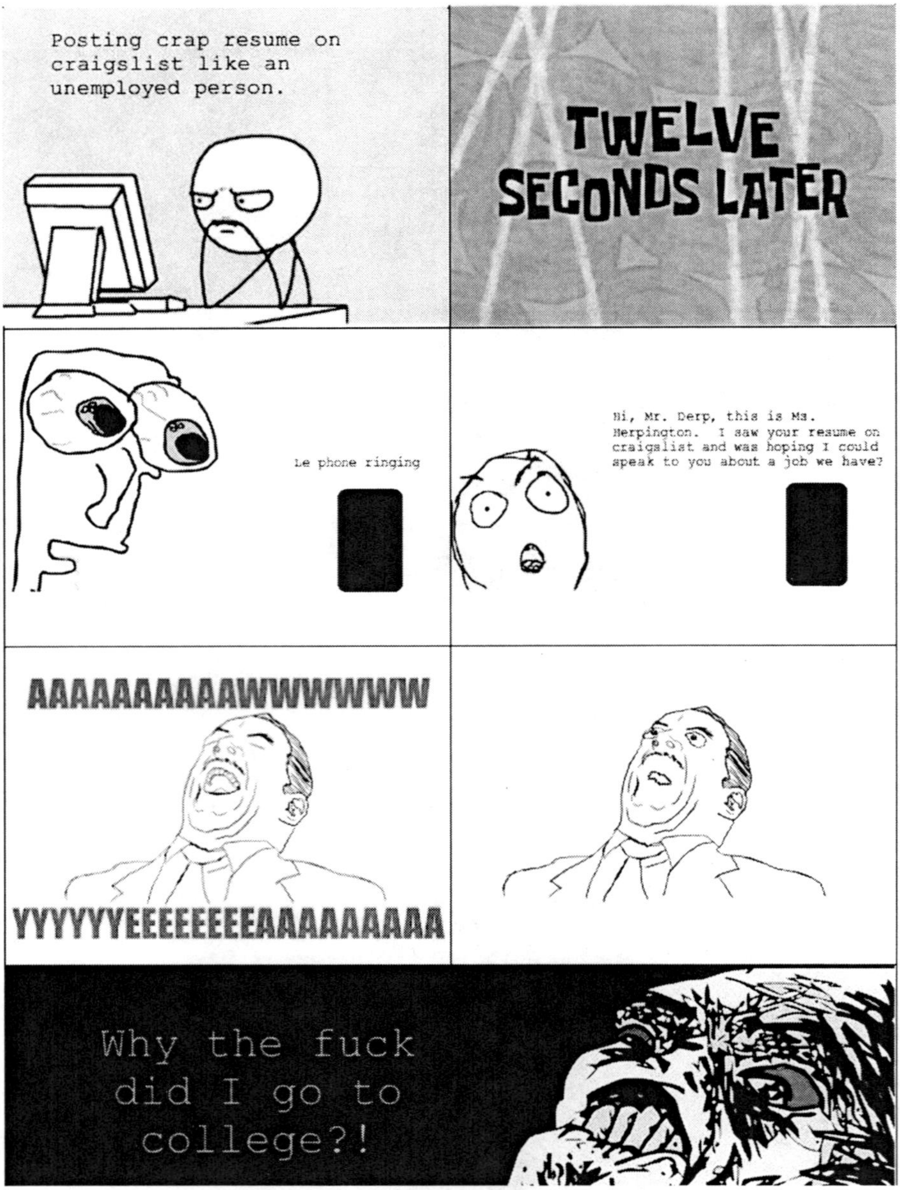
Posting crap resume on craigslist like an unemployed person.
TWELVE SECONDS LATER
Le phone ringing
Hi, Mr. Derp, this is Ms. Herpington. I saw your resume on craigslist and was hoping I could speak to you about a job we have?
AAAAAAAAAAWWWWWW
YYYYYYEEEEEEEEAAAAAAAAA
Why the fuck did I go to college?!

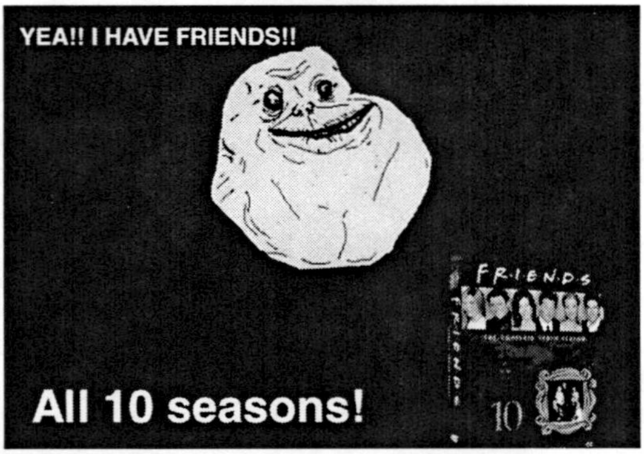
YEA!! I HAVE FRIENDS!!
FRIENDS
All 10 seasons!

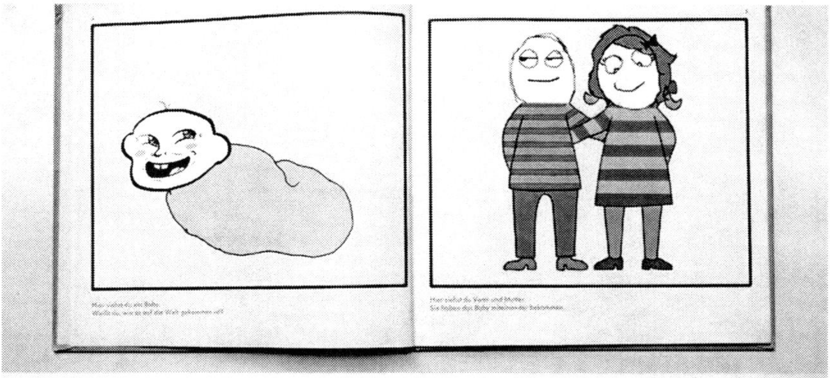

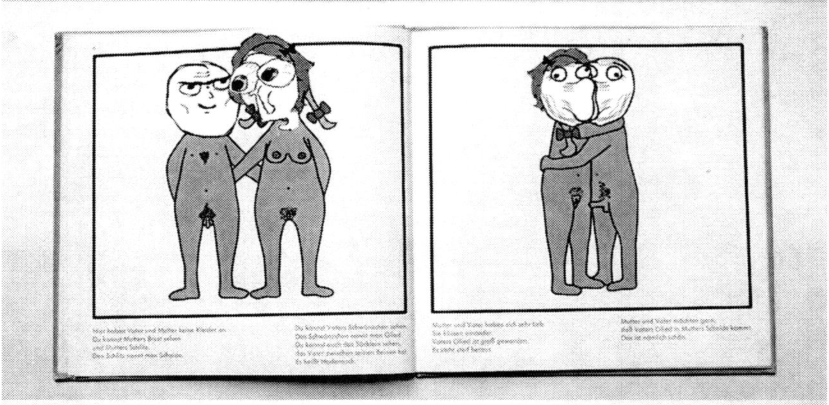

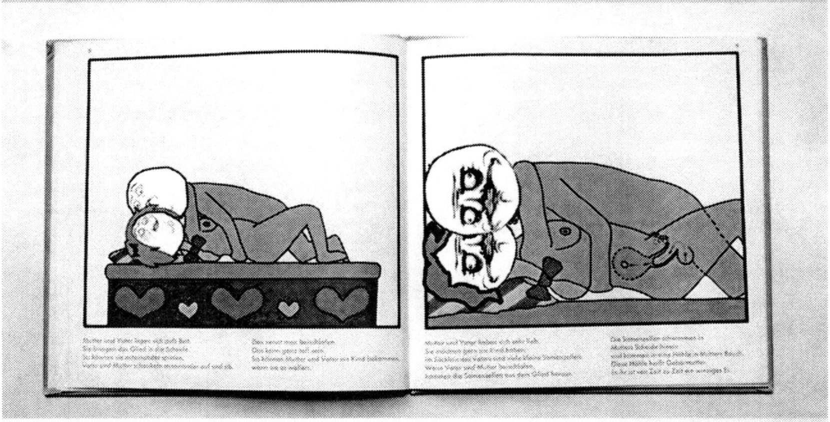

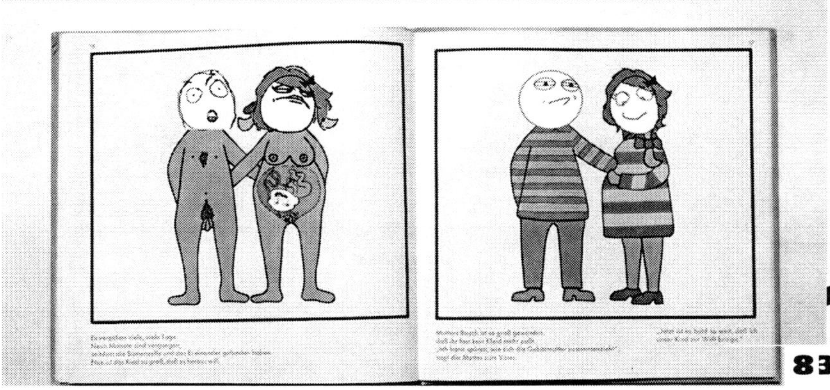

Klinik
!!!

84.

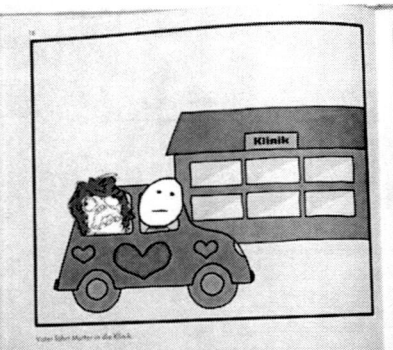

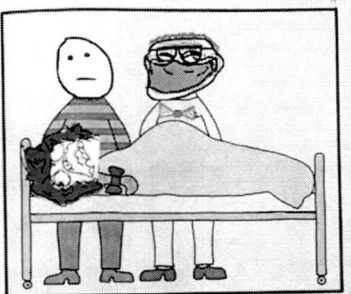

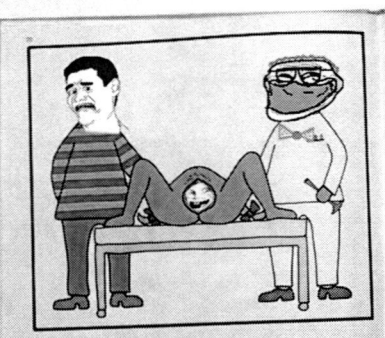

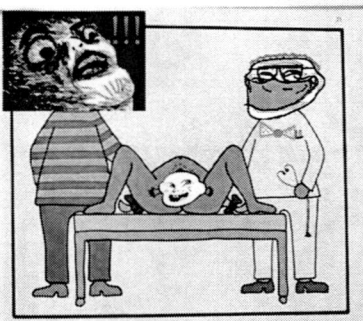

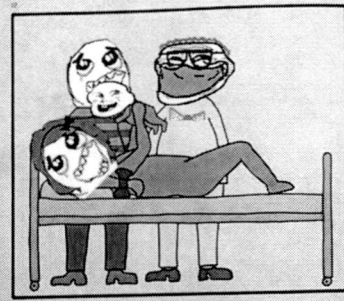

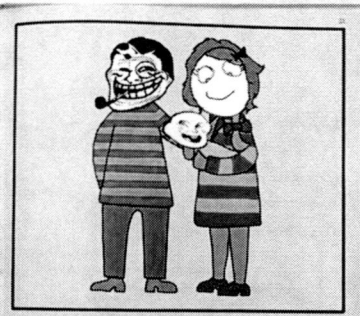

All my friends are dead.

Avery Monsen and Jory John

Forever Alone

MAKE DINNER FOR TWO

DON'T HAVE TO COOK TOMORROW

85.

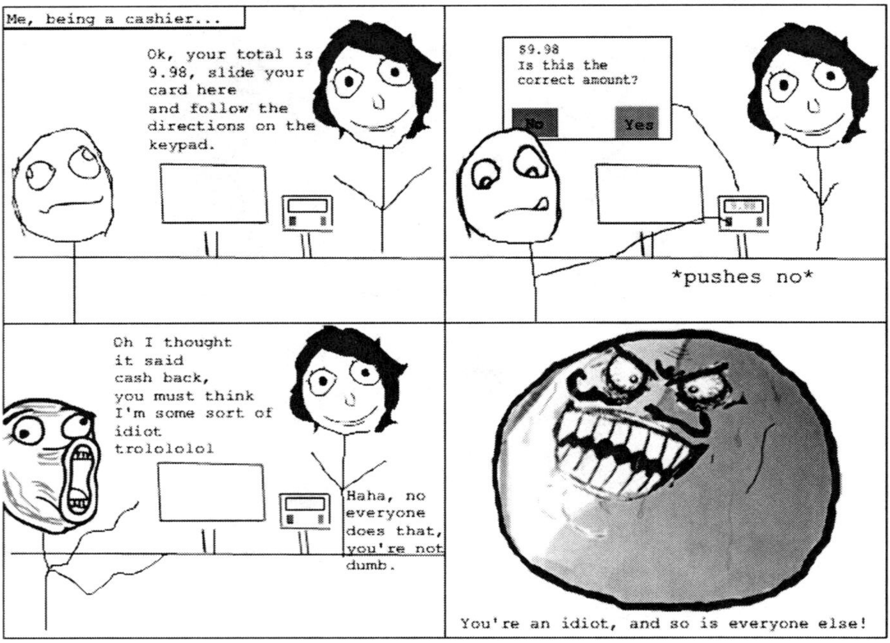

Me, being a cashier...
Ok, your total is 9.98, slide your card here and follow the directions on the keypad.
$9.98
Is this the correct amount?
No
Yes
pushes no
Oh I thought it said cash back, you must think I'm some sort of idiot trolololol
Haha, no everyone does that, you're not dumb.
You're an idiot, and so is everyone else!

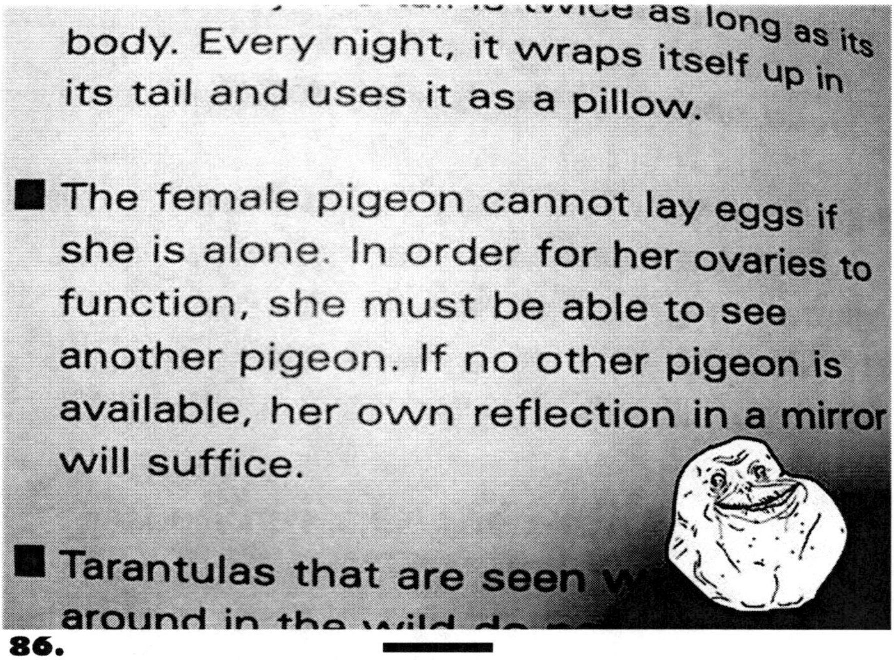
twice as long as its body. Every night, it wraps itself up in its tail and uses it as a pillow.

■ The female pigeon cannot lay eggs if she is alone. In order for her ovaries to function, she must be able to see another pigeon. If no other pigeon is available, her own reflection in a mirror will suffice.

■ Tarantulas that are seen

HOME ALONe
A FAMILY COMEDY WITHOUT THE FAMILY

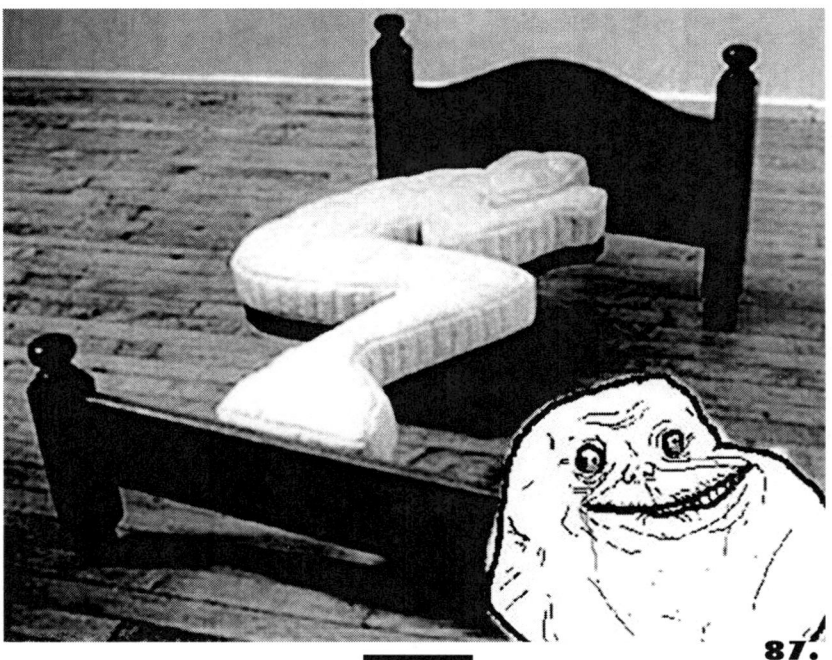

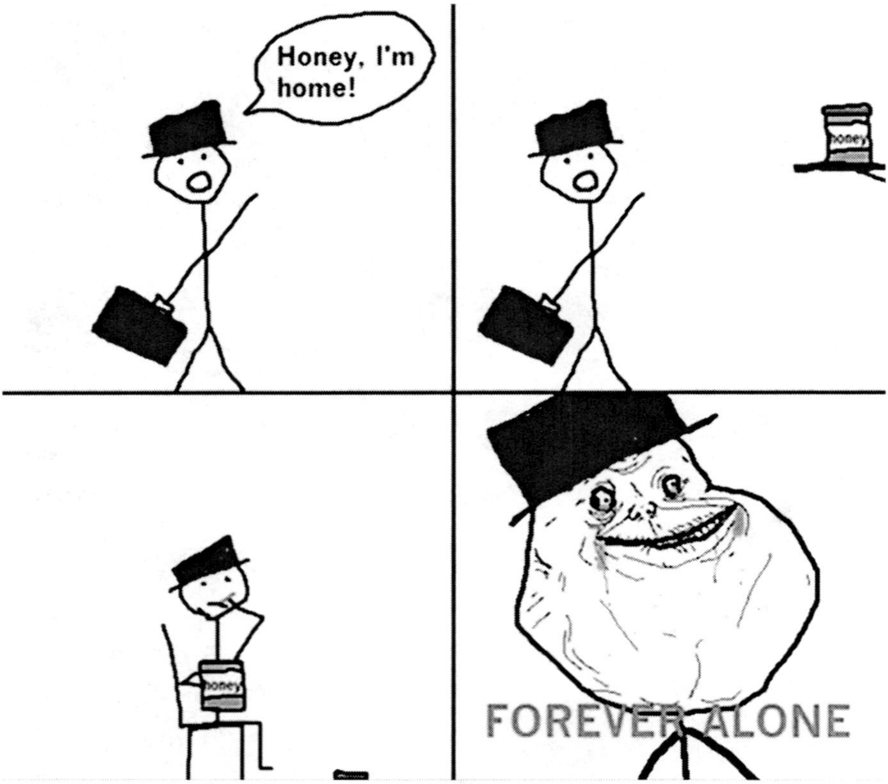
Honey, I'm home!
honey
honey
FOREVER ALONE

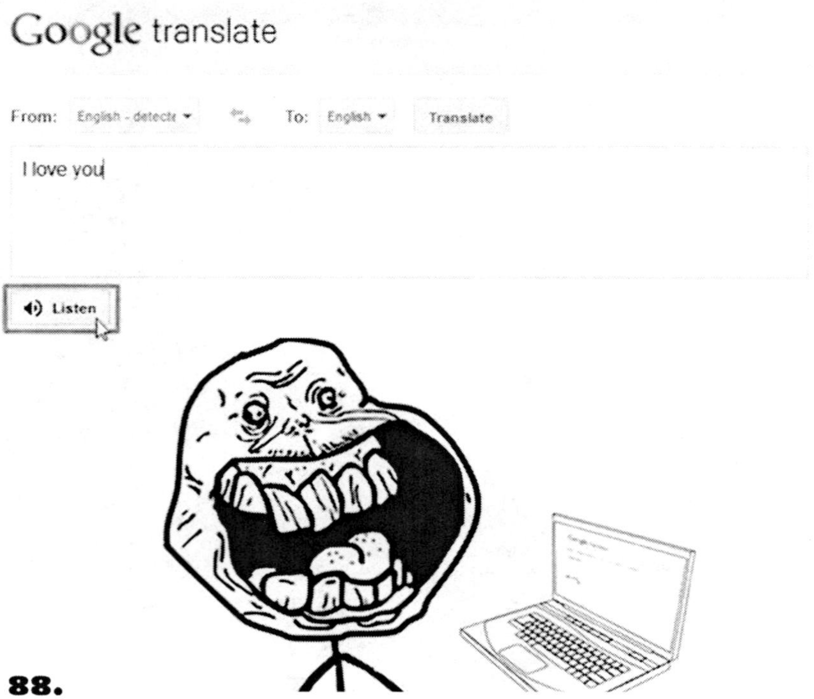
Google translate
From: English - detecte
To: English
Translate
I love you
Listen

1. Find a fresh status update with a mostly agreeable opinion.

John.the.Christian I have to say, the hatred that some of my people can cause are baffling and shameful. My apology on their behalf.
9 hours ago · Comment · Like

2. Say something outrageously disagreeable; make it something that will get a near immediate response.

John.the.Christian I have to say, the hatred that some of my people can cause are baffling and shameful. My apology on their behalf.
9 hours ago · Comment · Like

Todd.Trollington I agree with the Westboro Baptists and their cause.
8 hours ago

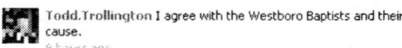

89.

3. Wait for the inevitable response of dissent.

John.the.Christian I have to say, the hatred that some of my people can cause are baffling and shameful. My apology on their behalf.
9 hours ago · Comment · Like

    Todd.Trollington I agree with the Westboro Baptists and their cause.
    8 hours ago

    Atheist.Steve ^Fuck you.
    8 hours ago

4. Delete your response.

John.the.Christian I have to say, the hatred that some of my people can cause are baffling and shameful. My apology on their behalf.
9 hours ago · Comment · Like

    Atheist.Steve ^Fuck you.
    8 hours ago

5. Sit back and enjoy the show.

John.the.Christian I have to say, the hatred that some of my people can cause are baffling and shameful. My apology on their behalf.
9 hours ago · Comment · Like

    Atheist.Steve ^Fuck you.
    8 hours ago

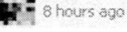

    Mary.Baptist You atheist scum; fuck you and your kind.
    10 hours ago

    Pete.the.Protestant pr00f that athe1sts hav no mor0ls!!1!
    9 hours ago

    Mr.Steve Son, we raised you better.
    8 hours ago

At my new doctor's office before a routine checkup...

OMG, they have Jelly Belly jelly beans, my favorite!!!

Grab a small handful, which flavor combination should I eat first?

I think I'll have Cherry and Watermellon!

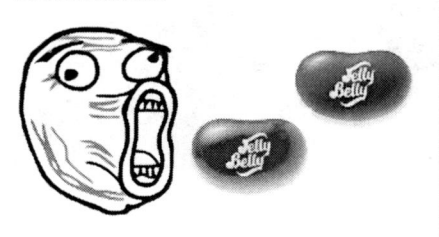

THEY WERE CINNAMON & JALAPENO

I have a husky-malamute mix named Kilo. He looks like a big red wolf.

Derping around with him playing fetch...

Whatchu got mommy's boy?

Dead sheep leg from sheep that got killed by mt. lion earlier that year.

Happily places it at my feet as an offering.

I AM THE ALPHA WOLF

Walking to *le supermarket* one fine day...

Pass under some overhanging branches.

Nonchalantly brush a few leaves off.

le cute girl at checkout can't help staring.

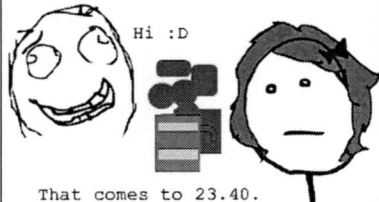

Hi :D

That comes to 23.40.

Hmm. Must be because I'm so devillishly handsome...

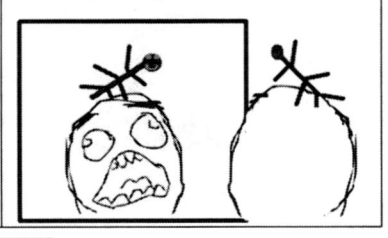

Get home and see honking great stick insect perched on head.

92.

*me, in a new house, going to turn off the light
Light switches....
everywhere
CHALLENGE ACCEPTED
I guess I'll just randomly pick one...
*switch off
nothing happens
I have no idea what I just turned on or off

Students cramming three hours before the first bioethics exam...

"Omg... Is that what I think it is?"

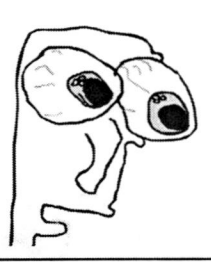

- Readings about the headless human clones
  - Using One's head
  - Of head less mice and human
  - Embryos pseudo-embryos and the headless human
  - Infant with anencephaly as organ donors
  - Headless Human Clones
- Week Seven (2/21-2/25)
  - Exam 1 Study Guide
  - Exam 1 Key - Version A
- Week Eight (2/28-3/4)
- Week Nine (3/7-3/11)

The professor must have uploaded it by accident!

Hmmm... This is an ethics class... Would it be wrong for me to see this before the exam?

FUCK THAT

le click

94.

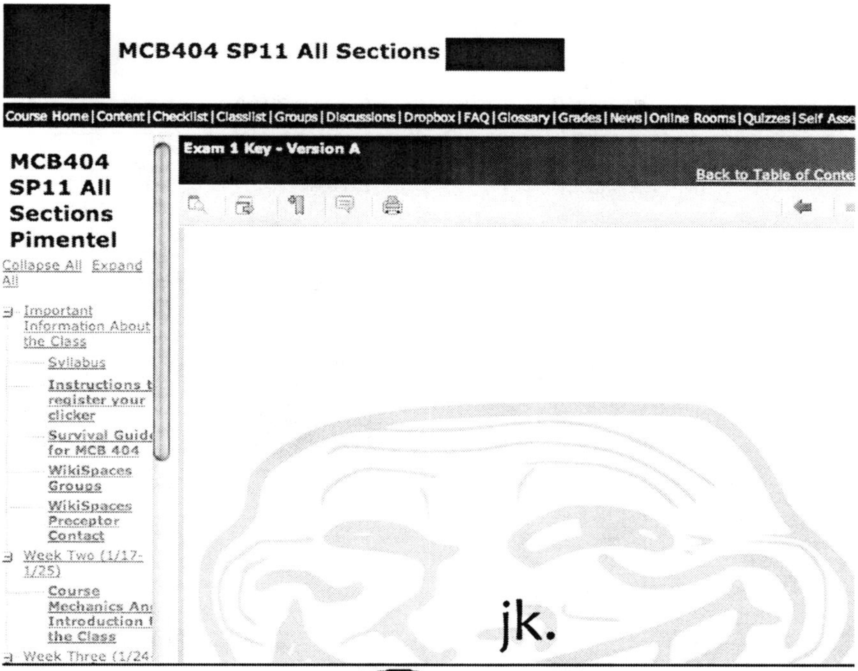
MCB404 SP11 All Sections [redacted]
Course Home | Content | Checklist | Classlist | Groups | Discussions | Dropbox | FAQ | Glossary | Grades | News | Online Rooms | Quizzes | Self Asse
MCB404 SP11 All Sections Pimentel
Collapse All Expand All
Important Information About the Class
Syllabus
Instructions t register your clicker
Survival Guide for MCB 404
WikiSpaces Groups
WikiSpaces Preceptor Contact
Week Two (1/17-1/25)
Course Mechanics And Introduction t the Class
Week Three (1/24
Exam 1 Key - Version A
Back to Table of Conte
jk.

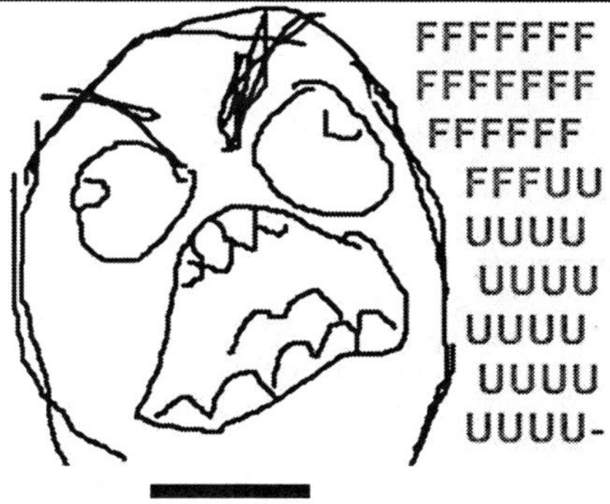
FFFFFFF
FFFFFFF
FFFFFF
FFFUU
UUUU
UUUU
UUUU
UUUU
UUUU-
[redacted]

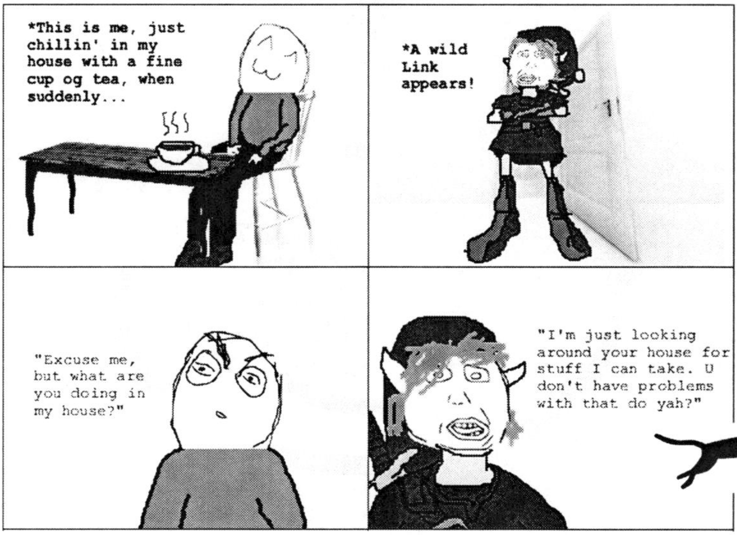
*This is me, just chillin' in my house with a fine cup og tea, when suddenly...
*A wild Link appears!
"Excuse me, but what are you doing in my house?"
"I'm just looking around your house for stuff I can take. U don't have problems with that do yah?"

"What?!
Of course I got problems with that! Get out of my house immediately!"
"Cool story bro... Hey! Look at this awesome pants I found in your warsrobe. I will definitely be keeping these.
"You can't just take my pants like that! It's stealing!"
"Hey! Watcha' keeping in this jar
"And now you are breaking my jars! What is the meaning of this?!"
"Wow, you had hidden this rupees very well, but I'm keeping these as well"
"Well, I'm off to save the world. Thanks for all the stuff. And btw, you wont ever get it back. It's mine now. See ya!"
FFFFFFF FFFFFFF FFFFFF FFFUU UUUU UUUU UUUU UUUU UUUU

Need to mail a letter but have no money? Yep...

1: Acquire envelope

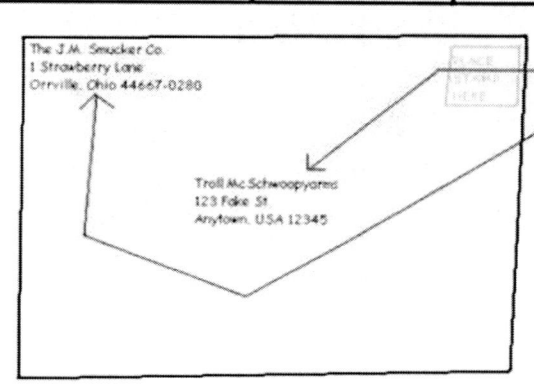

2: Put your address as the destination, and the destination as the return address.

The J.M. Smucker Co.
1 Strawberry Lane
Orrville, Ohio 44667-0280

Troll Mc Schwoopyared
123 Fake St
Anytown, USA 12345

3: Do not put a stamp on it so it is sent to the return address due to no postage paid.

Problem USPS?

*walking down hallway at university
*me
*le poster

*reading le poster

*le poster

Everytime someone reads this poster, somebody else in the world is diagnosed with AIDs. You can make a difference.

97.

I JUST GAVE SOMEONE AIDS!!
I HAVE THE POWER!!
*reads poster ten more times
PFFFTTTCHH
CHHCHHH
CHHPFFF
PFFFFTCH
PFFFFFTT
CHHTPF
PFFCHH
CHHHH
CHHCH
LOL
I'M A HORRIBLE HUMAN BEING!!

No more embarrassment in an elevator...
Next time I'm in a lift with four or more strangers, I'm going to turn around and say: "I'm sure you're wondering why I've gathered you all here..."
Oh man, I'm doing that today.
I'm sure you're gathered to wonder why you're here!

Uhh...pay me no mind. I was dropped on a baby when I was a head.
What the wrong is fuck with me?

Me and GF by ourselves in the elevator
GF
ME
Right before the doors closed an older gentlemen walked in.
He then turns and stares GF down
Um.....
Can I?......
Facebook you?

*Getting ready to eat lunch in elementary school

I hope my mom packed me something good today

*Open bag in total awe

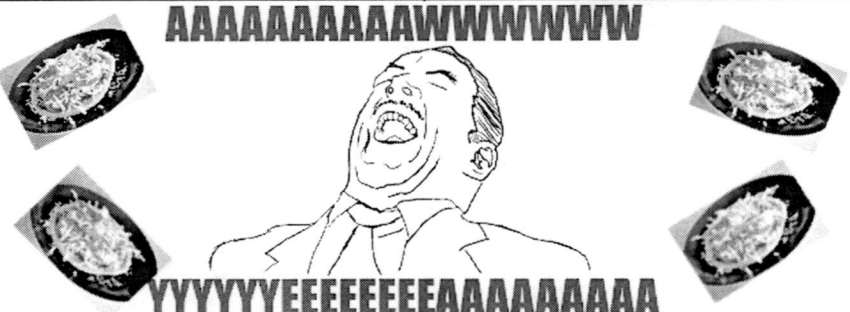

ENJOY!

AAAAAAAAAWWWWWW
YYYYYYEEEEEEEAAAAAAAA

I MAKE-A DA PIZZA

100.

Le me grilling like a boss
?????
= 8
=10
ACTUALLY...
okay
8x5=40
10x4=40
One Eternity Later
FFFFFFF
FFFFFFF
FFFFFF
FFFUU
UUUU
UUUU
UUUU
UUUU
UUUU-

OOhh look a Genie lamp!
I should rub it!
le rub
I AM GENIE DERPZAM.
YOU HAVE AWAKENED ME! YOU
HAVE 1 WISH, NAME IT NOW.
Ok! I wish for
all the girls
to like me!!!
VERY WELL, IT
SHALL BE
DONE!
POOF!
WTF DID YOU
DO TO ME?
LOL
FFFFFFF
FFFFFFF
FFFFFF
FFFUU
UUUU
UUUU
UUUU
UUUU
UUUU-

So let me get this straight....you're at this new college for ONE WEEK and you've already fucked some other guy?
Don't put it that way. It's part of the college experience, I'm trying new things and being social. Besides, you gave me permission!
Well guess what bitch? I met someone too! And I FUCKED HER IN THE BARNHOLE! She does stuff with me that YOU never would!
....God.....How did things fall apart so fast? We were supposed to stay together despite the distance...
Look....don't worry babe, it's gonna be okay.
Okay? OKAY!? How could things POSSIBLY be okay after what's happened??
Well, for one thing....I had Reeses for breakfast.
CANDY?
...For BREAKFAST??

NOT CANDY......REESES PUFFS CEREAL!!
JUST ONE BITE, AND MY TASTEBUDS ARE LOST IN A SEA OF CHOCOLATEY FLAVOR!!.
REESE'S PUFFS it's candy FOR BREAKFAST

*le me *le 3yo son	So, son make a wish and your toddlerish dreams will come true Hmm... I want to watch a movie!
Which one? How about...	Back to the Future!
*le proud father	The cowboy one!

FFFFFF
FFFFFF
FFFFFF
FFFFFF
FUUU
UUUU
UUUU
UUUU
UUUU
UUUUdge... (kids present)

Le me, trying to access facebook at my tiny high school

www.facebook.com
BLOCKED

m.facebook.com and the facebook iphone app
BLOCKED BLOCKED

BLOCKED
69.171.224.41
BLOCKED
BLOCKED

Le hot spot shield and proxy sites
BLOCKED BLOCKED BLOCKED

Well fuck this, I guess I'll work then

Le me, trying to access facebook during a trip to Vietnam

www.facebook.com
BLOCKED

m.facebook.com and the facebook iphone app
WORKS! WORKS!

...

106.

MY TINY HIGH SCHOOL IS BETTER AT BLOCKING FREE SPEECH, THAN A COMMUNIST ONE-PARTY STATE WITH 90 MILLION PEOPLE TO CONTROL!

night running

like a boss

when suddenly..

a mugger appears!

"yo man, give me your phone"

ignore

yes you fucking loser im not stopping for your shit

lock door

never leave home again

Comic 1

Panel 1: *Walking down the street when a wild hot femme appears.
- don't look stupid
- don't look stupid
- don't look stupid

Panel 2: *Suddenly our eyes meet
*le wind

Panel 3: *troll dust particle forces me to squinch my eye.

Panel 4: *she perceives it as a wink.
- Hey, you dropped something.
- huh?

Panel 5: My number.

Panel 6: FUCK YEA.

Comic 2

Panel 1: Just browsing Reddit when the wife pops in...
- Hey babe! Mind if I watch T.V.?
- Not at all!

Panel 2: She turns on her "stories".
- Ugh, how can you even watch this stuff? It's completely unrealistic.
- I know, but I love them!

Panel 3:
- Bah, no one's life is like this. Hasn't that lady been married like 10 times already?
- Okay then, smart guy, What do you like to watch?

Panel 4:
- Doctor Who, Torchwood, Breaking Bad, Firefly, lots of good stuff.
- What's Doctor Who about?

108.

Doctor Who is a guy with a time and space ship who travels all over the universe having adventures!
Okaaay... What about Torchwood?
Torchwood is about an immortal bi-sexual guy who works for a secret agency that's always saving the world!
...alright then. And Breaking Bad?
An ex-chemistry teacher turned meth dealer because he got cancer! He works for a guy who owns a chain of chicken joints!
Firefly?
SPACE-PIRATE COWBOYS!

*le big ass family going on vacation
*me
~Looks like there isn't enough room kids we'll just have to put one of you in the trunk
Good one mom
Your funny
Lulzz
Yeah, like that'd happen
ONE OF YOU BETTER BE IN THE TRUNK IN FIVE MINUTES OR SO HELP ME.
Not it.
Not it.
Not it.
You can't be serious, I'm the oldest and biggest out of you three, there is no way i'd fit in the truck.
Get in the damn trunk right fucking now or we'll leave you at your grannys!

But Dad you can't possibly agree to this
Listen to your mother, she's always right.
GET IN THE FUCKING CAR,
NOW!
True Story

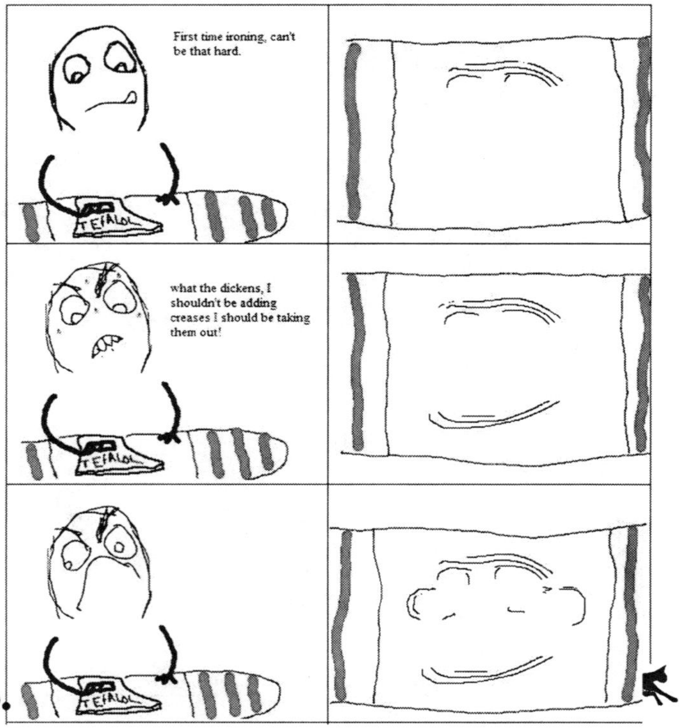
First time ironing, can't be that hard.
TEFALOL
what the dickens, I shouldn't be adding creases I should be taking them out!
TEFALOL
TEFALOL

Hello good friend, would you like to try some of my Jelly Derps?
Friend
Me
Sure...
Procedes to throw a handfull of jelly derps into his mouth.
What are you doing! You're supposed to eat one at a time!
Whatever bro, they all taste the same
YOU... WHAT HAVE YOU DONE?

AGELESS
DO NOT EAT
Oxygen Absorber
NE PAS CONSOMMER
NO ES PARA CONSUMO
NÃO INGERIR
Do Not Microwave

Smoking

finished smoking

now i have to get rid of that smell, so my mother won't find out that i smoke

washing hands like crazy

brushing teeth

using more deodorant than the guys from jersey shore

when suddenly i realize

WTF am I doing? I'm already 35

And my parents are already dead

And I'm actually a toilet

Honey, I think the toilette was smoking again

Volume 49%

Volume 51%

FFFFFFF
FFFFFFF
FFFFFF
FFFUU
UUUU
UUUU
UUUU
UUUU
UUUU-

Around 10-11 years old, my friend and I discovered dry humping and kissing (no tongue) and would occasionally do so on sleepovers
THREE WEEKS LATER
"Hey, Derpette, you feel like doing that stuff again?"
"Hmm... no, I'm okay right now."
"But I want to do the thing...."
"No, I don't want to."
le touch
"No!"
OH GOD
WHY

Le me, hard at work on my math homework with a group of classmates.
Math HW6
*Toilet paper roll for nose blowing
*Sick classmate
I've gone through a whole roll of toilet paper in 12 hours!!
Sounds like me when I first hit puberty.
*Me
*Me
POKER FACE
*Offended classmates
WHY DID I SAY THAT OUT LOUD?!?!

me, 11 years old
discover fapping recently
FAP
FAP
FAP
FAP
mom asks me to vacuum room
use vacuum hose to get dust behind bed

get bored so I put vacuum hose on face and make faces using the hose
"sweet jesus, this feels good"
have the brilliant idea of putting suction vacuum hose on dick
insane orgasmic feeling
start fapping with it
FAP
FAP
FAP
FAP
mom checks up to see how my room cleaning is going
i'm butt naked with the vacuum hose sucking my dick
stare at my mom with a poker face
mom slams the door yelling and is utterly disgusted
SLAM!
consider suicide
WORST.MEMORY.EVER
don't talk to my mom for a month
OH GOD
WHY

Let's make an awesome potion out of all these chemicals!
me, 12?
BLEACH
Now let's go dump it in a puddle in the field.
OH GOD
WHY

FFFFFFFF
FFFFFFFF
FFFFFF
FFFUU
UUUU
UUUU
UUUU
UUUU
UUUU-

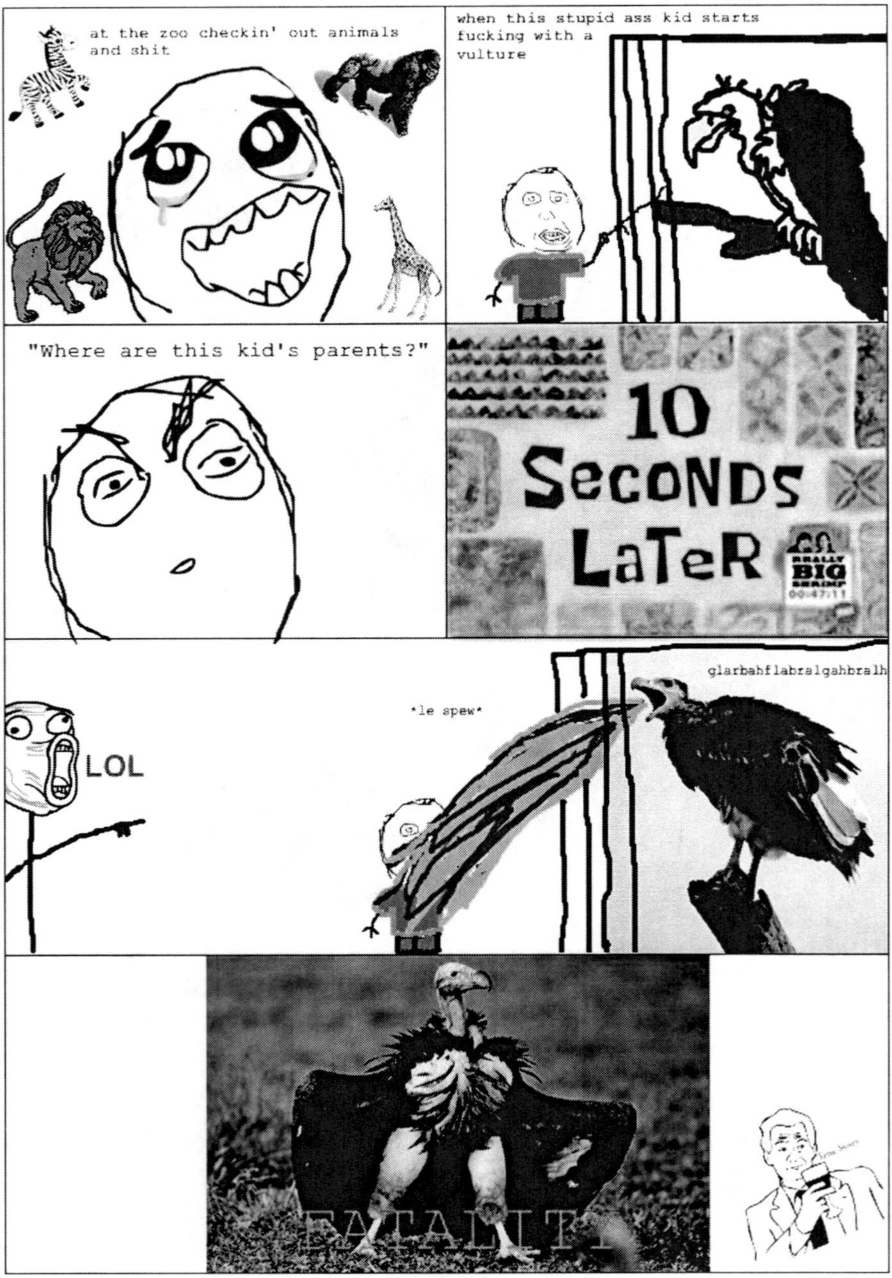
at the zoo checkin' out animals and shit
when this stupid ass kid starts fucking with a vulture
"Where are this kid's parents?"
10 SECONDS LaTeR
LOL
le spew
glarbahflabralgahbralh

Ugh I have to get my cat put down.

*"Friend"

Oh God I'm so sorry! Why?

*Me

She keeps puking and stuff it's so annoying.

Wait... You're putting your cat down because she pukes sometimes?

Yeah, I don't have time to clean that stuff. Plus that fucking cat is so ugly and stupid so I don't really mind.

*Le kitty

THAT KITTY IS THE NICEST CAT I HAVE EVER MET HER TUMMY JUST GETS UPSET EASILY AND YOU WANNA KILL HER BECAUSE OF THAT?! I WILL TAKE THAT KITTY AND LOVE IT AND TAKE CARE OF IT. ALSO, YOU'RE UGLY AND STUPID.

*Say hi to my new cat Elby

I love my gf alot

But she has this weird tendancy to hit me with random objects

LOL CHICKEN SLAP
*Bonk

LOL RAMEN SLAP
*Bonk

119.

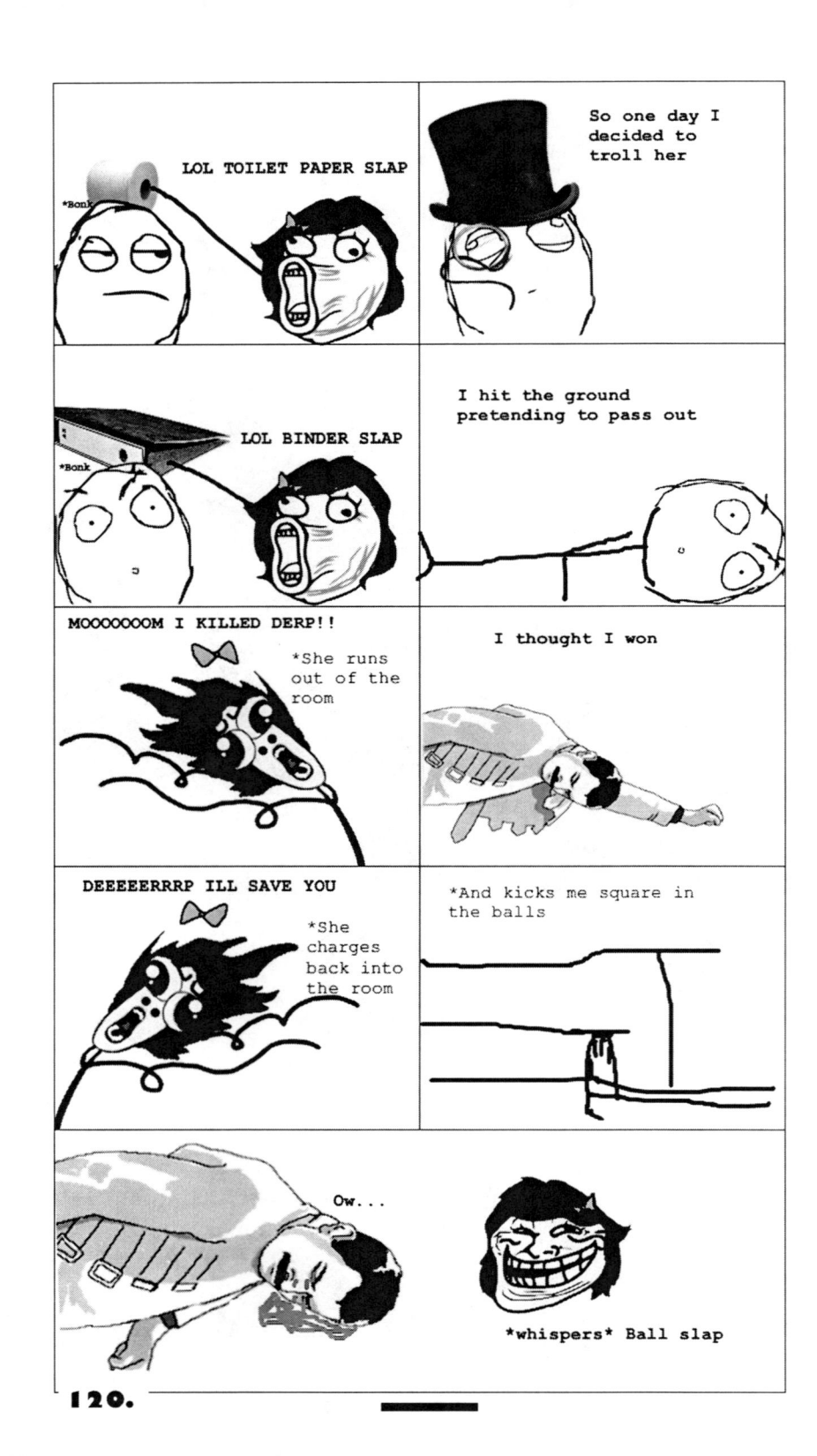

LOL TOILET PAPER SLAP *Bonk	So one day I decided to troll her
LOL BINDER SLAP *Bonk	I hit the ground pretending to pass out
MOOOOOOOM I KILLED DERP!! *She runs out of the room	I thought I won
DEEEEERRRP ILL SAVE YOU *She charges back into the room	*And kicks me square in the balls
Ow...	*whispers* Ball slap

*Derping down the street in New York City

*See pigeon down the block doing it's thing.

*Getting closer to Pigeon and it's not moving

Problem?

*Walk around Pigeon

Bitch

That pigeon just made me it's bitch.

You still want to marry me, even with my depression?

We'll deal with it together!

2 years later ...

I cheated, k thx bai

If it doesn't work out with him, I'll c.......

BANG
MURDER
MAN KILLS WIFE
R.I.P.
"It was worth it"

In the waiting room at the doctors office.
*me
*my mom
*nurse
Okay Derp, you can come back now so we can take a semen sample.
5 MINUTES LATER...

FAP
FAP
FAP
FAP
FAP
FAP
FAP
FAP
FAP
FAP
FAP
FAP
My mom knows I'm fapping
FAP
FAP
FAP
FAP
I'M THINKING
ABOUT MY MOM

le me, closing shop
after hard day of work
Press shutter key
* CluuuUNKk CluuNNKK*

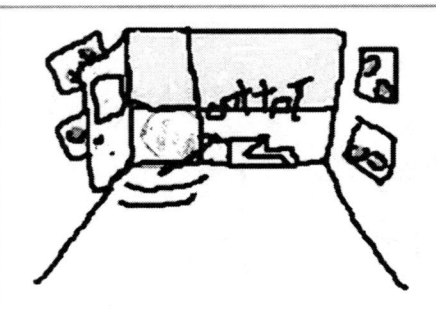

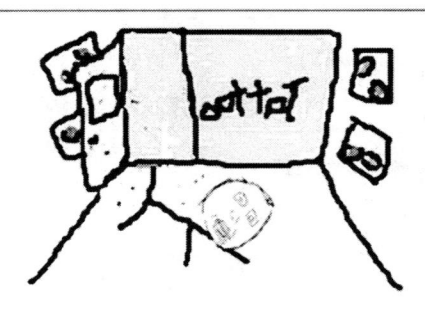

Are you guys still open?

---

me, hooking up with a girl I met online. Happens to be her birthday, so we go out with some of her friends

a lot of smooching and touching during the night

at one point, she looks at me and says: "Derp, I know we known each other for few hours, but I think I love you!

So, I fake a trip to the toilet and flee home!

NOTHING TO DO HERE

On my way home, I get a text from her: "You SOB, how could you leave me like that, I thought we had something special! I even wanted to share you with Herpette tonight!

I even wanted to share you with Herpette tonight!

How women see dancing:

How men see dancing:

125.

Looking through a drawer in my room for something I lost
"Hmm, an old birthday card. I wonder if there's money inside of it."
HoLy cow!
It's your birthday!
Have a MOO-gnificent one!
Love:
Gram-Gram
XOXO
No... Fucking... Way...
AAAAAAAAAAWWWWWW
YYYYYYEEEEEEEEEAAAAAAAAA

le older sister and mom derping around in the kitchen
le 10 year old me enters scene
le little brother
I think it's time we told Michael about Santa not being real.
Mom, kbakermemphis is right there!
Don't be silly. YOU don't STILL believe in SANTA CLAUS! Do you?
HELL NO
LOL
And That is How My Childhood Died

Panel 1: At the drive-up bank with Derpdog, mind elsewhere.

fucking loves her work

Panel 2: Awwww, your dog is sooooo cute. Here you go, you are all set.

Panel 3: OMNOMNOM

Panel 4: *(horrified face)*

Panel 5: Hello, this is the wireless broadband helpline, how can i help?

Yeah hi I just bought wireless internet and it's not working.

Panel 6: Okay, can you go to your modem and tell me which lights are on or flashing and which are off.

What do you mean? Modem? What?

Panel 7: It's the box that you originally bought and plugged in. Are you sure you have one?

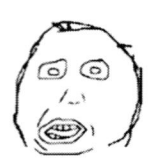

But...it's wireless, right? I just need to put the box I bought next to my computer, right?

Panel 8: *(Jackie Chan WTF face)*

128.

on skytrain, when suddenly a wild hot chick appears!
(trying not to stare)
(failing)
me
i should let this hot lady know i think she's hot - it's unexpected, and i could make her feel good about herself!
train stops at my station
hey! i have this sweater, too!
by the way, you look really hot.
turn to leave
bumps into someone entering the train
OH GOD THE DOORS ARE CLOSING
I CAN'T LEAVE
NOW WHAT?

8 year old me going to see Spider-Man at Wall-Mart
"OMG IT'S SPIDER-MAN"
GET YOUR PICTURE

After I got my picture I snuck away from my dad and followed SPIDER-MAN to the employee area then I saw this

"FUCKING KIDS! THEY ARE SO GOD DAMNED RETARDED! I'M PRETTY SURE ONE PISSED HIS PANTS!"

AND THAT IS HOW MY DREAMS WERE CRUSHED

ALSO HERE IS A PIC OF A PIC TO PROVE THIS IS A TRUE STORY

8 y/o Me --->
Penis buldge

My Thumb -->

click click click

damn.

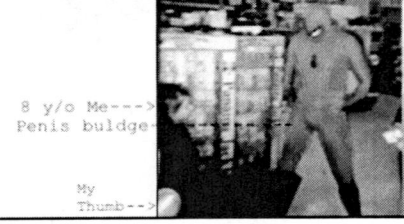

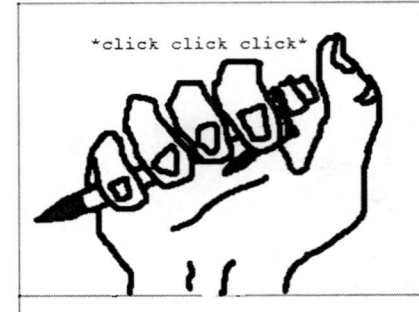

Hey melvin can i have some pencil lead

That's a common mistake. it's actually graphite.

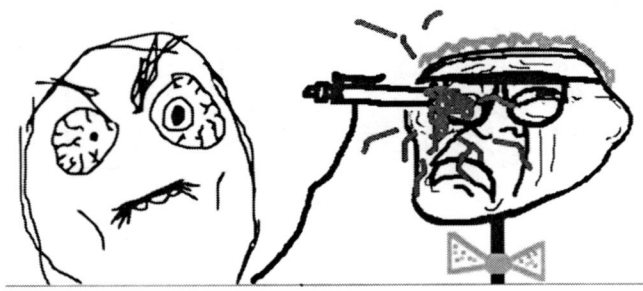

130.

Friend and i witness some serious road rage.
"Wow, i can smell the testosterone"
"Gross, how can you smell their semen?"
"What? No i said testosterone, thats not the same as semen"
"Yea it is, semen is another word for testosterone"
"What? No, semen is what you ejaculate. Testosterone is a hormone"
"Yea, semen is the hormone men have, like the way women have periods"
"Dude, thats like saying estrogen smells like your period"
"Estrogen does smell like your period, its fuckin gross"
derp

first ingredient:
bread
FFFFFFF
FFFFFFF
FFFFFF
FFFUU
UUUU
UUUU
UUUU
UUUU
UUUU-

Watching a movie with my parents
"Ah, shoot. The sex scene is coming up, better conveniently go to the bathroom..."
A FEW MOMENTS LATER
Hey son! We paused the movie for you!
... I think the good part is coming up!

working IT helpdesk at my school like a boss
IT Support
A hideous female appears carrying her laptop
IT Support
YOU NEED TO HELP ME FIX MY COMPUTER I HAVE LIKE A MILLION TROJAN SPYWARE SUPER VIRUSES AND EVERY TIME I TRY TO GO ON THE INTERNET IT SAYS SERVER NOT FOUND WHAT THE FUCK DOES THAT EVEN MEAN BUT I CAN'T GET TO MY WEBSITES WHERE I WATCH FREE TV SHOWS AND I HAVE TO SEE GREYS
Let's see that shit.

Mother of god...
POKER FACE
Server not found
Holy fucking 1998 what is this?!
POKER FACE
What the shit....
POINTER TRAILS!!!

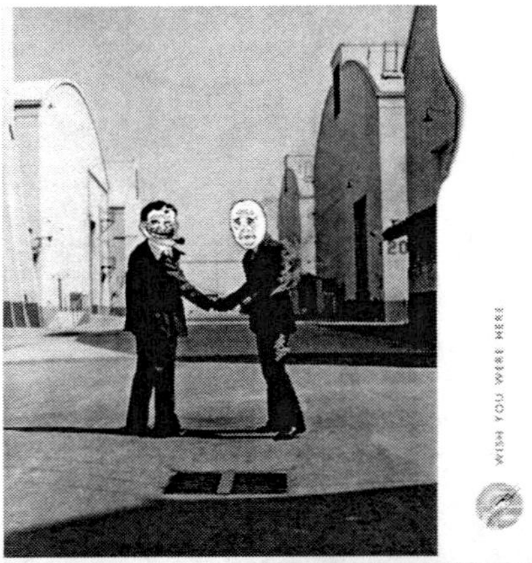
WISH YOU WERE HERE

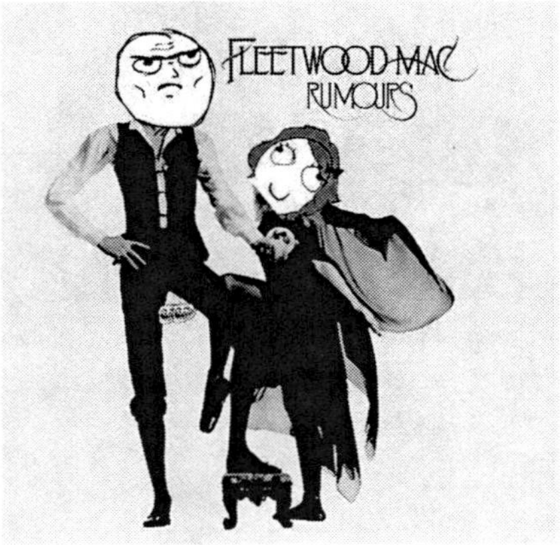
FLEETWOOD MAC
RUMOURS

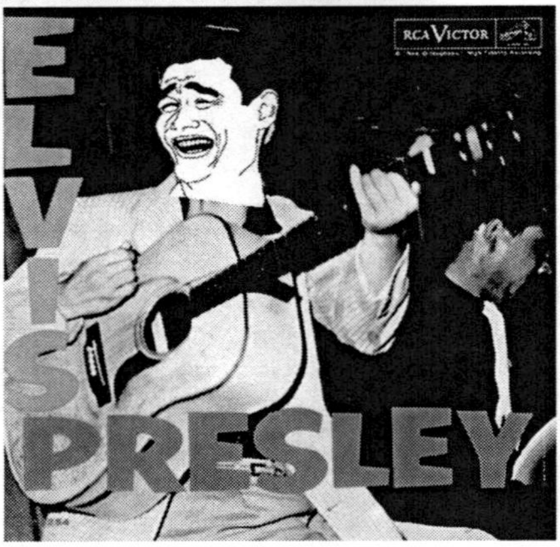
RCA VICTOR
ELVIS
PRESLEY

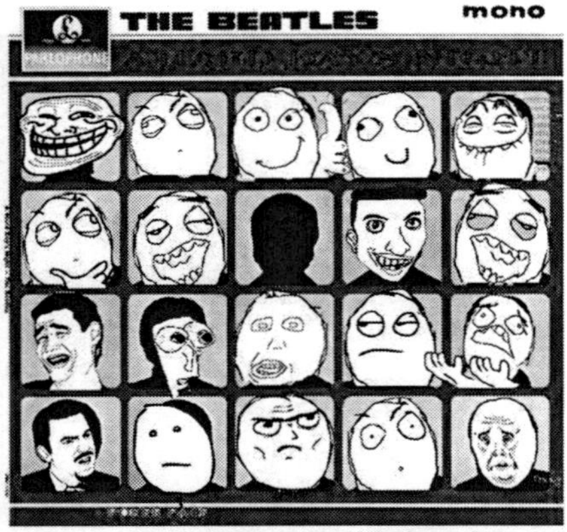
THE BEATLES
mono
PARLOPHONE

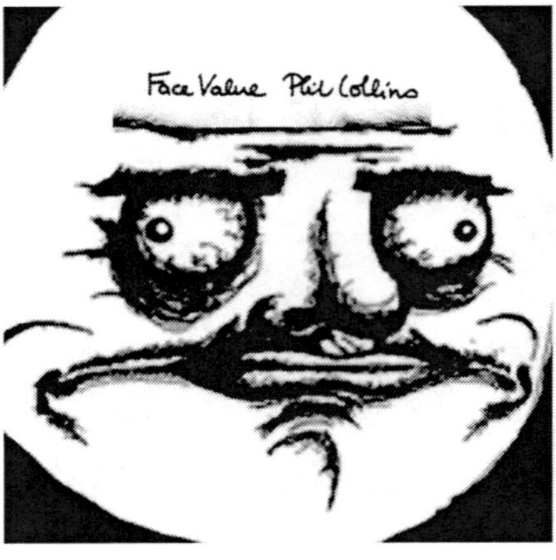
Face Value Phil Collins

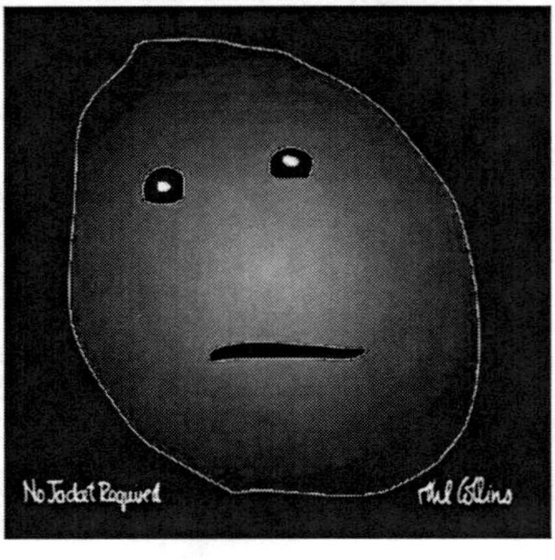
No Jacket Required
Phil Collins

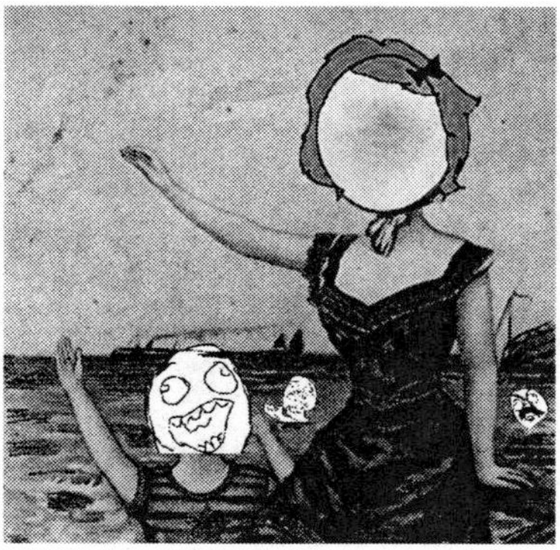

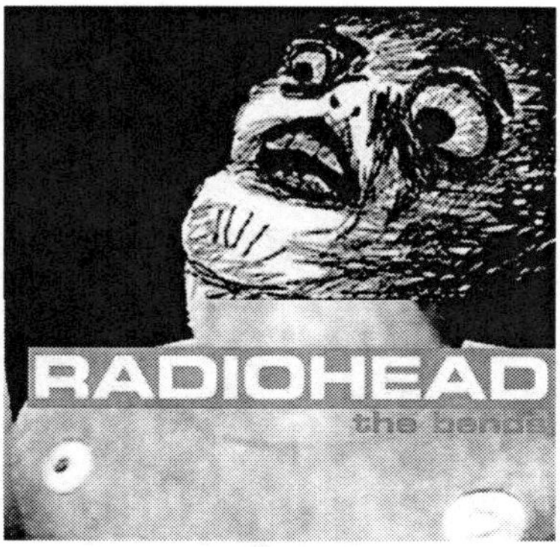
RADIOHEAD

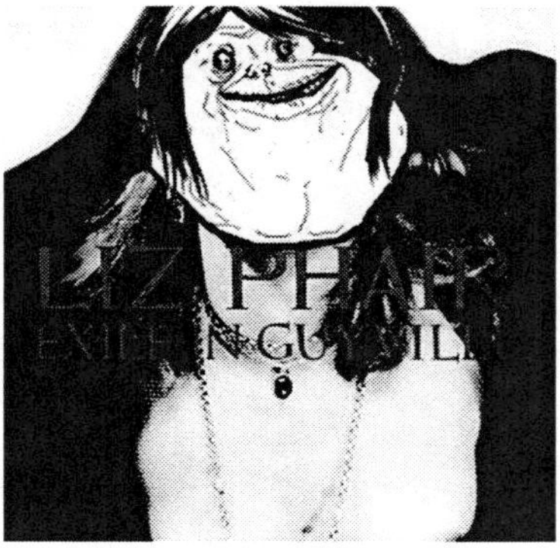

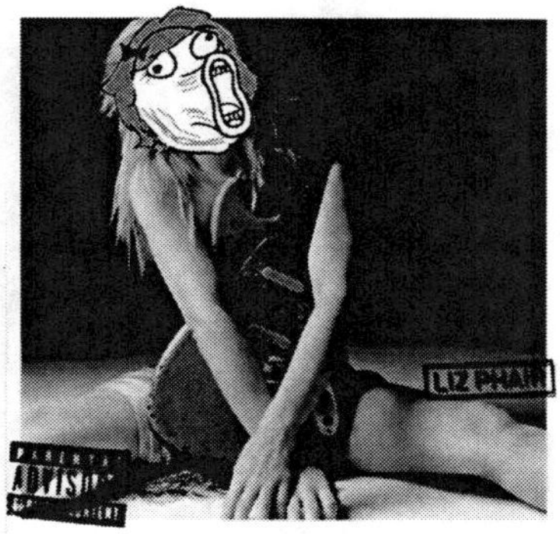

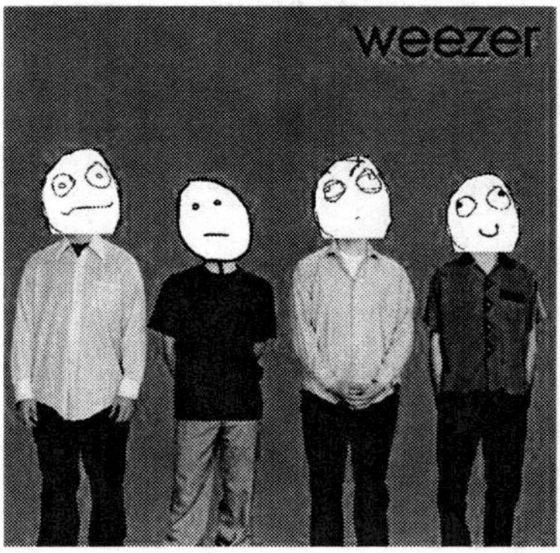
weezer

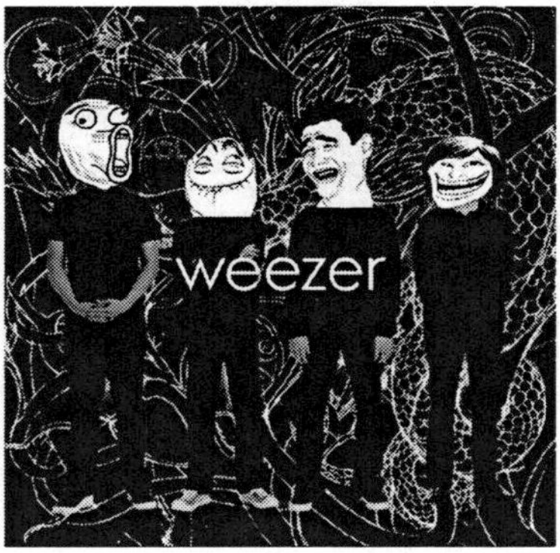
weezer

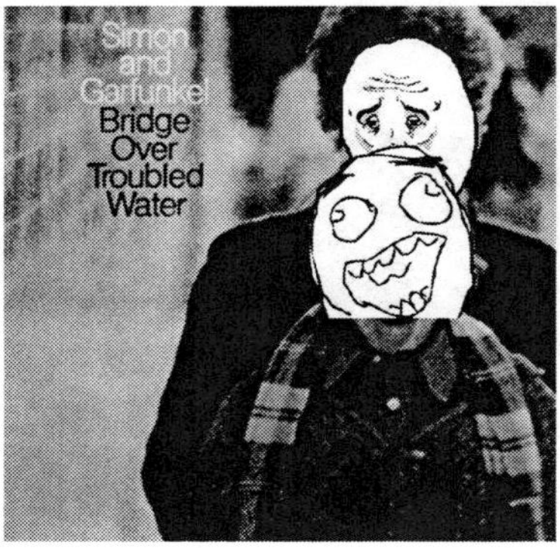
Simon
and
Garfunkel
Bridge
Over
Troubled
Water

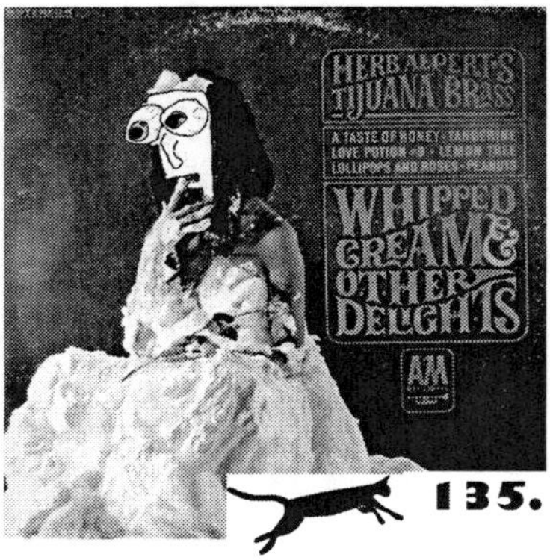
HERB ALPERT'S
TIJUANA BRASS
A TASTE OF HONEY · TANGERINE
LOVE POTION #9 · LEMON TREE
LOLLIPOPS AND ROSES · PEANUTS
WHIPPED
CREAM &
OTHER
DELIGHTS
A&M

DESCENDENTS

MILO GOES TO COLLEGE

136.

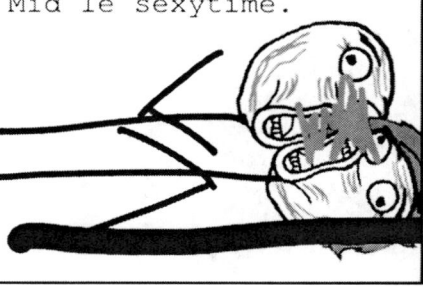

Sneezing. Ranked best to worst.	In a kleenex.
On your arm.	On your friend.
Mid piss.	Mid kiss.
Mid le sexytime.	

About to leave a party.

You aren't driving. You're completely pissed.

I'm not pissed at you. Derp might be, though.

Derp, why you pissed at my girlfriend?

Girlfriend? She's here?

He's not pissed. He's sad.

I mean piss drunk. You are piss drunk. You can't drive.

I can piss drunk. Want to see?

derpin' in the pool

push off pool wall

WOOOOSH

I AM A TORPEDO.

138.

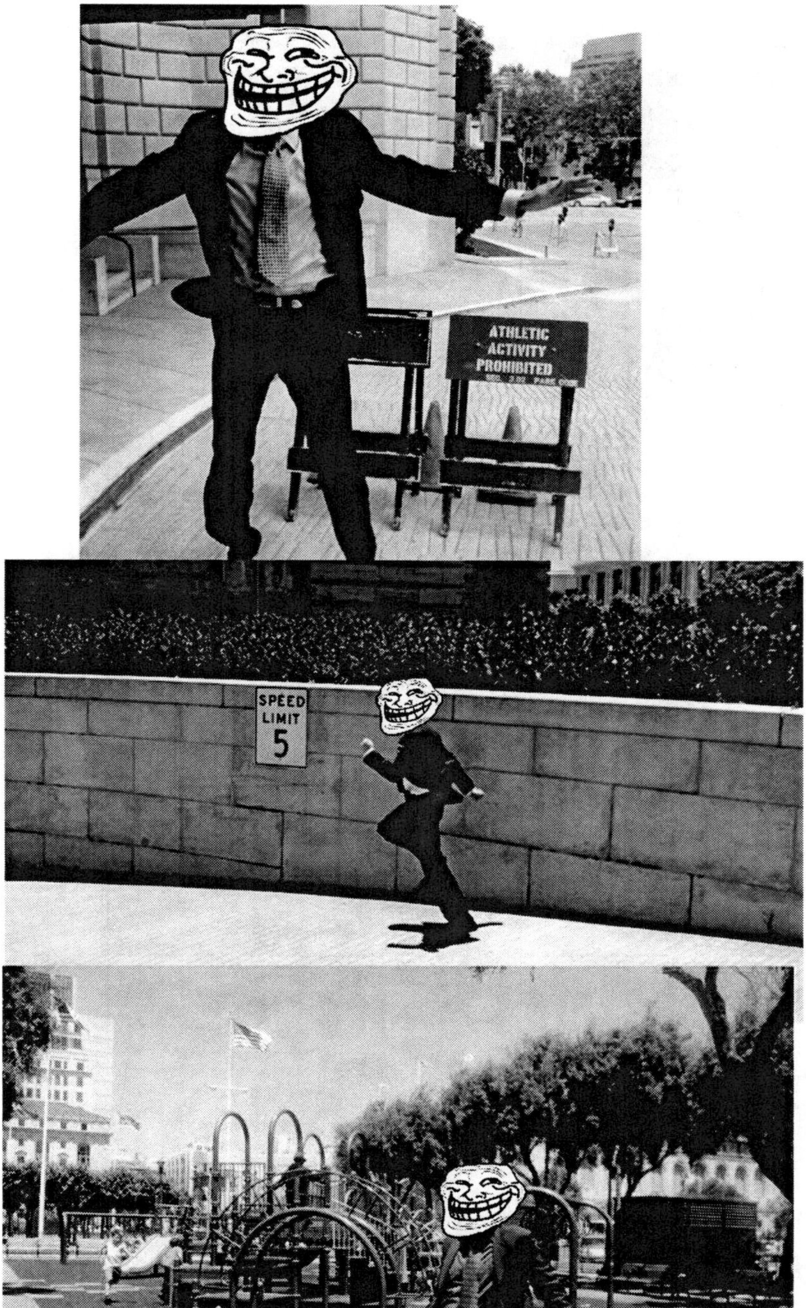
ATHLETIC
ACTIVITY
PROHIBITED
SPEED
LIMIT
5
NO ADULTS
ALLOWED UNLESS
ACCOMPANIED
BY CHILDREN

DO NOT
NTER
NO
LOITERING
POLICE
TAKE NOTICE
DO NOT
BLOCK
THIS DOOR

meow
scratch scratch
Hello kitty. Come in ^.^
frrrrr
15 seconds later....
Lemme out lol. Problem?
scratch
FFFFFFF
FFFFFFF
FFFFFF
FFFUU
UUUU
UUUU
UUUU
UUUU
UUUU-
OMFG, go out then.
15 seconds later...
Lemme in plz.
Problem?
FFFFFFF
FFFFFFF
FFFFFF
FFFUU
UUUU
UUUU
UUUU
UUUU
UUUU-

Casually doing homework one night	Don't notice my arm has been leaning on the spirals of my notebook for 30 minutes
Look at indent caused by spirals	I have **earned** my **stripes**

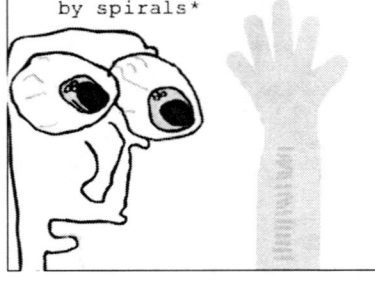

	- Here's your coffee, Sir.
	
	    Thank you! Say, does this road go to Annapolis?
	
	- Apple sauce?
	
	    Annapolis, is this the road to Annapolis...
	
	- Apple juice?
	
	    Annapolis. Annapolis, Maryland. This way?

- Apple Juice? You want Apple juice?
 	
    No, I'm sorry, I was just asking if Annapolis was this way...
 	
- Apple juice?
    Annapolis.
- Apple juice?
    Annapolis.
- Apple juice?
- Apple juice? You want?	

142.

Panel 1: me | guy eating mcdonalds

Panel 2: He gets up to leave, leaving the bag behind

Panel 3: Um, excuse me, do you mind not littering? There's a trash can right there.

Panel 4: It's not littering unless you leave it on the ground.

A few years ago I had an interview at a telephone company.

My father drove me to the interview. I had to read the map.

*perfectly drawn map

Unfortunately reading something while driving makes me sick.

We arrived at the company and I couldn't hold it anymore when I entered the lobby.

*lady at the reception

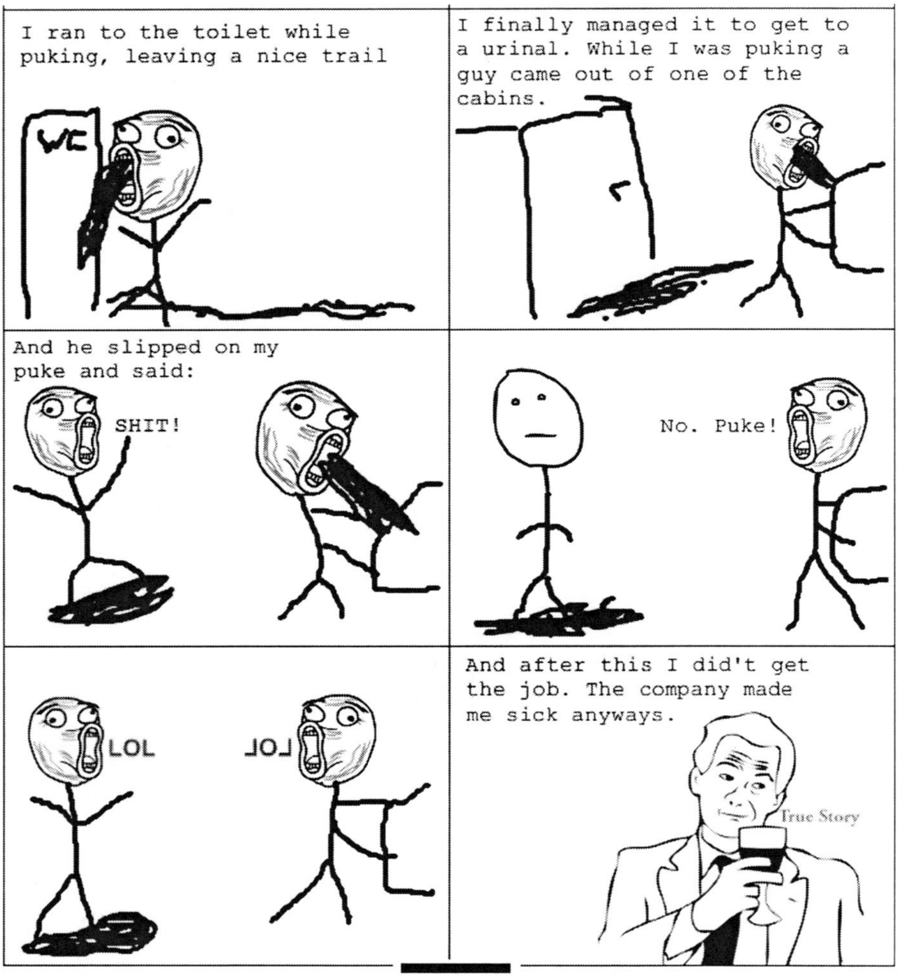
I ran to the toilet while puking, leaving a nice trail
WC
I finally managed it to get to a urinal. While I was puking a guy came out of one of the cabins.
And he slipped on my puke and said:
SHIT!
No. Puke!
LOL
LOL
And after this I did't get the job. The company made me sick anyways.
True Story

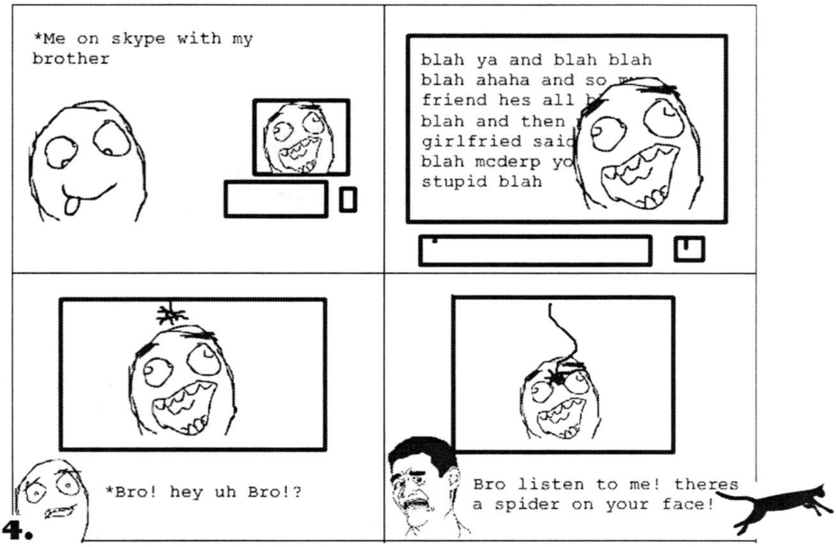
*Me on skype with my brother
blah ya and blah blah
blah ahaha and so m
friend hes all b
blah and then
girlfried said
blah mcderp yo
stupid blah
*Bro! hey uh Bro!?
Bro listen to me! theres a spider on your face!

*LE HUGE YAWN SUCKING IN SPIDER TOO

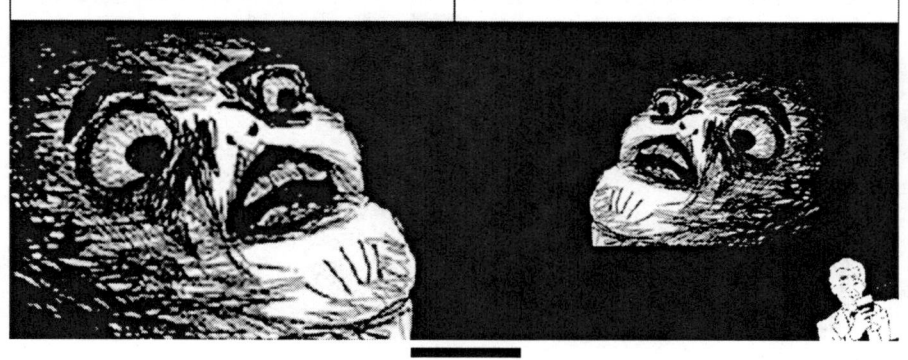

Its desperatly running trying to not be eaten

Swallows as a reflex

spider leg still twitching on his mouth

---

*Arguing with 1st grader in my class

GIVE ME BACK MY TOY CAR!

No, you threw it at a student so now it's mine

I'M SO MAD AT YOU!

You'll get it back at the end of the day

*Student reaches into eye

145.

*Pulls out a glass eye
*Student throws eyeball at me
WHAT THE FUCK IS GOING ON?

me and my buddy, hanging out
"hey dude, want a poke?"
"the fuck is a poke?"
"here, try it."
"so many wasted years..."

Getting drunk at a fair with a friend when..

..we decide to go ride the Enterprise.

What I ate/drank that evening:

So logically, I get sick and have to throw up (in the cup I'm holding - good drunk aim I guess).

My friend looks into the cup and in his drunk state he says: "Hey, it's pink, it looks like a milkshake. I dare you to drink that, I'll give you 50 CHF if you do it!"

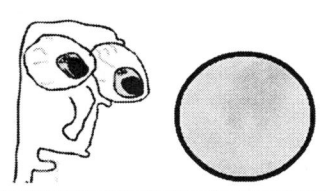

CHALLENGE ACCEPTED

The next morning:

"Wait..did I drink my puke yesterday? That's disgus..wait, did i get paid to do it??"

I REGRET NOTHING!

147.

*me, working like a retail slave.
When throughout the day, I keep getting customer after customer giving me shit so they can get discounts:
"they were mislabelled!!!"
"it was on the SALE rack!"
"CRYYYYYYYYY!!!!!!!!!!!!"
THOUSANDS OF TEARS LATER
*finally get home after the shittest day of work ever.
*chillin'. Watching TV
*tv
*today tonight is on
"......... encourage you to complain to staff so you can get great discounts....."
"encourage you to complain"
DAMN YOU "TODAY TONIGHT".

me shopping for new glasses
2 pair for $99
I know! I'll buy one regular pair and one creepy-old-man pair for my own amusement
One week later
destroyed glasses
At school
le hot girl
Wow your glasses are hilarious. i love them! Want to go for a coffee sometime?
Haters gonna hate

*Returning home from le best bike ride ever, listening to loud music
*In the back room
DISARM SYSTEM NOW!
BEEP
BEEP
BEEP
BEEP
BEEP
BEEP
*Bedroom, getting undressed, still listening to loud music
BEEP
BEEP
BEEP
BEEP
......
*BEEEEEEEEEEEEEEEEEEEEEEE
EEEEEEEEEEEEEEEEEEEEEEEEE
EEEEEEEEEEEEEEEEEEEEEEEEE
EEEEEEEEEEEEEEEEEEEEEEEEE
EEEEEEEEEEEEEEEEEEEEEEEEE
EEEEEEEEEEEEEEEEEEEEEEEEE

NEVER GONNA GIVE YOU UP NEVER GONNA LET YOU DOWN
THIS IS THE POLICE! OPEN THE DOOR!
NEVER GONNA RUN AROUND AND DESERT YOU
My gun is bigger
FFFFFFF FFFFFFF FFFFFF FFFUU UUUU UUUU UUUU UUUU UUUU-
True Story

*eating glodfish like a bau5

*when i notice the ingredients

does it really say...

MADE WITH SMILES

Hey baby, how many girls have you had sex with?

Yeah, let's not go there.

Why not? I want to know!

I'd just rather not go into it. I don't want to know how many people you've been with.

151.

FIVE! Now you have to tell me how many you've been with!
FINE! THREE...
Oh, that's not bad at all! I thought that it was going to be a lot mo-
...times as many people as you.
FFFFFFF
FFFFFF
F
FFFUU
UUUU
UUUU
UUU
UUUU
UUUU-

Little brother and dad
dad, what was the British Invasion?
It was when a bunch of rock bands from the UK came to the US. Like the Beatles.
me
and the Rolling Stones
and the Kinks

and the Animals	And the Troggs
the who?	Ya, them too.

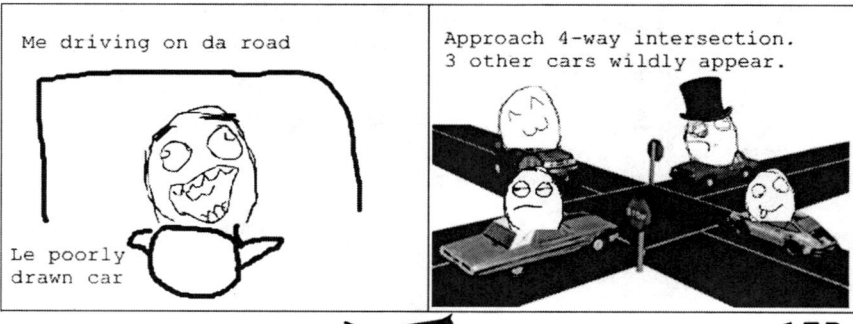

Me driving on da road

Le poorly drawn car

Approach 4-way intersection. 3 other cars wildly appear.

IT'S TIME.
le standoff
le wind
le wave the others on
True Story

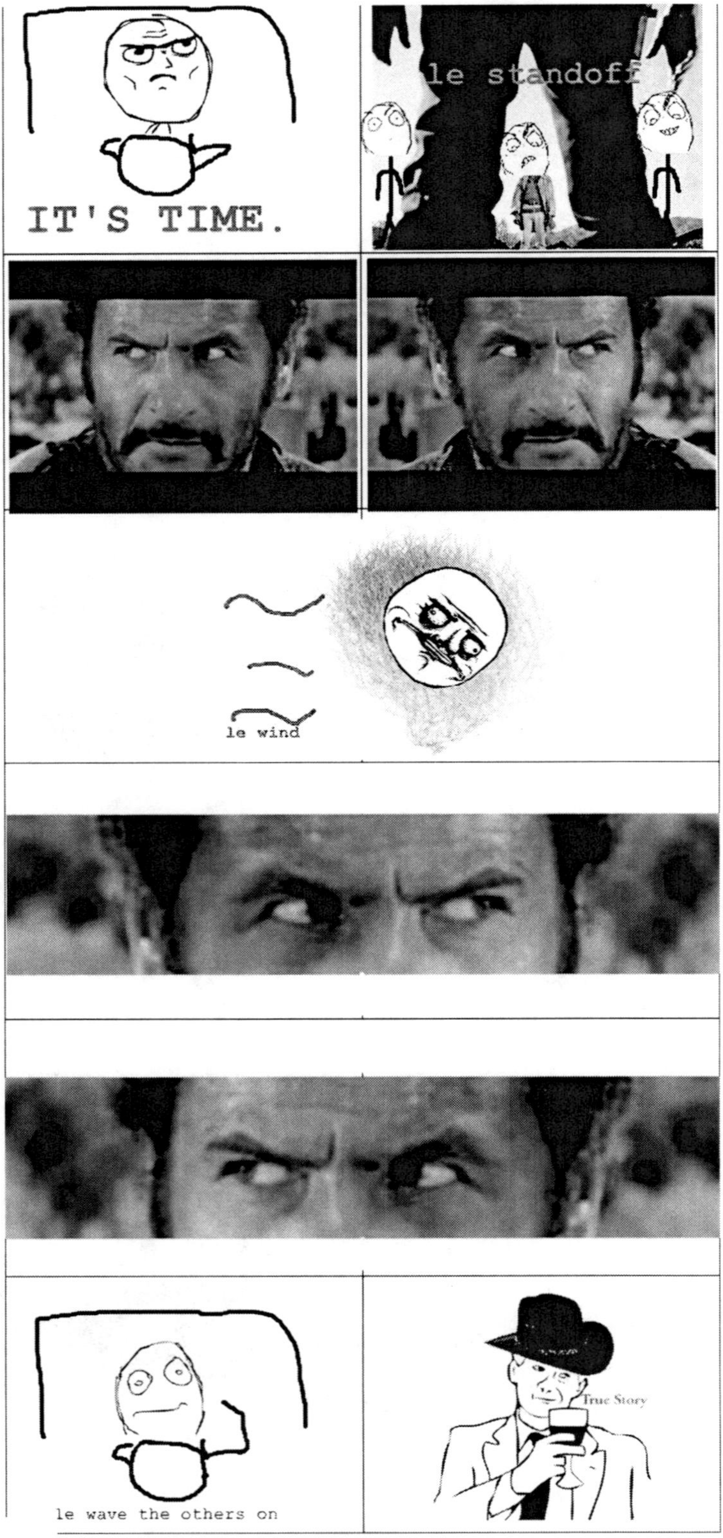

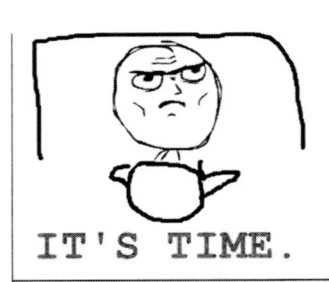

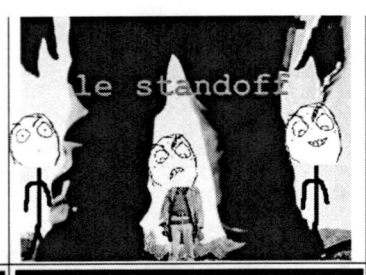

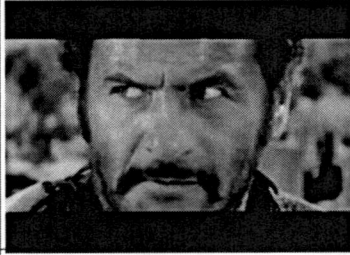

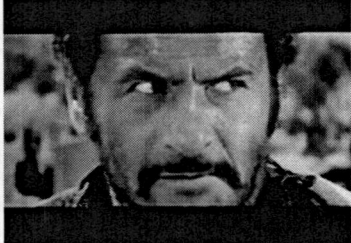

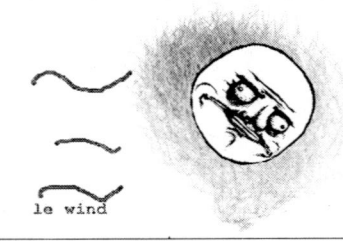

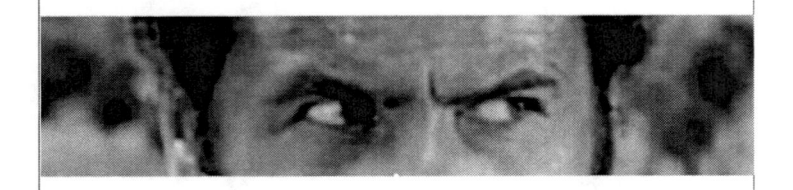

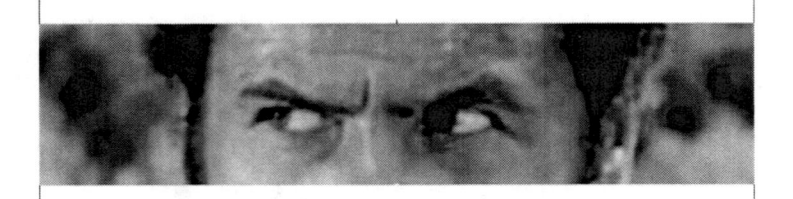

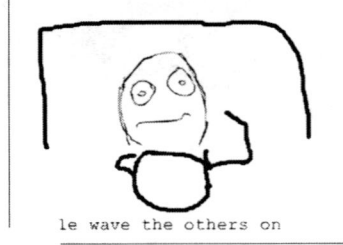

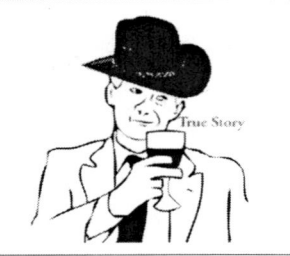

Panel 1: *le me watching Saving Private Ryan

Panel 2: *le gets hit in the helmet with bullet

Panel 3: *takes off helmet in shock

Panel 1: Pesticides are too harmful to the environment

Panel 2: They should use something else to kill mosquitos, like dropping spiders from the sky or something

Panel 3: Spiders? Falling from the sky?

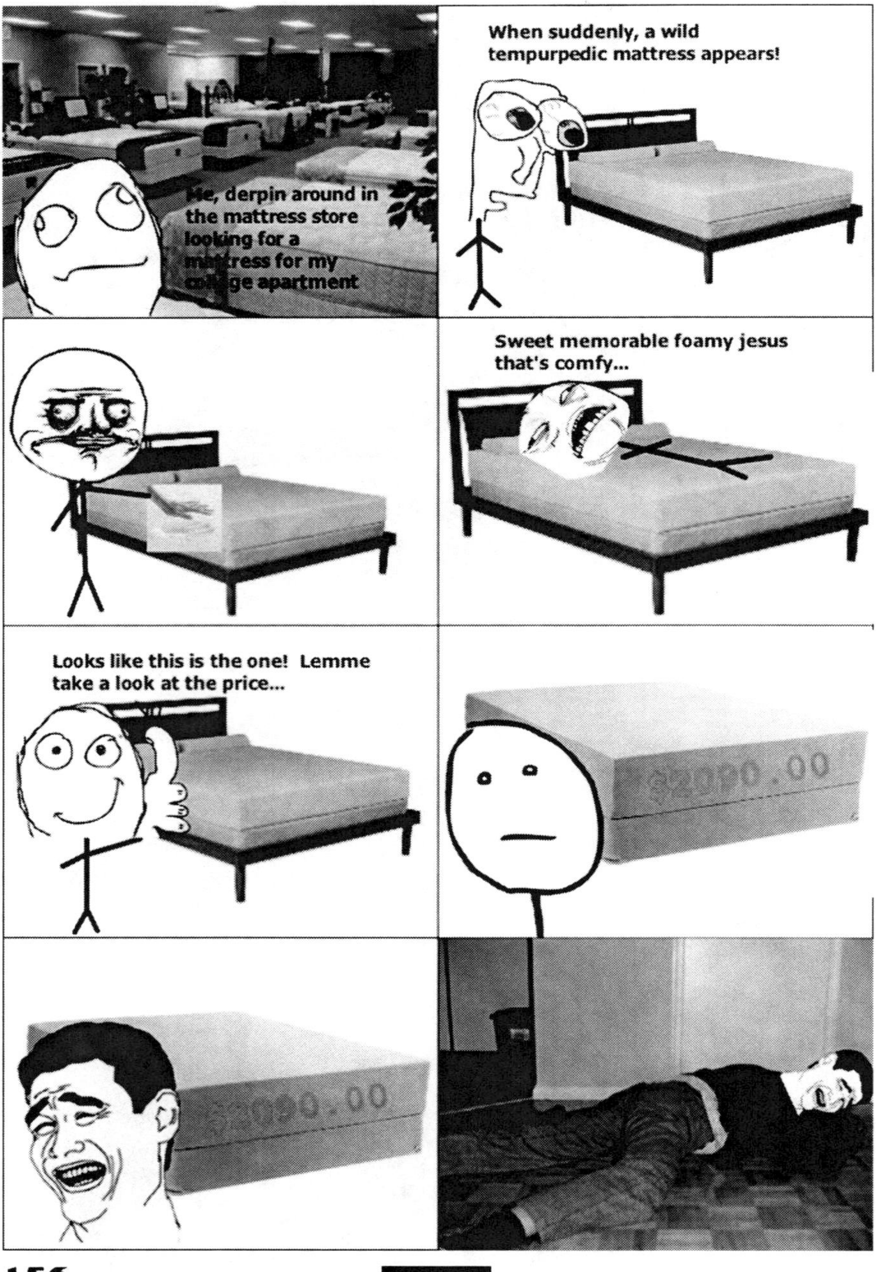
Me, derpin around in the mattress store looking for a mattress for my college apartment
When suddenly, a wild tempurpedic mattress appears!
Sweet memorable foamy jesus that's comfy...
Looks like this is the one! Lemme take a look at the price...

In care after going to a HS dance with my buddies.

One of my buddy's parents is driving us home and his mom asks us how the dance was.

- so how was the dance boys? meet any cute girls?

The son of the parents driving car

Ya mom! There was this one chick there that me and derp (me) wanted to dance with and ask out but we figured we better not, to be fair to each other.

Well that's nice of you boys but you could have just split her half and half, one gets the top of her and the other gets the bottom.

Retarded me

Haha, I would totally just take the bottom half! It's the only good part.

POKER FACE

What in the fuck did I just say?

157.

Honey, have you seen my broom?	Why? Are you going somewhere?
FFFFFFF FFFFFF FFFF FFUU UUU UUU UU UUU UUUU-	

Saturday Morning Cocoa Puffs	Pokemon all day

I haven't aged in ten years

158.

I have no money again!
Solid!
Except for this change
ive been collecting for
many years..
actual jar much larger
let's cash this bitch
yepppppppp
bank.
wussup fresh,
how can
I help
you today?
BANK OF
DERP
I need this
change
counted please!
quite a
load you've
got
BANK OF
DERP
be back in a
bit!
BANK OF
DERP
3000
YEARS
LATER
well
youre all set
BANK OF
DERP

there were also some.. foreign coins.. in.. your jar.

here ya go..

bag of foreign coins

alright thanks.

BANK OF DERP

bank.

160.

ASIAN CONSPIRACY

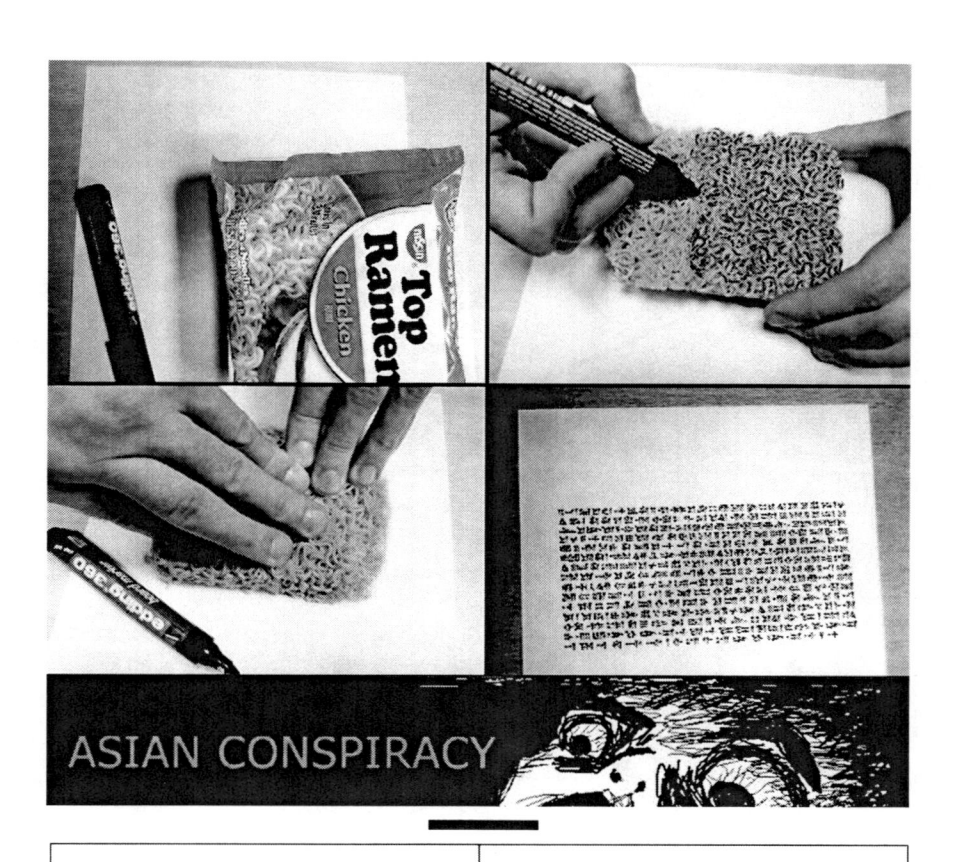

"Ha! Found my old fake moustache. Wonder if it still works..."

"Hey Derpette!"

"Um do I know you?"

NOT BAD

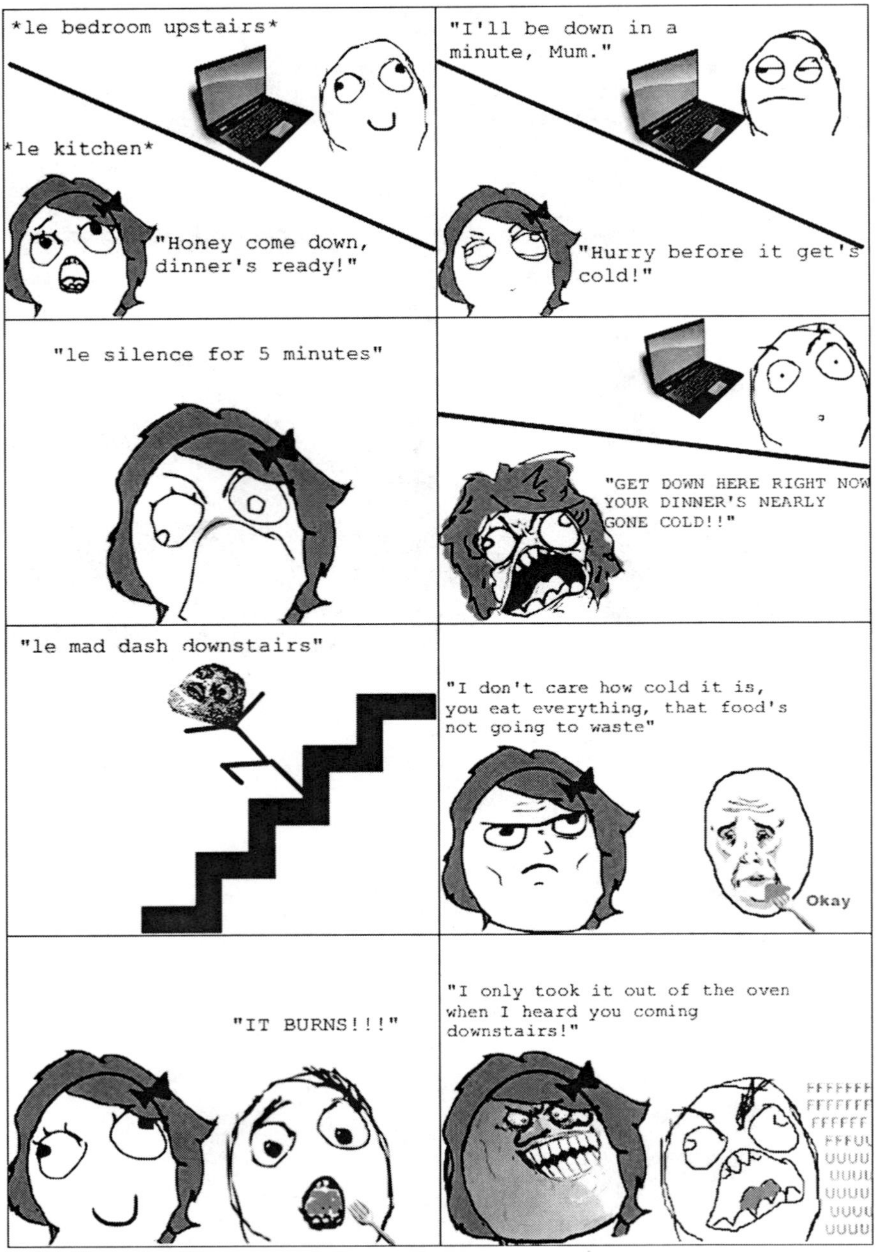
le bedroom upstairs
le kitchen
"Honey come down, dinner's ready!"
"I'll be down in a minute, Mum."
"Hurry before it get's cold!"
"le silence for 5 minutes"
"GET DOWN HERE RIGHT NOW YOUR DINNER'S NEARLY GONE COLD!!"
"le mad dash downstairs"
"I don't care how cold it is, you eat everything, that food's not going to waste"
Okay
"IT BURNS!!!"
"I only took it out of the oven when I heard you coming downstairs!"
FFFFFFF FFFFFFF FFFFFF FFFUU UUUU UUUU UUUU UUUU UUUU

"knit-knit" "knit-knit" "knit-knit" "knit-knit" "knit-knit" "knit-knit" "knit-knit" "knit-knit"

I'm worried about my son...

...mmm

I read an article on the importance of a strong male role model in a young boy's life. You know, his father left us before he was even born...

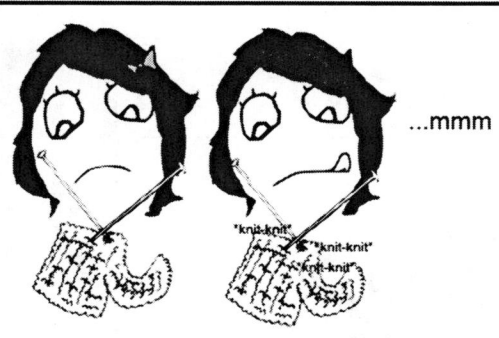

...mmm

...and so I worry about him!

All he does is sit in there playing his "mario box" all day long. Where is he going to find a father figure?

...mmm

knit- knit- knit-

163.

PEPPY
Never give up.
Trust your instincts.

snacking on chex mix when suddenly...

chex with excess seasoning detected!

sweet hypertension that's salty

164.

*me
6:00
Holy crap, forgot about that 20page report due for 11am today
7:00
8:00
9:00
10:00
10:30
All this work and ive only done 4 pages! I'm never gonna make it
Insert 16 blank pages behind 4 pages of work and staple together
tear out all blank pages, purposely leaving the corners still under staple.
Drop in Homework Box
rip
One Eternity Later
*teacher
Herp derp, it seems someone has stolen part of your homework, have a weeks extension if you deleted the file
What kind of sick person steals homework? ...yes...deleted...
*me
AAAAAAAAAWWWWWW
SUN
TUE
WED
THU
YYYYYEEEEEEEEAAAAAAAAA

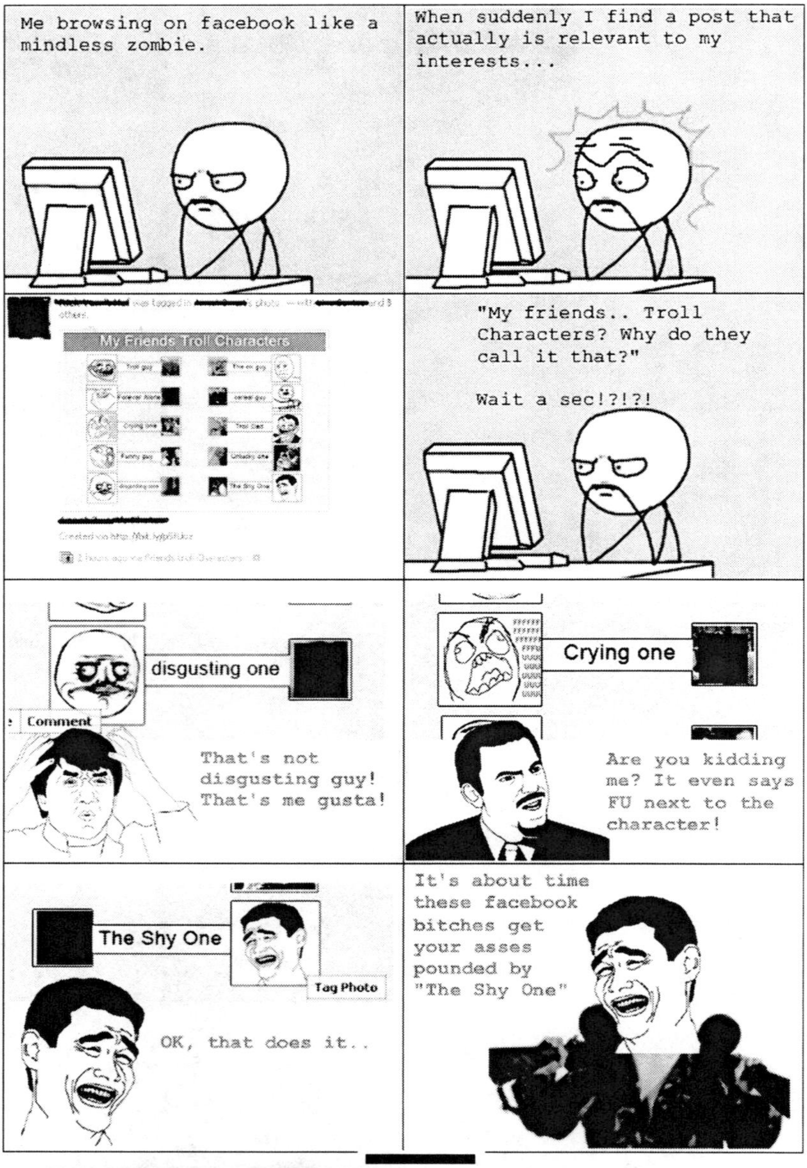
Me browsing on facebook like a mindless zombie.
When suddenly I find a post that actually is relevant to my interests...
My Friends Troll Characters
"My friends.. Troll Characters? Why do they call it that?"
Wait a sec!?!?!
disgusting one
Comment
That's not disgusting guy! That's me gusta!
Crying one
Are you kidding me? It even says FU next to the character!
The Shy One
Tag Photo
OK, that does it..
It's about time these facebook bitches get your asses pounded by "The Shy One"

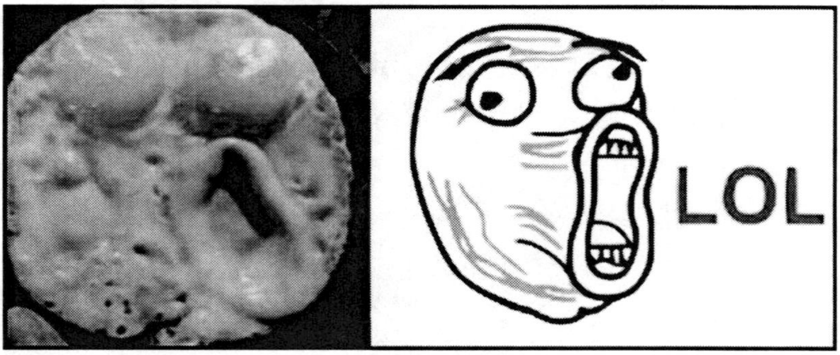
LOL

me just walking and derping along
suddenly see a female in the distance walking towards me
"I can't tell if she's hot or not.."
15m away
"Mmm yeah I think she actually might be."
10m away
"Yeah she's a babe. And she's totally checking me out."
5m away
"..."
1m away
TIME TO UPGRADE MY CONTACT LENSES!!!
*le me in 4th grade
Okay class! Today we are going to be going over the questions on the homework
*le teacher

*me

eh, okay nothing too special just another day at school

and if you answer the question correctly - you get a jolly rancher!

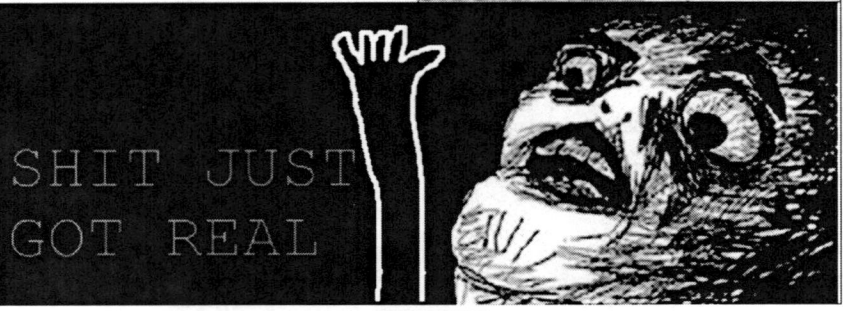

SHIT JUST GOT REAL

le me, bored as fuck so I decide to randomly search for 'weird food' on Google Images

"What the...?!"

"It actually might be worth a try..."

* le order Giant toasted ants online *

a few days later the ants arrive

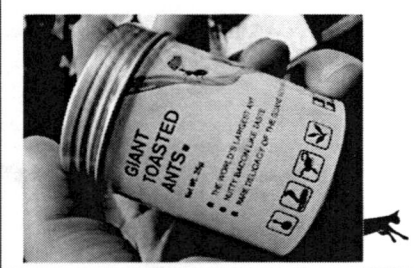

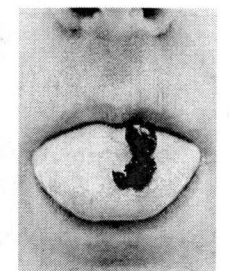

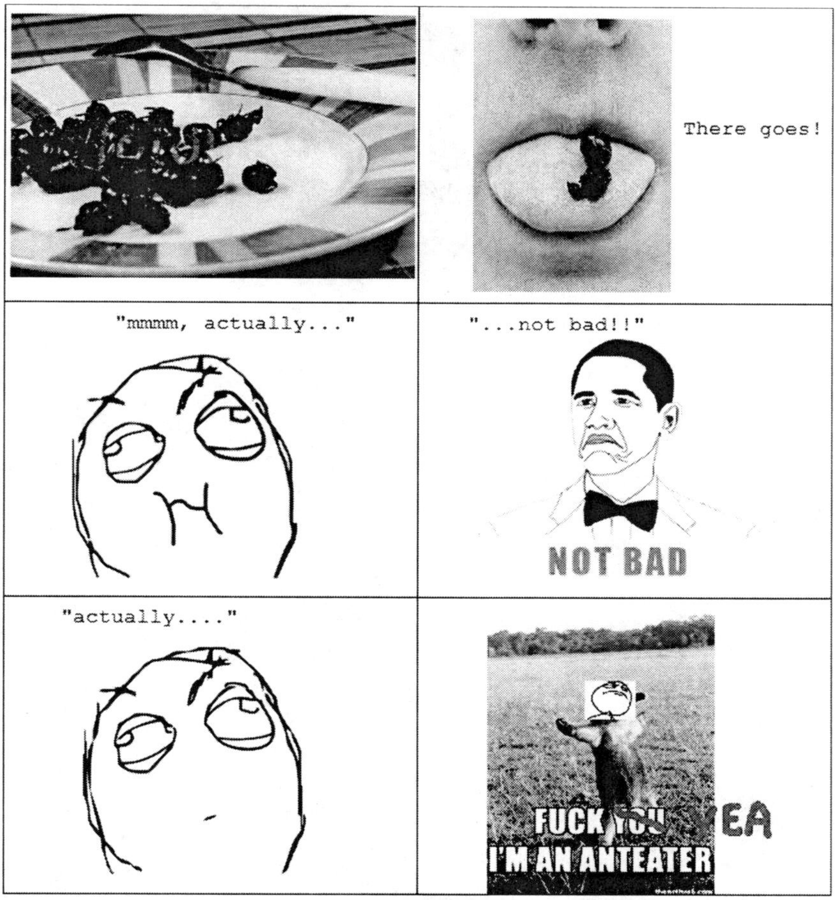

There goes!

"mmmm, actually..."

"...not bad!!"

NOT BAD

"actually...."

FUCK YEA
I'M AN ANTEATER

here you go son, happy 6th birthday

ferociously opening le present

Thanks!

169.

20 years LATER...
at 26th birthday in front of couple of friends

Here you go son, happy 26th birthday. I kept this for you in the attic for 15 years...

Wow, thanks mom, what can this be?

---

*le 6 year old me watching people hang-gliding on tv.

way too much sugar

I MUST HANG GLIDE!

*le begging my mom to let me hang glide.

I'm on the phone! Yes, whatever, Yes, GO!

*not even listening

YEEEESSSSSSSS, she approves! Now to get the equipment necessary!

170.

Hmmm, but I don't have a hang glider..
*LE RATIOS
*le kite
CLOSE ENOUGH!
*on le roof
FFFFFFFFFF
FFFFFFFFFF
FFFFFFFFFF
FFFFUUUUUU
UUUUUUUUUU
UUUUUUUUUU
UUUUUUUUUU
UUUUUUUUUU
UUUUUUUUU
PROBLEM?
*le broken legs
*month after getting casts off.
Coke
Coke
Coke
Coke
MARY POPPINS
OF COURSE...

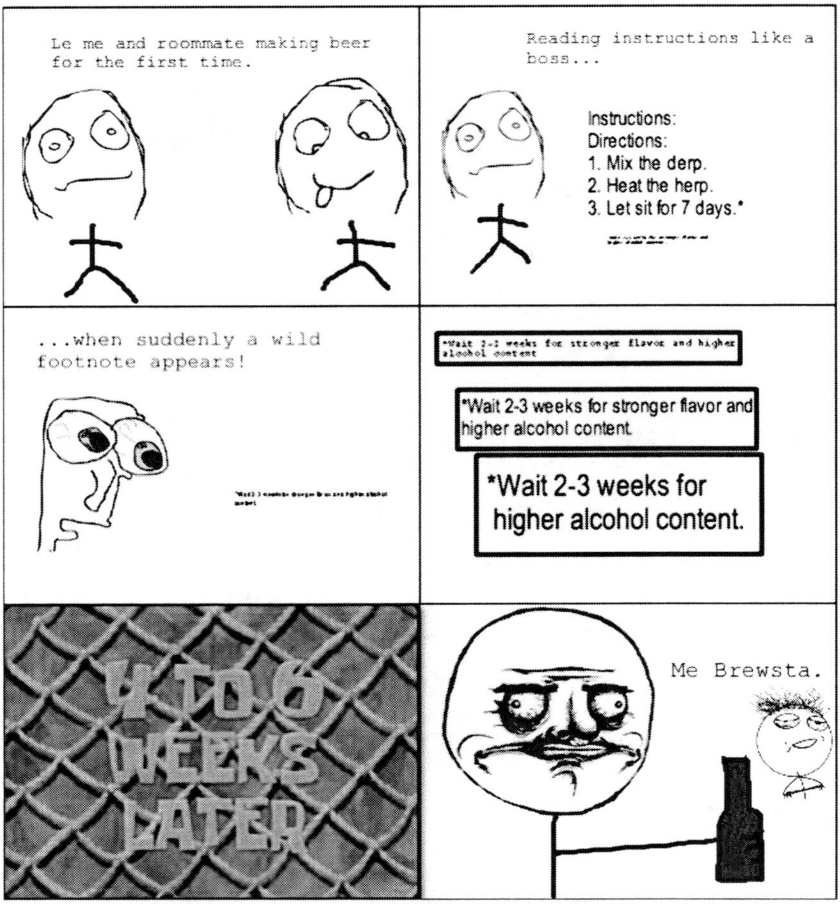

Le me and roommate making beer for the first time.
Reading instructions like a boss...
Instructions:
Directions:
1. Mix the derp.
2. Heat the herp.
3. Let sit for 7 days.*
...when suddenly a wild footnote appears!
*Wait 2-3 weeks for stronger flavor and higher alcohol content
*Wait 2-3 weeks for stronger flavor and higher alcohol content.
*Wait 2-3 weeks for higher alcohol content.
4 TO 6 WEEKS LATER
Me Brewsta.

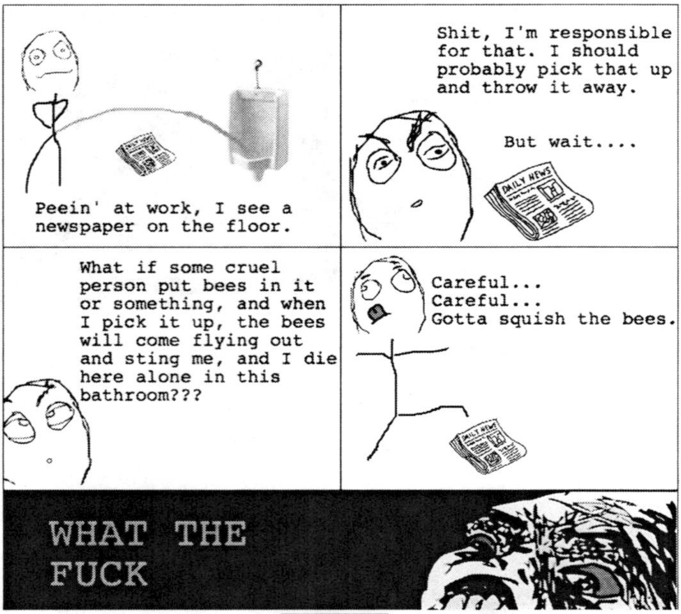

Peein' at work, I see a newspaper on the floor.
Shit, I'm responsible for that. I should probably pick that up and throw it away.
But wait....
DAILY NEWS
What if some cruel person put bees in it or something, and when I pick it up, the bees will come flying out and sting me, and I die here alone in this bathroom???
Careful...
Careful...
Gotta squish the bees.
WHAT THE FUCK

Me, playing with LEGO bricks. Probably building something fucking awesome.
Notices the missing piece
That's okay! I'll just sift through the massive box in front of me! It's bound to be in there somewhere!
I'll just dump it all.
CHALLENGE ACCEPTED
A FEW MOMENTS LATER
Found it!
Wait a damn minute...

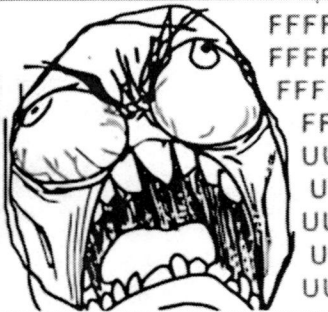

Buying le two items at Walgreens.

Clerk bags item.

"No bag for me today!"

Throws unused bag in trash.

174.

MENS
Going to Men's room
Dude already there, okay
plenty of room
MENS

*playing some CoD4
with friends over
Xbox live*
*Get put on
opposite team
as friends*

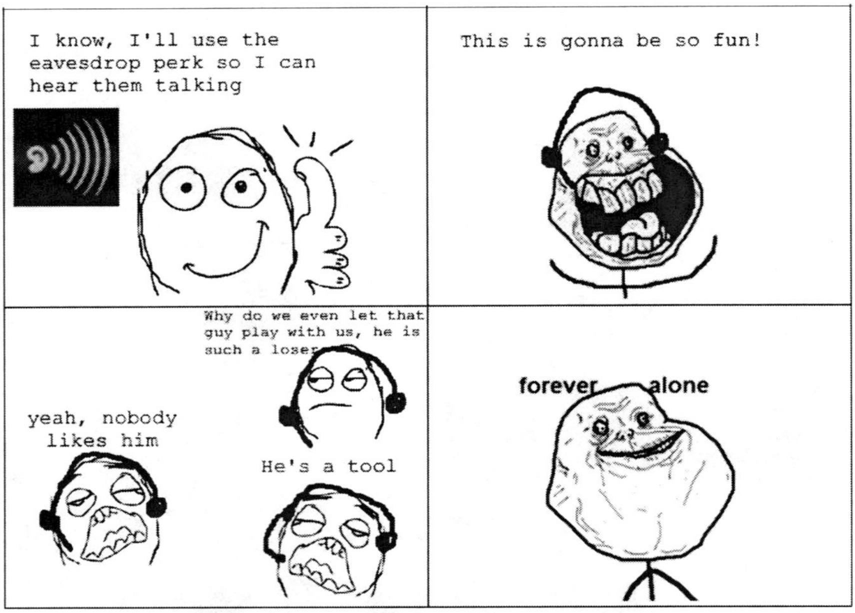
I know, I'll use the eavesdrop perk so I can hear them talking
This is gonna be so fun!
Why do we even let that guy play with us, he is such a loser
yeah, nobody likes him
He's a tool
forever alone

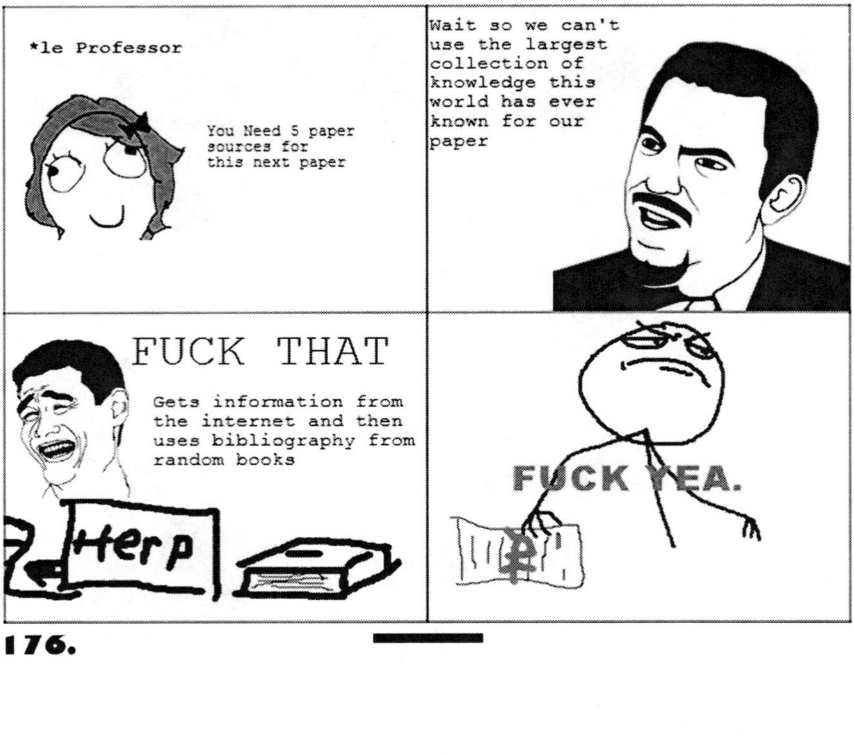
*le Professor
You Need 5 paper sources for this next paper
Wait so we can't use the largest collection of knowledge this world has ever known for our paper
FUCK THAT
Gets information from the internet and then uses bibliography from random books
Herp
FUCK YEA.

My girlfriend talks in her sleep, sometimes I mess with her to see what she says.
ZzZz
Hey Derpette, what's my favorite color?
Green.
Hey Derpette... what's Richard Nixon's favorite color?
ZzZz
Peach Mint
...
IM-Peach Mint
Impeach...
ZzZz
ZzZz
LOL

THE NEVERENDING CYCLE OF CHIPS & SALSA
AT THE GROCERY STORE...
AAAAAAAAAWWWWWW
YYYYYYEEEEEEEEAAAAAAAAA
BACK AT HOME....
OM NOM NOM NOM NOM NOM NOM NOM NOM NO
SALSA RUNS OUT...
BAG OF CHIPS STILL HALF FULL.
OM NOM NOM NOM NOM NOM NOM NOM NOM NO
RUN OUT OF CHIPS...
LOTS OF SALSA LEFT...
OM NOM NOM NOM NOM NOM NOM NOM NOM NO

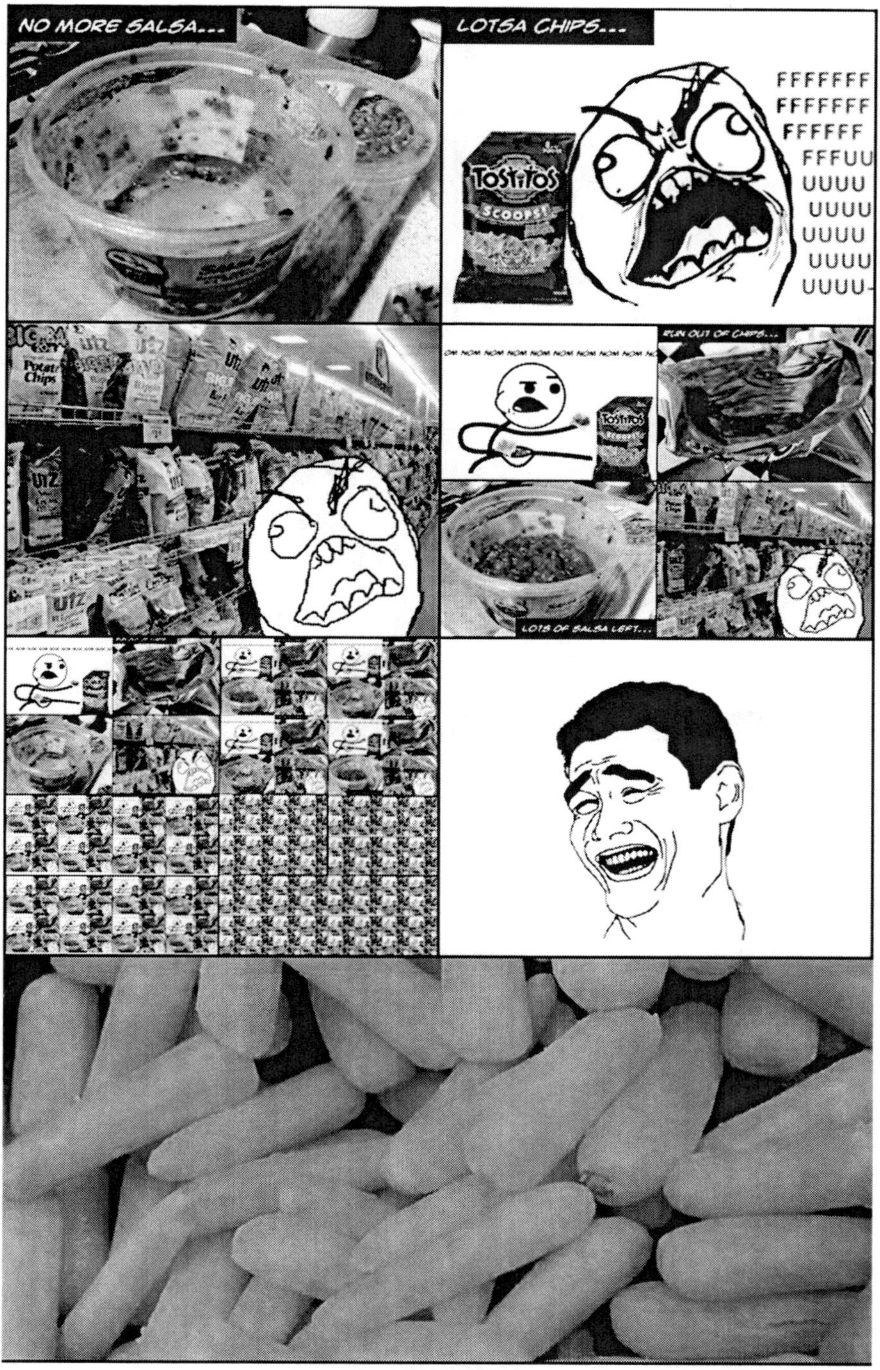
NO MORE SALSA...
LOTSA CHIPS...
FFFFFFF
FFFFFFF
FFFFFF
FFFUU
UUUU
UUUU
UUUU
UUUU
UUUU-
OM NOM NOM NOM NOM NOM NOM NOM NOM N
RUN OUT OF CHIPS...
LOTS OF SALSA LEFT...

Me! (7)	Older Sister (9)	Did you ever see daddies movies? The ones where the boy puts his thingy in the girls thinggy?
Daddy said we should never watch those movies.	We should try that. It looked like it felt good.	
CHALLENGE CONSIDERED	**CHALLENGE ACCEPTED**	
Attempted prepubecent sexytimes. *FAP FAP FAP*	INSTANTLY THROW UP.	

180.

I HAD SEX WITH MY SISTER WHEN I WAS 7!

I HATE THAT BITCH! .... AND IM GAY! THIS EXPLAINS SO MUCH!

It's yummy!!!!

It's yummy!!!!

It's yu....

Oh my gooooooooooooood!!!!!

*My husband and me at Wendy's. He has been awake for 36 hours and we have been moving and cleaning all day.

*I give him the sour cream packet for my potato, out of habit.

*30 seconds later, he's sucking on the packet with a blank stare on his face.

"Herper, I was going to give you my potato skin! Why don't you save the sour cream for that?"

"Indeed. How barbaric of me."

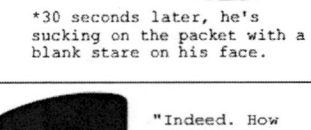

"Here you go, Herper! One potato skin!"

*Proceeds to fill the potato skin with vanilla frosty.

"Yes, quite."

"The hell....?"

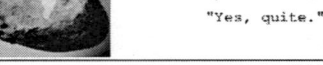

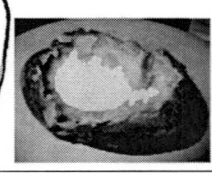

182.

REDTUBE VIDEO
REDTUBE VIDEO
*LE SWIPE
can't find remote...
OMG! WTF! HOW THIS SHIT GET ON!
HONEY ! CHANGE THE CHANNEL NOW!!!
OH OH OH! AAHHH YA! OH OH OH!
OMMG!FEELS SOO GOOD! AAHHH!!!!

Where am I?
I am being cooked..!
What can I do?
I don't know what to do!
However,no problem if I'm delicious.

le changing in car after to work to go on a date	Woman Driver (reversing to park) sorry I hit your car and damaged the front of it.
Me : Well we're going to have to call the NYPD for a report, I won't pay for this out of pocket. Girl : No, this is not my car my bf will kill me. *SHE SPEEDS AWAY*	*Me thinking : WTF now.. I have her plate number but no proof.
	* A WILD CRACKHEAD APPEARS* Random Crackhead : dude I saw everything, and I'll be glad to back you up when the police arrive, but first I have.. to.. uhh.. meet someone.. POKER FACE
Me : thanks man.. I appreciate it, hurry back please.	* POlice Arrive* NYPD : I see the, damage but you have no proof and you stated to 911 you had a witness which is not here. We'll take the report but something is not right and we're going to report that also.

184.

Me : no the guy said he'd be right back.. I swear!! * Police are about to drive away..	HE APPEARS from other side of the block
* Le crackhead explains EVERYTHING and then drops THE BOMB* Crackhead : Also, the lady who hit him, is now parked down this same block! I can show you!!!	Police : Lets walk there and see if this all checks out. * WE SPOT THE CAR AND PROCEED*
Police : thats the exact car you described and the lady you described.. this checks out.. And for you lady.. Here's 2 summons and I need all your info to put on this report so this guy gets his car fixed.	FUCK YEA. * *Hand the druggy 20$ for all his help and he's forever greatful WIN WIN*

185.

Its a Boy!	First steps...
	Middle-school **One Eternity Later**
Gonna have to keep them on for a little longer... Orthodontist*	High school **MUCH MUCH LATER....**
blah blah blah blah blah "JUST FREINDS" blah blah...	

186.

EVENTUALLY...
Nick.com
That will be 855 dollars please...
college books*
Now Broke...
Just for this...
A FEW MOMENTS LATER
Im pregnant...
LOL

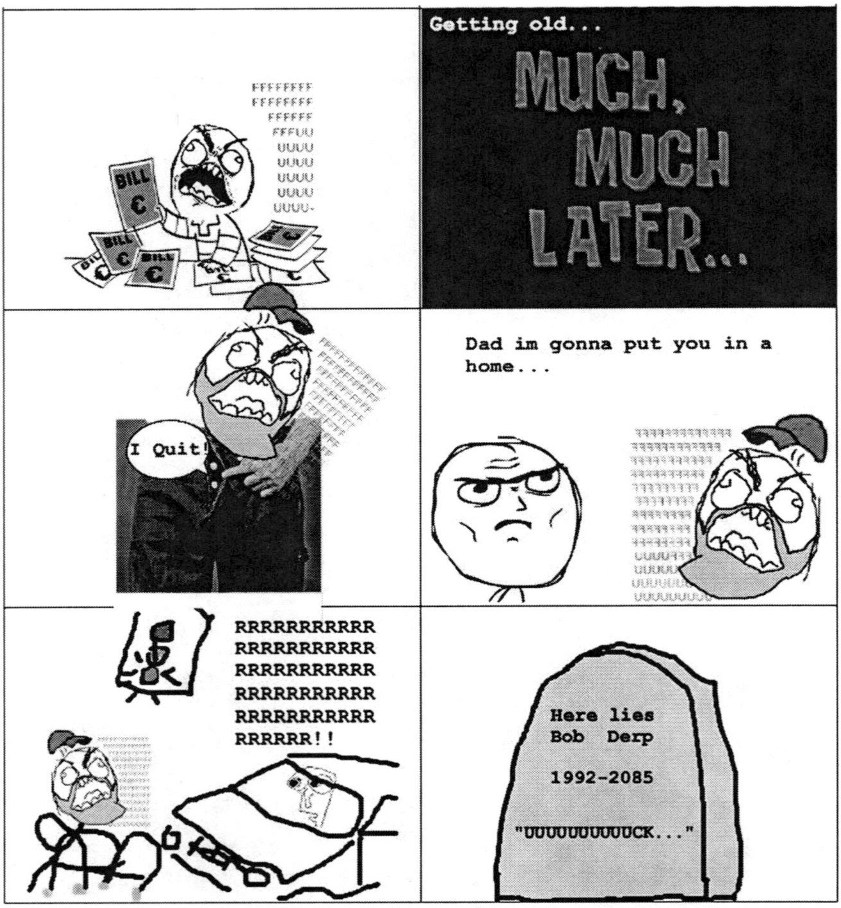
FFFFFFFF
FFFFFFFF
FFFFFF
FFFUU
UUUU
UUUU
UUUU
UUUU
UUUU-
BILL
Getting old...
MUCH, MUCH LATER...
I Quit!
Dad im gonna put you in a home...
RRRRRRRRRRR
RRRRRRRRRRR
RRRRRRRRRRR
RRRRRRRRRRR
RRRRRRRRRRR
RRRRRR!!
Here lies
Bob Derp
1992-2085
"UUUUUUUUUUCK..."

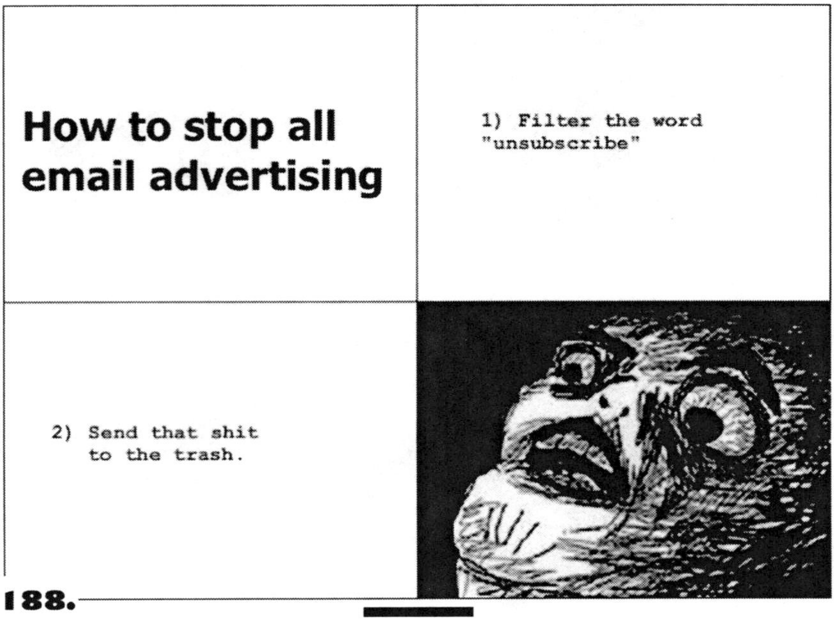
How to stop all email advertising
1) Filter the word "unsubscribe"
2) Send that shit to the trash.

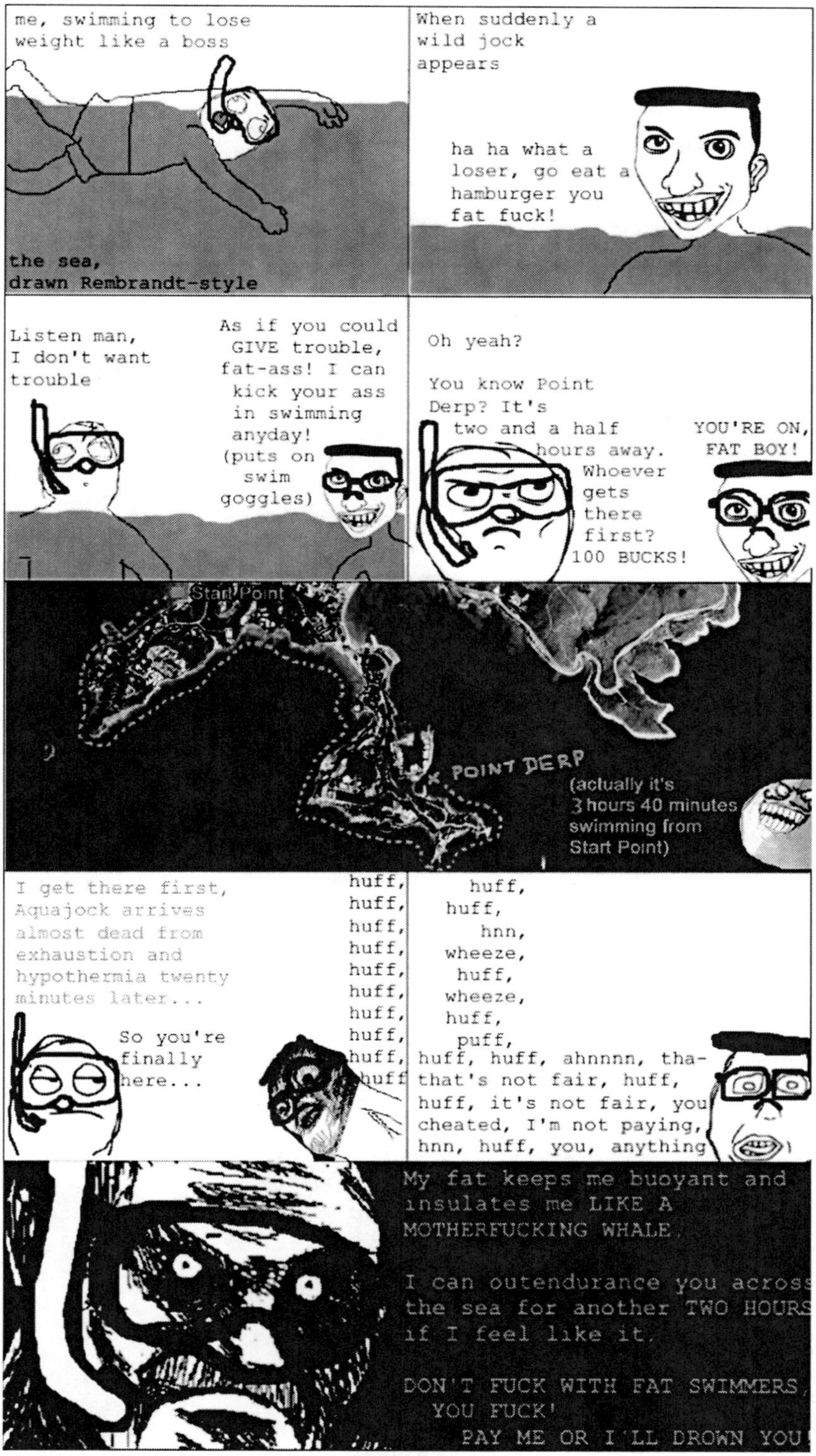

me, swimming to lose weight like a boss
the sea, drawn Rembrandt-style
When suddenly a wild jock appears
ha ha what a loser, go eat a hamburger you fat fuck!
Listen man, I don't want trouble
As if you could GIVE trouble, fat-ass! I can kick your ass in swimming anyday! (puts on swim goggles)
Oh yeah?
You know Point Derp? It's two and a half hours away. Whoever gets there first? 100 BUCKS!
YOU'RE ON, FAT BOY!
Start Point
POINT DERP
(actually it's 3 hours 40 minutes swimming from Start Point)
I get there first, Aquajock arrives almost dead from exhaustion and hypothermia twenty minutes later...
So you're finally here...
huff, huff, huff, huff, huff, huff, huff, huff, huff, huff
huff, huff, hnn, wheeze, huff, wheeze, huff, puff,
huff, huff, ahnnnn, tha-that's not fair, huff, huff, it's not fair, you cheated, I'm not paying, hnn, huff, you, anything
My fat keeps me buoyant and insulates me LIKE A MOTHERFUCKING WHALE.
I can outendurance you across the sea for another TWO HOURS if I feel like it.
DON'T FUCK WITH FAT SWIMMERS, YOU FUCK!
PAY ME OR I'LL DROWN YOU!

Merry christmas,
Santa Claus!
I was looking
forward to you.
Thanks.
Have you been
a good girl?
Maybe YES...
But I ate my brother'S
pudding yesterday.
Am I a bad girl??
Oh,
I have nothing to
give such a bad girl.
Sorry~~
What?
I can't hear you.
Give
me
a present.

Le getting ready for BAMF
camping trip
OFF!
Yes, I finally found my
sleeping bag!
wait a tick...
Le puts
arm in
I am Samus.

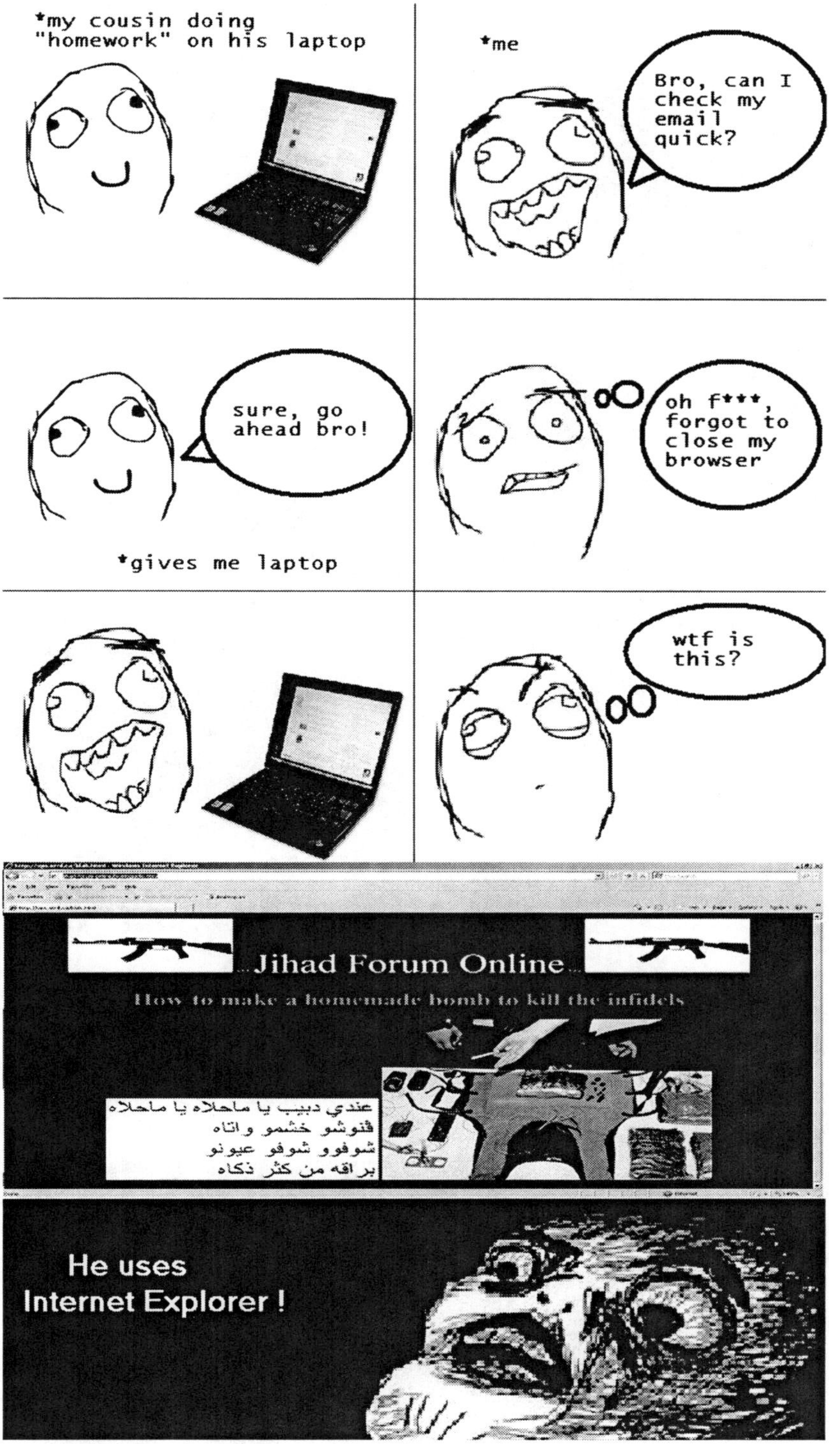

*my cousin doing
"homework" on his laptop
*me
Bro, can I check my email quick?
sure, go ahead bro!
*gives me laptop
oh f***, forgot to close my browser
wtf is this?
..Jihad Forum Online..
How to make a homemade bomb to kill the infidels
عندي دبيب يا ماحلاه يا ماحلاه
قنوشو خشمو واتاه
شوفوو شوفو عيونو
براقه من كثر ذكاه
He uses
Internet Explorer !

Playing darts on my roof terrace...

At first I was like...

"YAY THIS IS FUN!!11!!!ONE!"

But then a dart fell off the board, and went down this gap between the fence and the roof, falling a whole storey...

And then I was like...

"This is the worst thing that ever happened to anyone!"

But then I was like...

CHALLENGE CONSIDERED

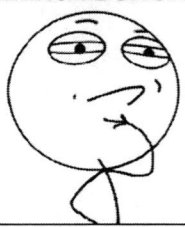

THE NEXT DAY

Having recovered from yesterday's rage, I thought about solutions...

CHALLENGE ACCEPTED

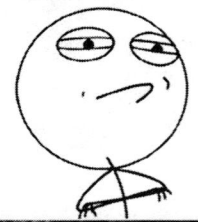

until eventually...

I own a fridge magnet whose name is Key Pete.

He holds my keys for me.

He has a strong magnet on each arm.

A FEW MOMENTS LATER

192.

A long piece of string is attached, and Rescue Pete is ready!

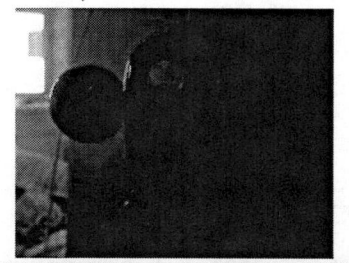

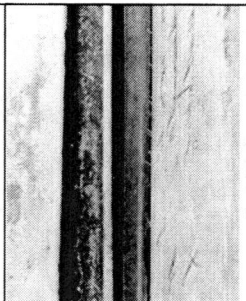

I peered down the gap and managed to see the dart.

I helped little Pete into the gap and started to lower him down.

ONE MINUTE THIRTY SEVEN SECONDS LATER...

MISSION ACCOMPLISHED

**playing scrabble with my grandma

*I look at my letters during my turn

I, E, P, I, N, I, S

Hmm, to play it or not to play it?

193.

(*My brother, Herp, chatting with a single woman.) (*Le laptop)	(*He knows I'm single too, so he offers me to continue the chat with the lady...) Hey Derp! Would you like to chat with a single woman?
OK! (*Le me, Derp)	(*Le me, continuing le chat with le single woman. We say nothing to her about this change, so she still thinks she's chatting with my bro)
(*Le single woman asks me where do I work. I tell my bro...) She wants to know where do I work...	(*My bro tells me...) Don't tell her the truth. That bitch is probably a single slut that wants your money. You might find her one day in your office telling lies about you...

(*Suddenly, I see on the laptop's screen she writes the following answer...)

> Tell your brother one should always tell the truth...

(Laptop screen)

Andromeda galaxy 2.5 million light-years far

194.

*Le Milky Way

LE LAPTOP'S MICROPHONE WAS ON AND OPEN

Me, texting a close guy friend

Derp: i wanna ask this girl to homecoming but im afraid she'll say no

*le phone

My response: well if she says no then fuck her, who cares just ask her

Derp: okay... Wanna go to homecoming with me?

Oh hi honey, what were you and jenean talking about?
you know how we all get a 'one',the one person that you're each allowed to have sex with but it wouldn't count as cheating...
.. and hers is BRAD PITT and his is ANGELINA JOLIE! Isn't that crazy?? Mine is BRAD PITT too. Is yours ANGELINA JOLIE?
THAT WOULD BE SO CRAZZZY!!!!
No, my one is definately Beth Grimshaw.
Who's she?
Oh just some new chick at work.
Sleeping on the couch
FUCK YEA.

Planning my trip to the Grand Canyon, I need a good camera.
This looks promising, Canon SLR camera
SALE
$1,000
Camera

Mom coming home from the store
"Hey honey, there was a 2 for 1 sale on those frozen pizzas you like so I bought you a couple!"
AAAAAAAAAAWWWWWW
YYYYYYEEEEEEEEEAAAAAAAAA
"Thanks mom!
So how many did you buy?"
"Five"

Oh hey, would you like a soda?
troll dad
me
Yeah, that'd be great!
Ok, get me one too while you're at it
FFFFFFF
FFFFFF
FFFFF
FFUU
UUU
UU
UU
UUUU
UUUU-

Goddamn it is hot in here...
TO THE FREEZER!
*le boss enters
Woah what the... Derp, what are you doing in here?

*le me at my parents' house during my vacation

*see the cherry tree that I always climbed on when I was a kid.

*decide to climb it again to see if I'm still as badass as I used to be. Of course the tree became much higher in the meantime and I became least 100lbs heavier.

CHALLENGE ACCEPTED

How it felt

How it looked

*le finally in the tree, climbing around and enjoying the landscape view over the neighbourhood

FUCK YEA.

How it felt	
How it looked	
*eventually I become bored and decide to jump off the tree.	
How it felt	
How it looked	

200.

My overall experience	
How I looked	Harp, I climed tree lolz
How I felt	

Working like a boss (actual spelling) at day care. Watching them color with what looks like coloring crayons on the table.

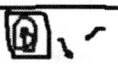

SUDDENLY. One child says to the other: You're coloring outside the lines.

The tyke replies: It doesn't matter because I'm cutting it out anyways.

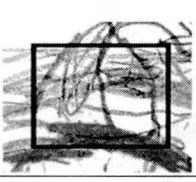

Kids a genius

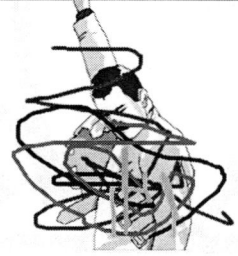

Problem?

201.

Thank you for calling Derpnet support, how may I help you? *awesomely drawn headset	I forgot my password and I need to get into my email right now! le customer
Ok, just answer the security question and I can reset that for you. Where did you go on your honeymoon?	Oh that's easy, Florida!
Um, that's not what it says here. **POKER FACE**	What? My husband set this up but that's where we went. Wait, does it say Hawaii?
Yes ma'am. **POKER FACE**	That's where he went with his FIRST wife! I'm gonna need to call you back! *click*
Did I just cause a divorce?	True Story

202.

*Le new friend an me in my car, about to drop him off at his place
friend
me
*friends turns to my side to grab his stuff from backseat
... I misinterpret the gesture, thinking he wants to give me a good bye hug
SPREAD OUT ARMS, READY FOR INCOMING HUG! ...
me!
... friend
"Bye Derp, thanks for giving me a ride"
"No problem, see you then!"
POKER FACE
POKER FACE
*leaves car, door slams...
forever alone
*le awkwardly empty seat

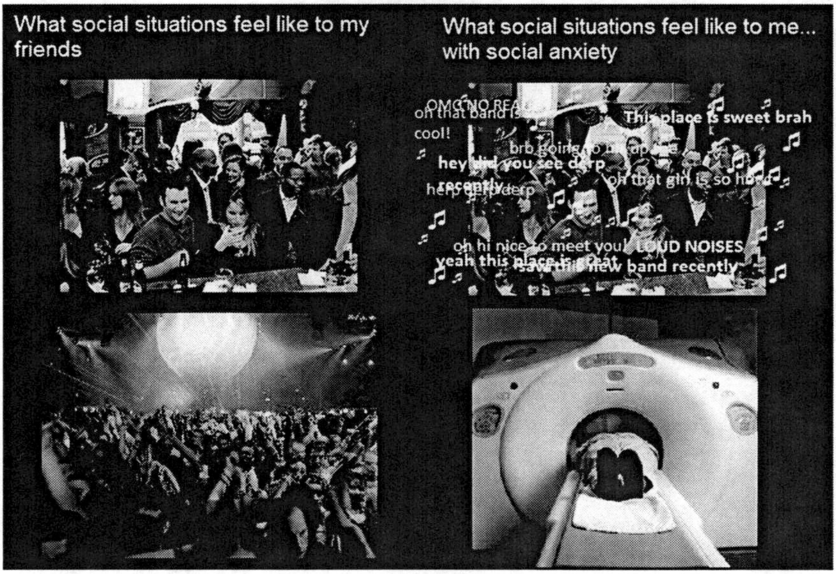
What social situations feel like to my friends
What social situations feel like to me... with social anxiety
This place is sweet brah
cool!
oh that girl is so hot
oh hi nice to meet you!
LOUD NOISES
band recently

Video games on a friday evening? Totally gay.

Video games on a friday evening? Sweet!

NOM NOM NOM...

Oh hi everybody!

*Me try to type 'Me gusta!' in a german phone
*typing
Me G
*autocorrect kicks in
MS Gustav
okay
ACTUALLY...

forced to talk with my stupid co-worker
"If you had a time machine, where would you go?"
*me
"Jamaica"

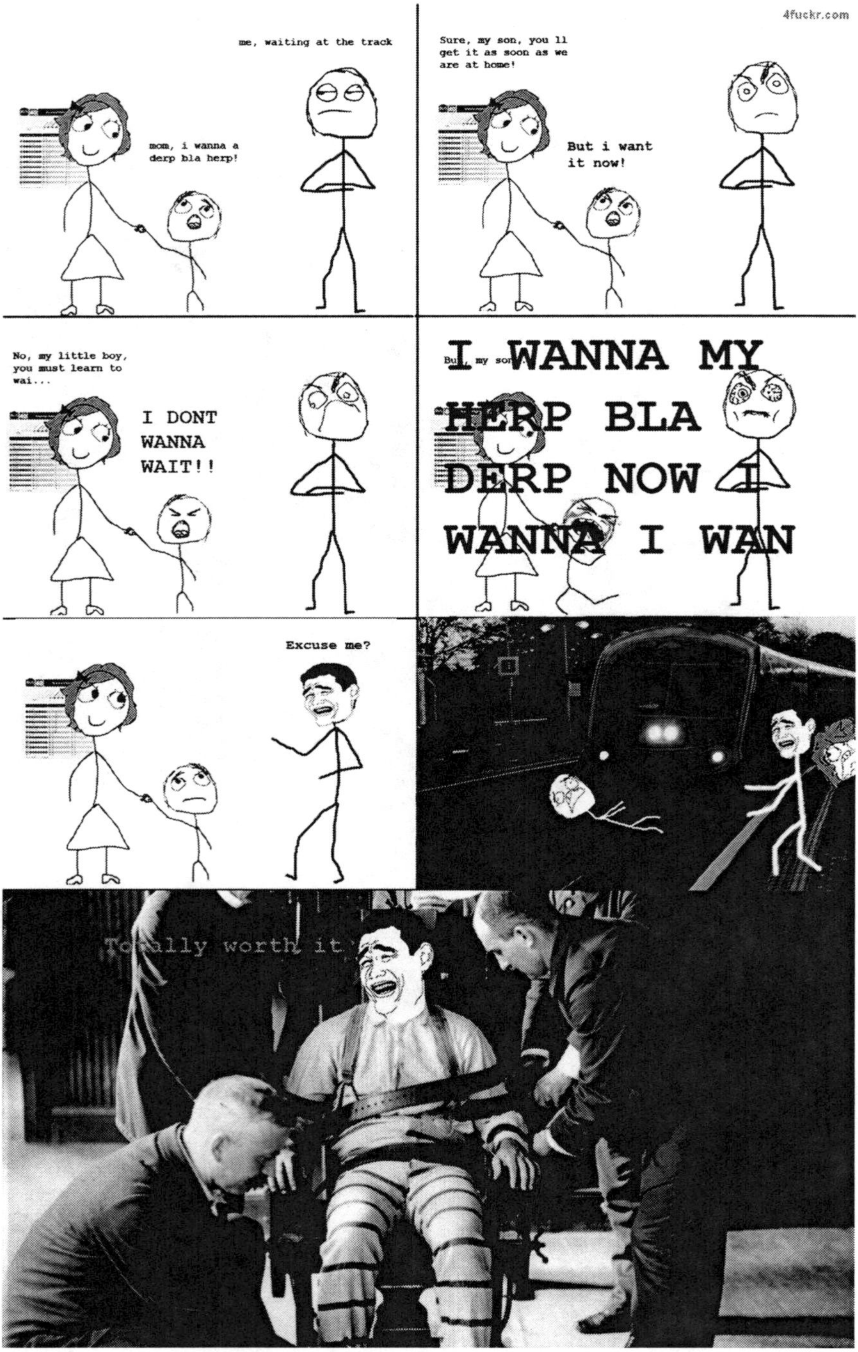
4fuckr.com
me, waiting at the track
mom, i wanna a derp bla herp!
Sure, my son, you ll get it as soon as we are at home!
But i want it now!
No, my little boy, you must learn to wai...
I DONT WANNA WAIT!!
I WANNA MY HERP BLA DERP NOW I WANNA I WAN
Excuse me?

11 years old.
"What's this strange feeling I'm getting? I feel like something bad is about to happen."
Later that day...
"I'm sorry to be the one to tell you but your best friend Derp passed away."
13 years old.
"I'm getting this foreboding feeling again. Uh oh."
Two days later...
"Say goodbye to your grandma. She's leaving us."
"Okay..."
17 years old.
"Oh no. That feeling. AGAIN. Except it's not as strong...maybe it'll go away."
4 days later...
Indian Dad: "We know about you and Derp dating."
hell breaks loose for months
19 years old.
"Oh joy. That feeling again. It's been growing for a while. I think it has to do with Derp. I know it."
5 days later...
"We have to break up. There's this other girl that I've been dating for a week."
"Alright."
21 years old.
"I've been feeling weird all week. Herp is going to break up with me. On Friday. Time to grow some ovaries of steel.."
One week later (Friday)...
"I'm just not feeling it anymore. We need to break up."
"I understand. That's fine."

"I have an amazing sense of intuition. Or maybe even a second sight!"

I AM MISS CLEO
Try a Reading Yourself
1-800-997-5219
www.MISSCLEO.com

Shopping one night like an employee...

When suddenly...

Cinnamon Toast Crunch

This is me, realizing I don't have to ask mom's permission.

Oooh, I see you're already planning ahead for breakfast tomorrow.

yep

*beep

A FEW MOMENTS LATER

208.

First day of classes. My elective class starts at 10:45! Better be there at 10:35 to get a seat.	10:35

Gah, I'm going to have to wake up so early every morning to get a seat! | Show up at 10:45, second week of classes.

Third week of classes. | *beep* *beep* *BEEP* *BEEP*

209.

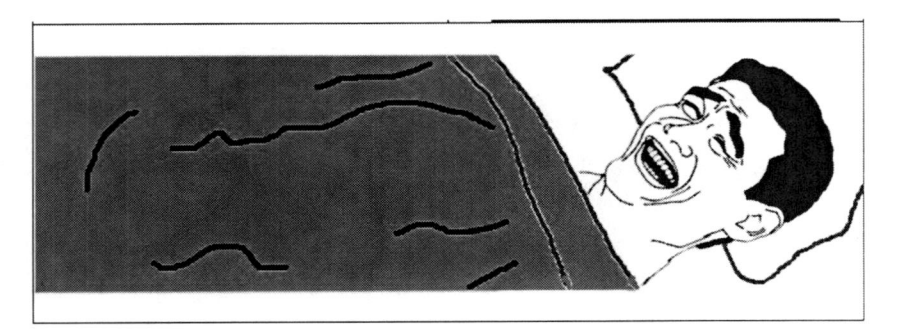

"Jus derping on Reddit, nomming on some chocolate shells, when all of a sudden...."

*le check notification

invited you to the event
"Please read girls only."

"I'm not a girl... so I really should ignore this..."

SWEET.
BABY.
JESUS.

COULD IT BE???

Please read girls only
invited you · Private Event

Time — Wednesday, March 16 at 1:30pm – March 31 at 11:30pm

Location — Now – the end of march

Created By — Ida Boyd

More Info

READ READ READ THEN YOU WILL SEE IT'S NOT THAT KIND OF INVITE TO GO SOME WHERE IT'S... A INVITE TO SHOW YOU CARE!!!!

We are playing a game. Someone proposed that we GIRLS do something special on Facebook to help with Breast Cancer Awareness. Its easy, and Id like you to join us to help it spread. Last year it was about writing the color of the bra that your were wearing in your Fb status and it left men wondering for days why the girls had random colors as their status. This year it has to do with your relationship status. You will where you are, by posting one of the codes below. Remember DO NOT REPLY JUST POST IN YOUR STATUS ON YOUR WALL TO CONFUSE THE GUYS. Then invite female friends to join this event

+ Select Guests to Invite

687,403 Attending   See All
Britt Watt
Aanzhenii Starr
Ariana Cisneros
Carmen Gonzalez
Iyrandaa Alvarez

210.

I'M A SPY

me arriving at work with new hat and beard
Hey Fidel Castro, nice hat!
POKER FACE
co-worker
takes off hat while boss who has never seen me with beard walks in
Okay
boss
Hey Osama, I thought you were dead?
boss

forever a terrorist

Hello Derpetta, may I have your number?
Sure! It's (717)867-5309
3 DAYS LATER...
Derpetta! Would you like to go with.....
Sorry man, this is Pizza Hut
ONE HOUR LATER

wife
me
SWEET! Wife made me cake with extra icing!
MUCH MUCH LATER....
standing in line at store
random bitches
Would you do that guy infront of us?
no, too fat

TOO FAT???

Clever Girl

On the way home from the store, I decided to try the derper king drive-thru...

Uh, hi, I'll have the large number derp with herp to drink. That's it.

Okay, that'll be $7.28

Hand cashier $12.28

Yeah, man, you handed me way too much money. Have the two singles back.

Not entirely sure how to explain it

Just... put $12.28 into the computer for the cash you took.

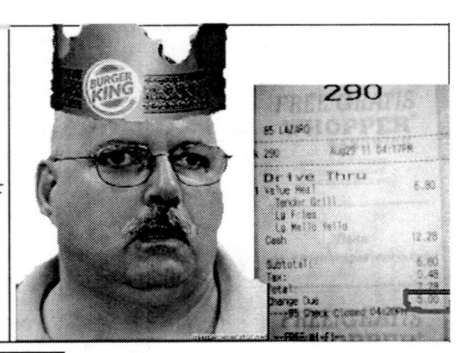

---

my friend and I walking down the street like 2 poorly drawn stick figures.

suddenly he stops and grabs at his chest.

"you okay bro?"

*suddenly he falls to the ground, gripping his chest and mouthing a silent yell."

214.

"dude, the fuck? are you ok? what was that?"
"oh that's nothing, it happens all the time. no big deal."
"How can you call that no big deal?"

"Okay kids, I want to have a peaceful vacation, so nobody stress out over anything."
"Sure thing, Mom!"
DAY BEFORE TRIP
OH MY GOD! WE HAVE TO GET READY OR ELSE WE'RE GOING TO HAVE TO PACK IN THE MORNING AND WE'LL BE LATE!
"We're all packed!"
MORNING OF THE TRIP
"Mom, let's go!"
"Just wait... I have to pack my clothes."

IN THE CAR
"Remember kids, this is my vacation, too. So, I don't want to rush around when we get there!"
AT THE HOTEL
FIRST, WE
TO GO SEE
YOUR
WE'LL GO
THE
O'CLOCK
WE
AND WE
COLLEGE
COME
ON! THERE'S NO TIME TO SIT DOWN!!!
"We thought you wanted to relax..."
NO, NO, NO... WE HAVE TO GET EVERYTHING DONE ON THIS TRIP! I DON'T WANT TO MISS OUT ON ONE THING! WE HAVE TO ENJOY OUR TIME HERE!

Hey, I was thinking it'd be fun if we took a bath together later!
Sounds good!
*le gf
*getting undressed
Water's ready! Be careful though, I like it really hot!
Heh, I think I can handle a little hot water, babe.
Hot. Hot. Fucking hot water. How can anyone be comfortable in this. I'm going to die for sure.

Panel 1:
Hey, are you okay? If the water's too hot I can add some cold.

Nope. This is great.

Panel 2:
Are you sure? You don't look so well.

....

Panel 4:
*De Mij, a dutchman for first time on vacation in USA, about to pick up girlfriend from airport

Panel 5:
hmm, haven't had lunch yet, and I'm kinda hungry

Panel 6:
A Ta-co bell? We don't have those in Holland, and I'm pretty early so let's get some TA-CO'S

*my car

Panel 7:
Well, here goes nothing!

Panel 8:
Crunch!

Panel 9:

217.

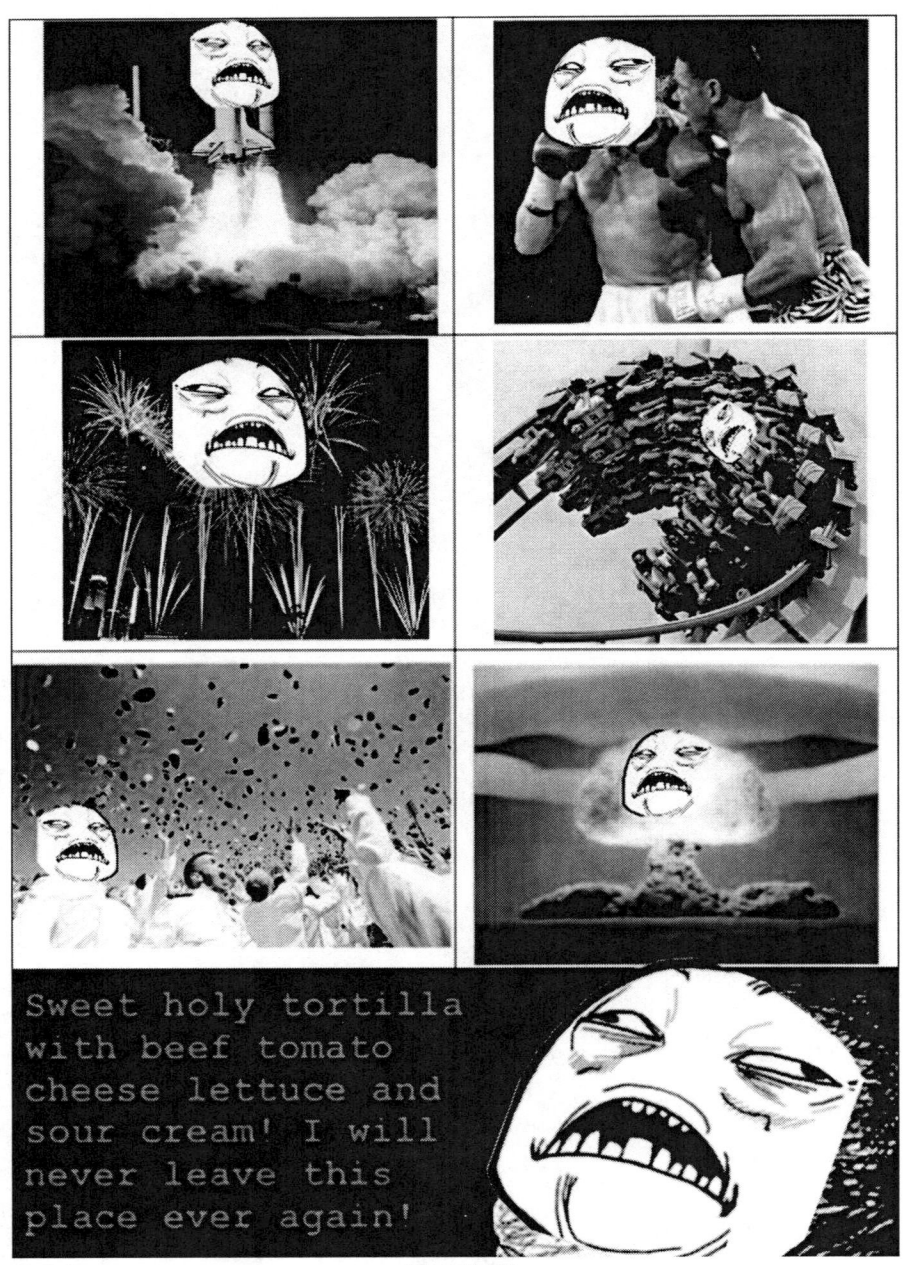

Sweet holy tortilla with beef tomato cheese lettuce and sour cream! I will never leave this place ever again!

218.

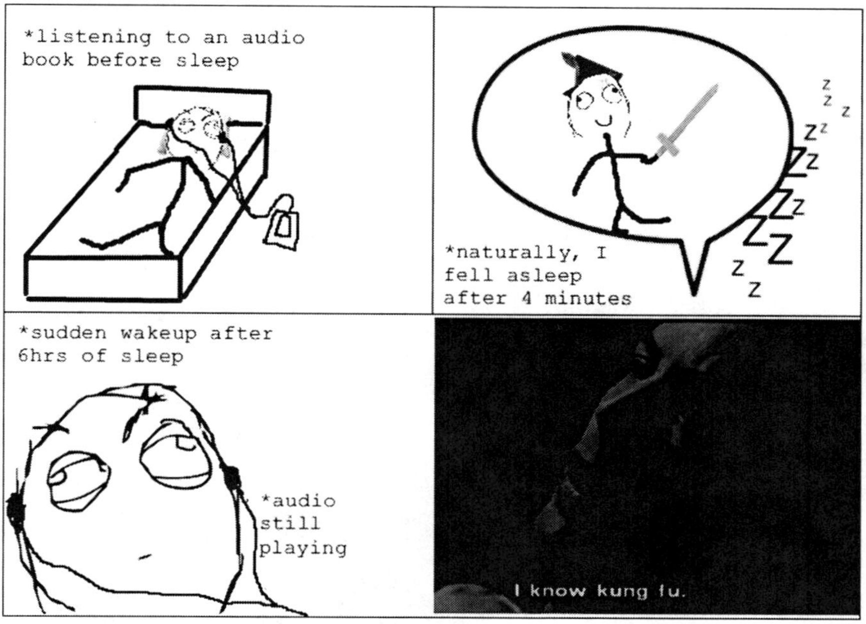
*listening to an audio book before sleep
*naturally, I fell asleep after 4 minutes
z z z
*sudden wakeup after 6hrs of sleep
*audio still playing
I know kung fu.

le texting the girlfriend...
DERPETTE:
Idk why, but I find it sexy that you make rage comics.. im odd, lol.
URHGAAUGH!!!
MUST MAKE COMICS FASTER!!

Me, checking Cragslist for possible apartments
Hmm, this one looks promising.
click
Looking for third roommate, we are:
•College students
•Liberal
•Play music
•Drug free, including alcohol
•No drinking allowed in our living space.
alcohol.
•No drinking allowed in our living space.

checking out at Derp Mart
do you want this now?
oh no, heh. You can bag it.

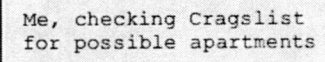

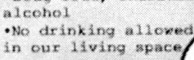

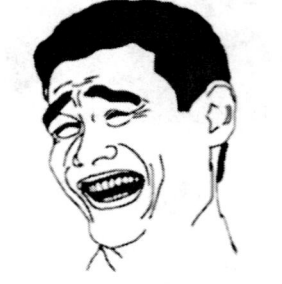

How I eat spaghetti in public
*le twirl
How I eat spaghetti alone...
*der SHOVEL

(my kindle)
(not my kindle)
FFFFFFF
FFFFFFF
FFFFFF
FFFUU
UUUU
UUUU
UUUU
UUUU
UUUU-

Dude, i definitely can't pass this exam, i'm going to fail!
?
*me
random classmate*
I don't know, just pretend your sick and go to the infirmary
But... What am I supposed to say?
Er... just say you have a stomach ache
and don't forget to scream if she touches your belly!
Thank you! *running to the inrmary*
So, does it hurt if i push here?
nope
and here?
nope
and don't forget to scream if she touches your belly!
And here?
AAA AAAAAA
AA AAAA
AA AAAA
AAA AAA
AAAA AAAAA
RRRRR RRRRRRRRF
RRRRRR RRRRRRRRRR
HHHHHH HHHHHHHH
DARPH HHHHHHHH
HHHHH HHHHHHHH
Oh my God, it's the colon! go see doctor Herp right now!!
just try to calm down, kid!
FFFFF
FF
F
U
UU
UUU
UUU UUUU

Guess what, Derp? We're getting a pool this weekend!

Me, just got back from surgery still REALLY high on pain killers.

"Think I'm gunna go take a walk."

CUE BLACK OUT

*Turkey sandwich

223.

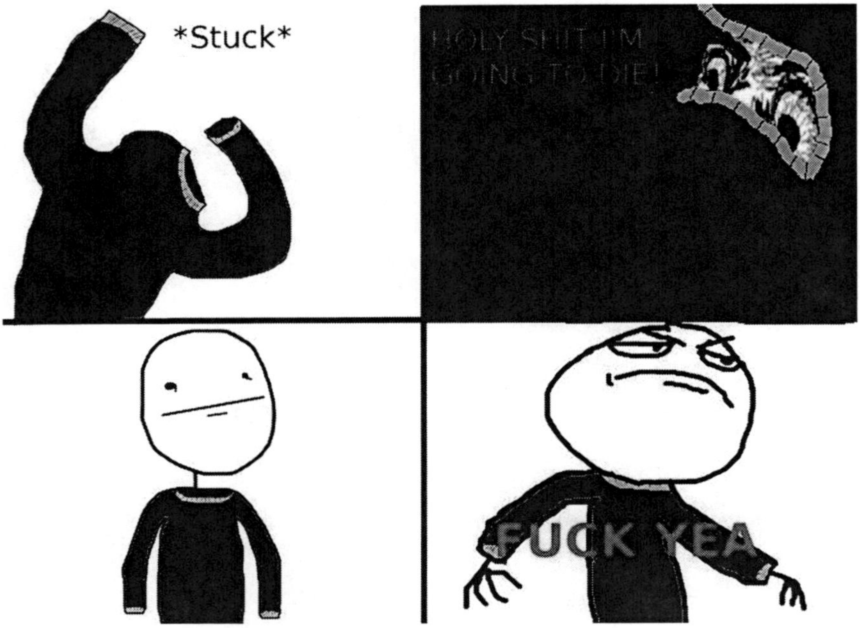
Stuck
HOLY SHIT I'M GOING TO DIE!
FUCK YEA

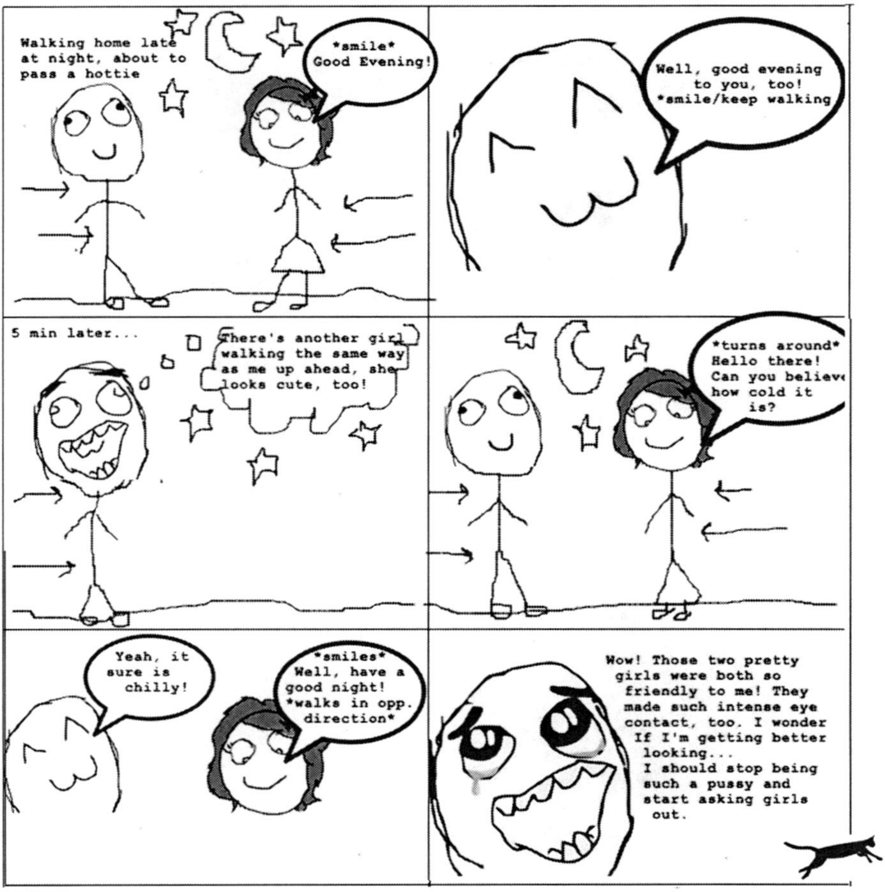
Walking home late at night, about to pass a hottie
smile Good Evening!
Well, good evening to you, too! *smile/keep walking
5 min later...
There's another girl walking the same way as me up ahead, she looks cute, too!
turns around Hello there! Can you believe how cold it is?
Yeah, it sure is chilly!
smiles Well, have a good night! *walks in opp. direction*
Wow! Those two pretty girls were both so friendly to me! They made such intense eye contact, too. I wonder If I'm getting better looking...
I should stop being such a pussy and start asking girls out.

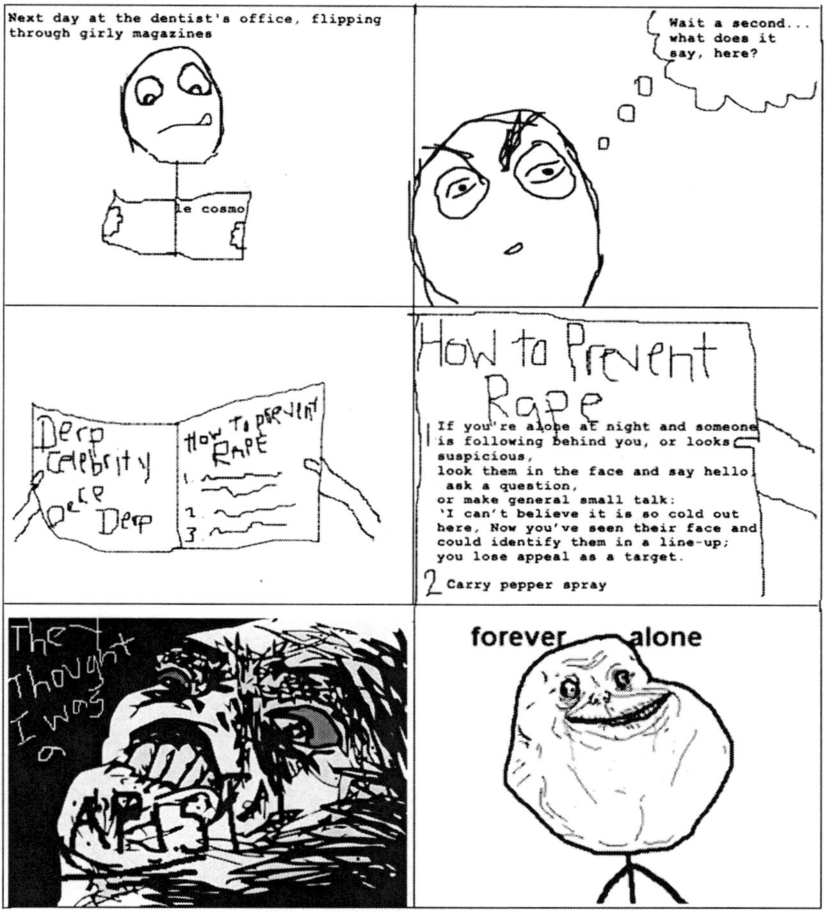

Next day at the dentist's office, flipping through girly magazines
le cosmo
Wait a second... what does it say, here?
How to Prevent Rape
1 If you're alone at night and someone is following behind you, or looks suspicious,
look them in the face and say hello.
ask a question,
or make general small talk:
'I can't believe it is so cold out here, Now you've seen their face and could identify them in a line-up; you lose appeal as a target.
2 Carry pepper spray
They thought I was a
forever alone

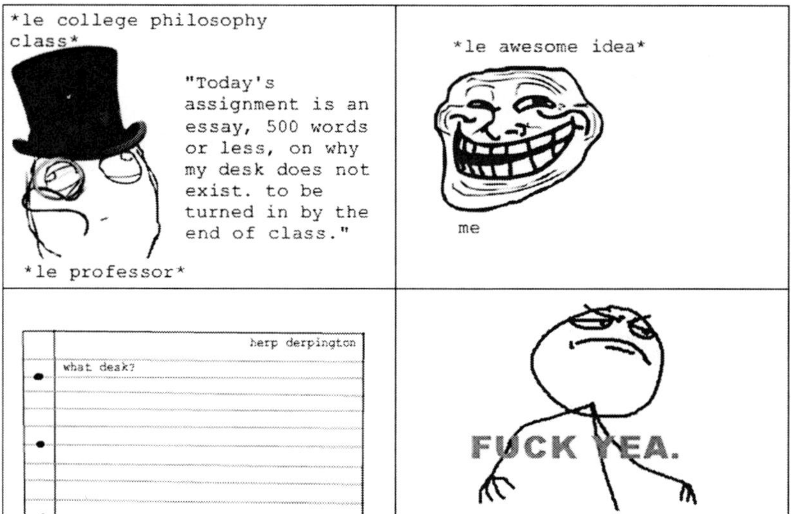

le college philosophy class
"Today's assignment is an essay, 500 words or less, on why my desk does not exist. to be turned in by the end of class."
le professor
le awesome idea
me
herp derpington
what desk?
FUCK YEA.

*me, eating pizza with friends

*when suddenly there is only one slice left

"so. uhh.. do any of you guys want the last slice?"

BAD POKER FACE

"i'm full" "it's all you bro!"

"nope!"

Me, walking through the park on a sunny day, feelin' fine.

Me: Is that a lollipop on a string..?

226.

I notice the weird 13 year old from down my street is the one dangling the lollipop.
Me: Herp, what are you doing up there?
Herp: FISHING!!!
(Thinking: Awww, heh. Kids can be so cute. Things like this make me wanna have kids someday.)
Me: Say Herp, what are you trying to catch using that big ol' lollipop?
Herp: Gonna catch me some bitches.
Never having kids.

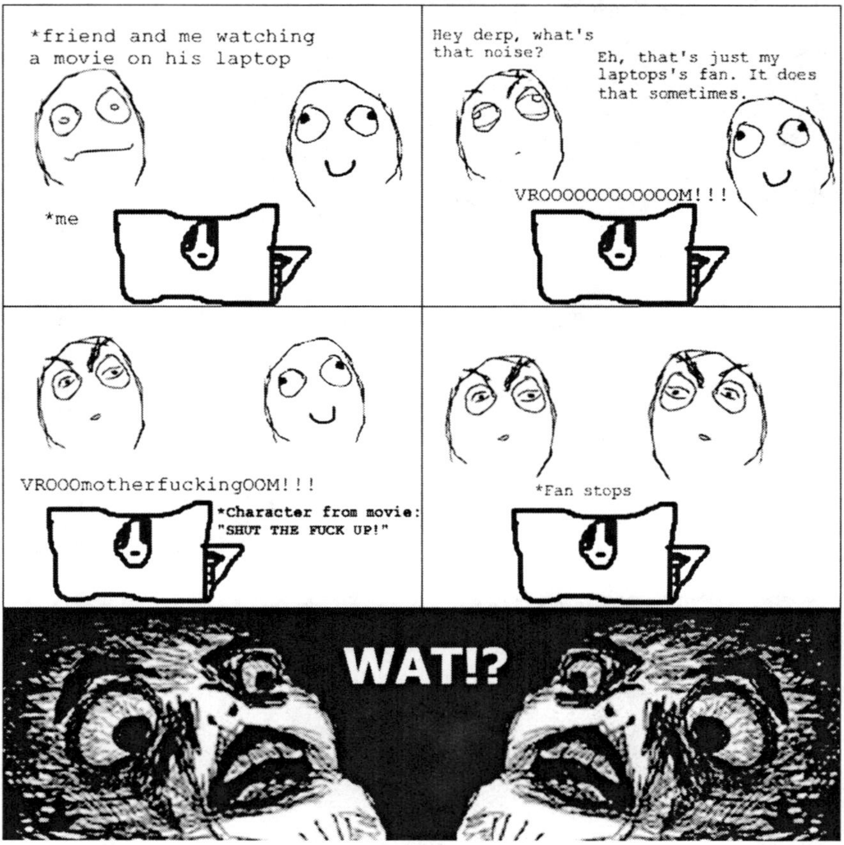
*friend and me watching a movie on his laptop
*me
Hey derp, what's that noise?
Eh, that's just my laptops's fan. It does that sometimes.
VROOOOOOOOOOOOM!!!
VROOOmotherfuckingOOM!!!
*Character from movie: "SHUT THE FUCK UP!"
*Fan stops
WAT!?

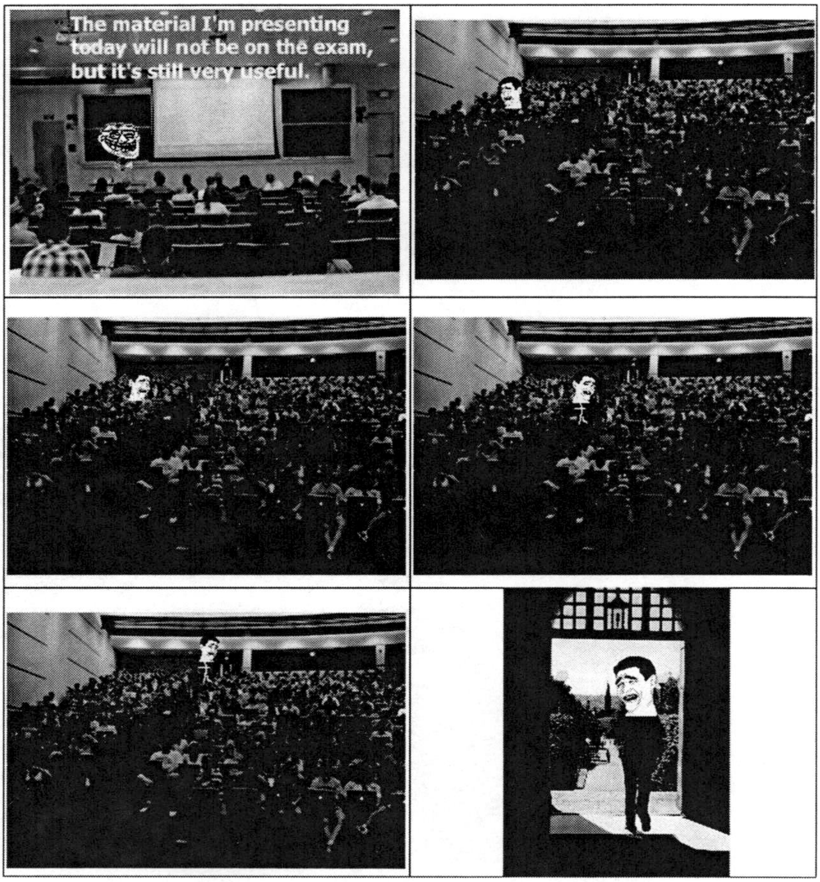

The material I'm presenting today will not be on the exam, but it's still very useful.

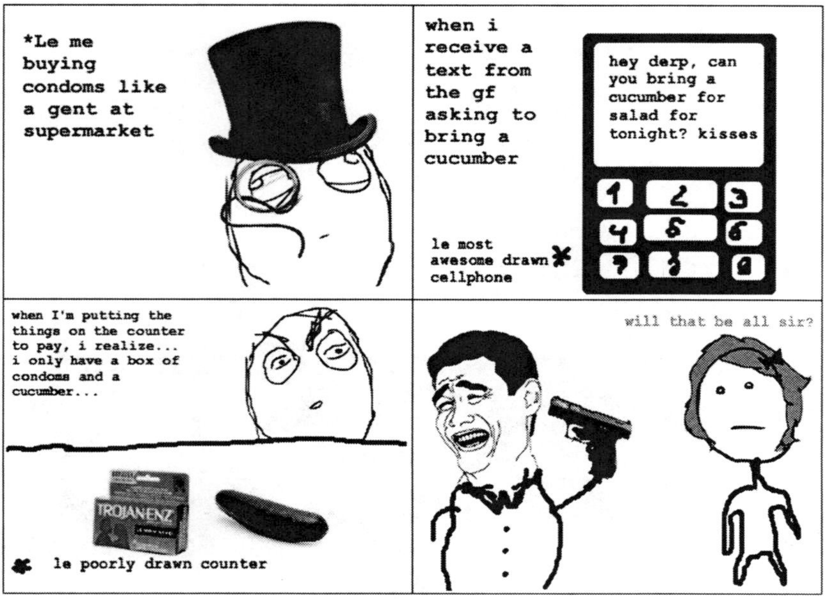

*Le me buying condoms like a gent at supermarket
when i receive a text from the gf asking to bring a cucumber
hey derp, can you bring a cucumber for salad for tonight? kisses
le most awesome drawn cellphone
when I'm putting the things on the counter to pay, i realize... i only have a box of condoms and a cucumber...
TROJANENZ
le poorly drawn counter
will that be all sir?

MECHOOSTA
MASSEUSETA
ME GOOSTA
ME SHOESTA
ME MOOSTA
ME BOOSTA
ME JUICETA
FFFFFFF
FFFFFFF
FFFFFF
FFFUU
UUUU
UUUU
UUUU
UUUU
UUUU-

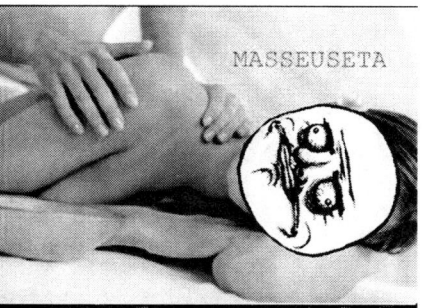

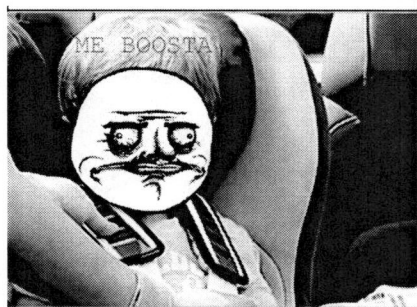

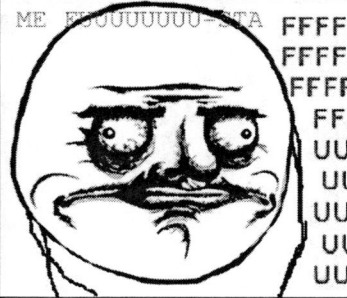

Hi. What can I get for you? / Are...are you a vampire? / *waiting tables at Applebees	Well, my dad is half-vampire he he / Please, don't bite me
Ma'am, I'm not going to bite you / Don't put any blood in my food either. I don't want to be a vampire	Ma'am, I'm not going to put blood in your food. I'm not a vampire. We serve regular food here. / Let me speak to your manager
A FEW MOMENTS LATER	What seems to be the problem? / Is your vampire waitress going to bite me? / -the manager

Only if you don't tip her well

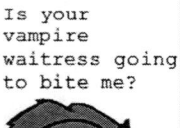

Finally done with college!

Time to go home and clean out my room.
Got to get a job and move out.

230.

I haven't cleaned my room since the end of high school.

I only have a weekend to clean out my room and 24 years of junk.
CHALLENGE ACCEPTED

Playing with my old toys!

Old, ugly clothing.
GTFO

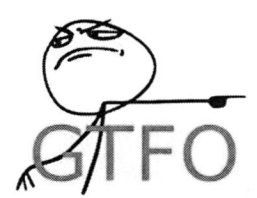

Box of pictures and love notes from my ex of 7 years.

5 minutes later...
She was ugly, boring, dumb, and cheated on me anyways.
Burned that shit.

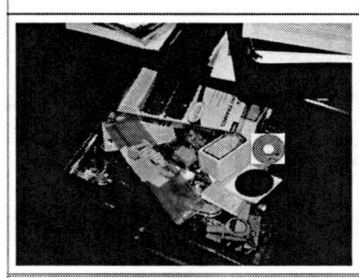

What is that?

Yes.

Just work that body, work that body, make sure you don't hurt nobody

231.

So I work in a store where kids come in to paint and have parties.

*le me

Alright, kids! Who's ready to paint?!?

I make minimum wage and am not allowed to take tips.

Thanks for all of your help! Here's a little extra!

I'm sorry, ma'am. I appreciate the offer, but I can't accept any monetary tips...

...but I'll take a piece of cake and a juice box, please!!

In the Library..

"Hi, I'd like a book on "How to survive in the wild without Toilet paper"

"No problem!"

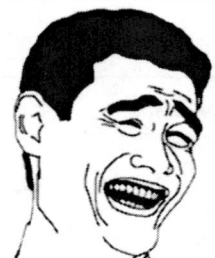

"Terribly sorry, Sir. Someone seems to have ripped the pages out of the book"

Me sitting in my English 092 class like a tool
When suddenly the professor hands out graded essays
actual words on graded essay
Derpia, your essay way great! I have never had so much fun reading an essay. It was byfar the best one out of all the essays turned in to me!
"Wait..if he loved my essay why did I get a failing grade on it? I should go talk to him after class"
TWO HOURS LATER
"Professor Derpner, I had a question about the mark I recived on my essay. You stated in your comments that you enjoyed it, but I have recived a failing grade for it. Might I ask why?"
"Ah yes Derpia! You're essay was a joy to read. The best on in the class no doubt. Your grammer and spelling and word usage were spectacular and I am actuall wondering why you're not in an English 101 class."
"I think its mosty because I was a bit ill when I took the placement test and wasn't thinking too clearly, but I choose to take English 092 to polish up before I take English 101. May I ask though, why I recived a failing mark if my essay was so amazing?"
"You're essay was too wordy and to advanced for this English level. I had to mark you down because of that."

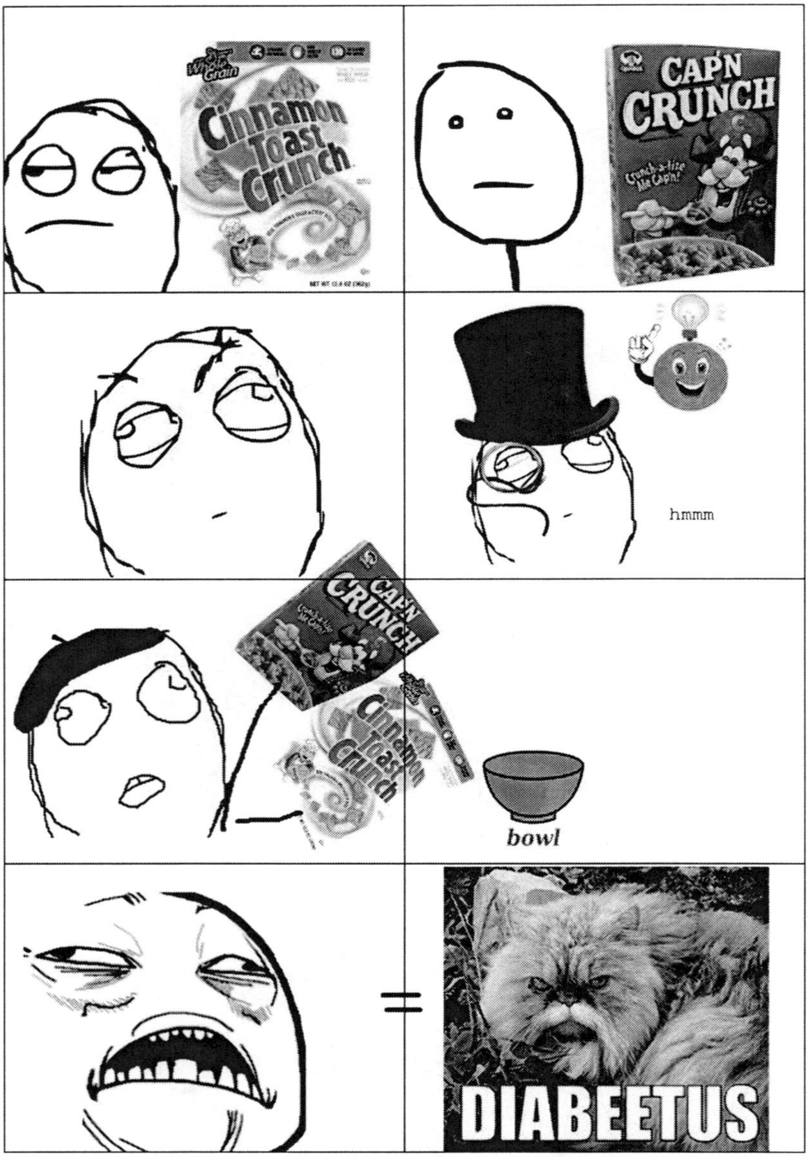
Cinnamon Toast Crunch
CAP'N CRUNCH
hmmm
CAP'N CRUNCH
Cinnamon Toast Crunch
bowl
DIABEETUS

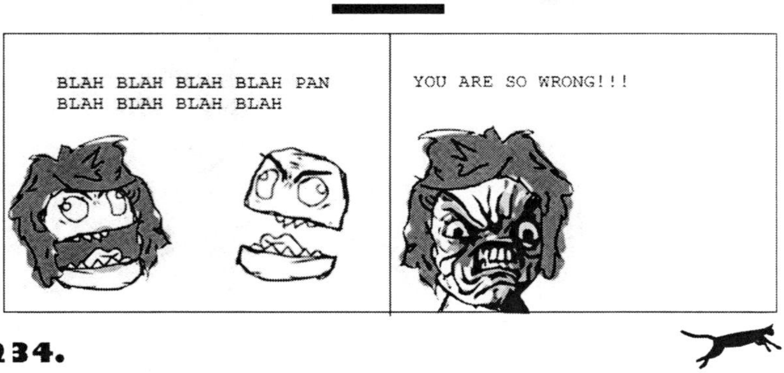
BLAH BLAH BLAH BLAH PAN
BLAH BLAH BLAH BLAH
YOU ARE SO WRONG!!!

WOMAN! I CAN PROVE IT!!
Prove it then!
when
Suddenly
my wall! OMG
why Leonard Nimoy,
why?
stand back...
I got this bro!
OMG! What is wrong
with your eyes?
What is happening?
Quick Derp!
Take cover!
Okay Mr. Nemoy,
I go call police now
LOGIC!!!!

I must go now derp. Goodluck with your woman...

I did nazi that coming

*le me, working as a cashier at a gas station
*le counter
that'll be $3.59, sir. do you need a bag?
milk
obviously not. don't you see the milk has its own handle?
I SEE THE HANDLE YOU IDIOT. SOME PEOPLE LIKE BAGS.
oh, okay. have a nice day!
*remembering handle = no bag
that'll be $3.59, sir.
milk
ahem
i'm sorry! is there something else i can help you with today?
a bag for the milk, miss. i don't like when the condensation touches my skin.
THE CONDENSATION ISN'T THAT BAD IF YOU USE THE HANDLE
of course. here, let me bag it for you. have a nice day!
*realization: the bag provides a handle AND keeps the condensation from touching you

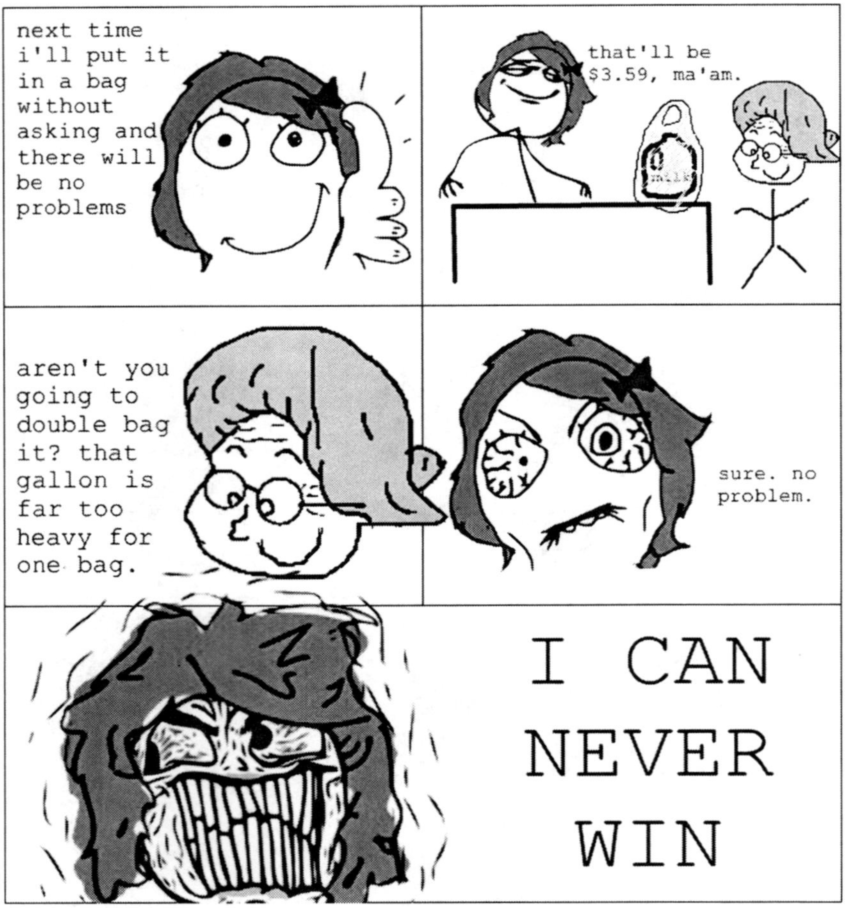
next time i'll put it in a bag without asking and there will be no problems
that'll be $3.59, ma'am.
milk
aren't you going to double bag it? that gallon is far too heavy for one bag.
sure. no problem.
I CAN NEVER WIN

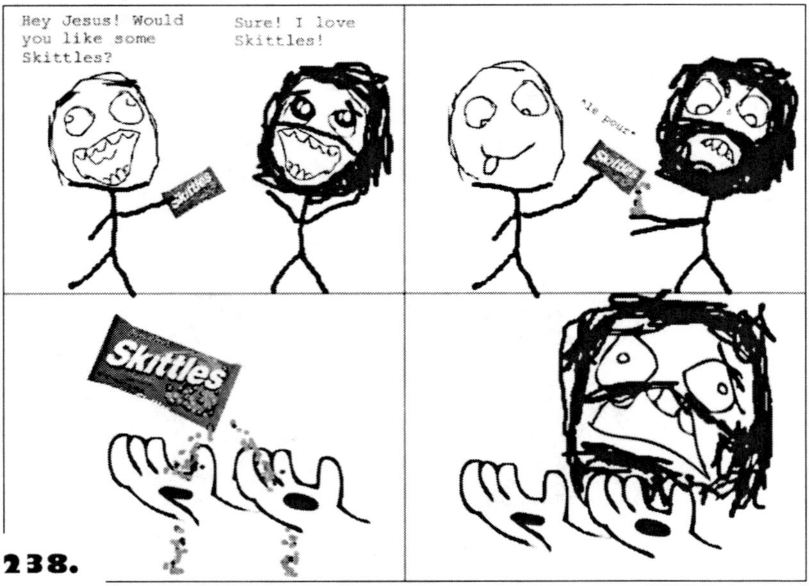
Hey Jesus! Would you like some Skittles?
Sure! I love Skittles!
le pour
Skittles

Backstory time:
My sister, herpette, just got a new boyfriend, herp. My mother and grandfather discuss...

So where did you say herp was from?

TrollGramps

He's American, but his parents are from Korea

Mom

Korea
Korea
Korea

You know, I fought in Korea

Yeah...

Which means...

He could be my grandson

LOL

True Story

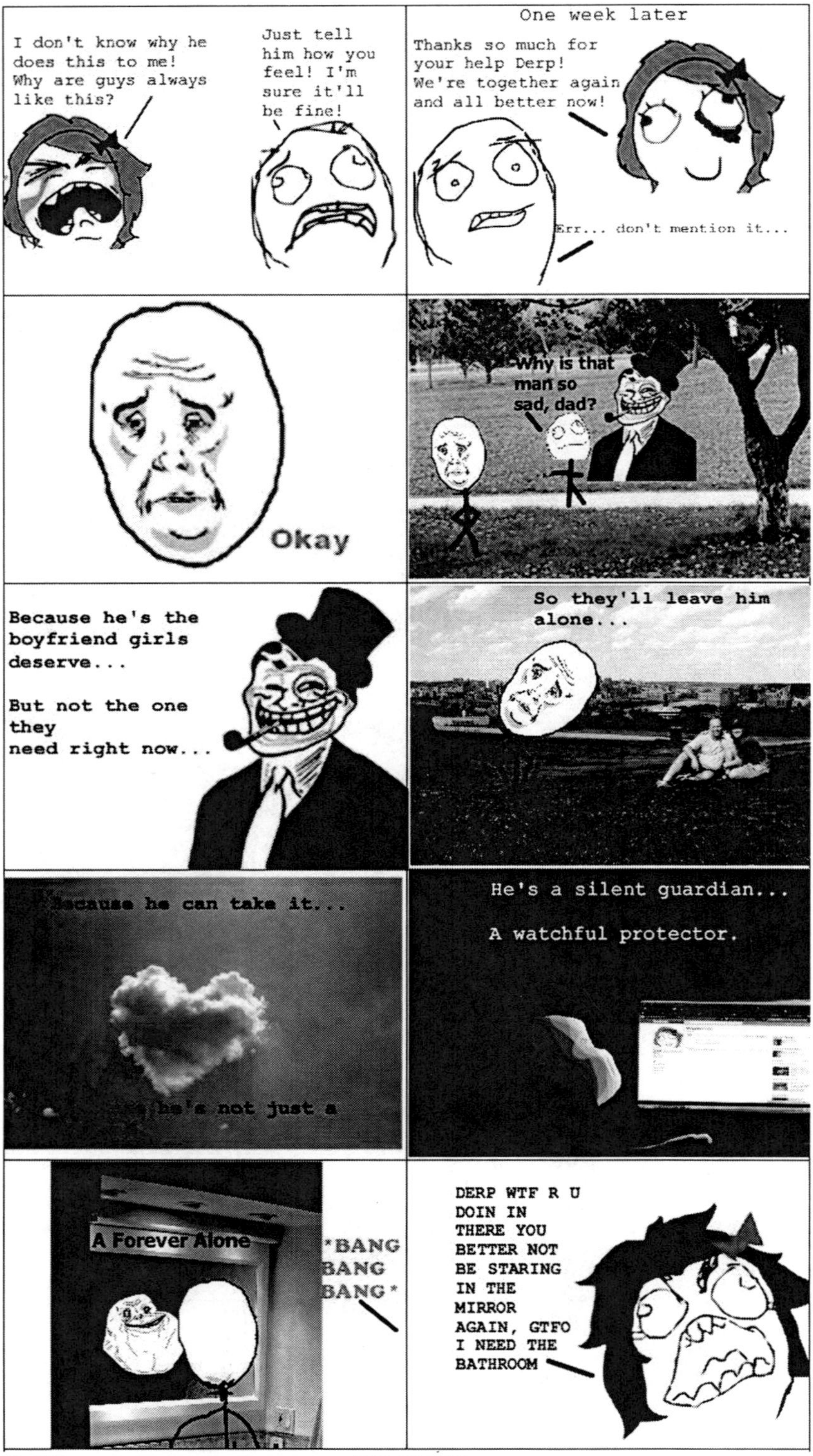
I don't know why he does this to me! Why are guys always like this?
Just tell him how you feel! I'm sure it'll be fine!
One week later
Thanks so much for your help Derp! We're together again and all better now!
Err... don't mention it...
Okay
Why is that man so sad, dad?
Because he's the boyfriend girls deserve...
But not the one they need right now...
So they'll leave him alone...
Because he can take it...
he's not just a
He's a silent guardian...
A watchful protector.
A Forever Alone
BANG BANG BANG
DERP WTF R U DOIN IN THERE YOU BETTER NOT BE STARING IN THE MIRROR AGAIN, GTFO I NEED THE BATHROOM

Coming up! Your chance to win $100,000!

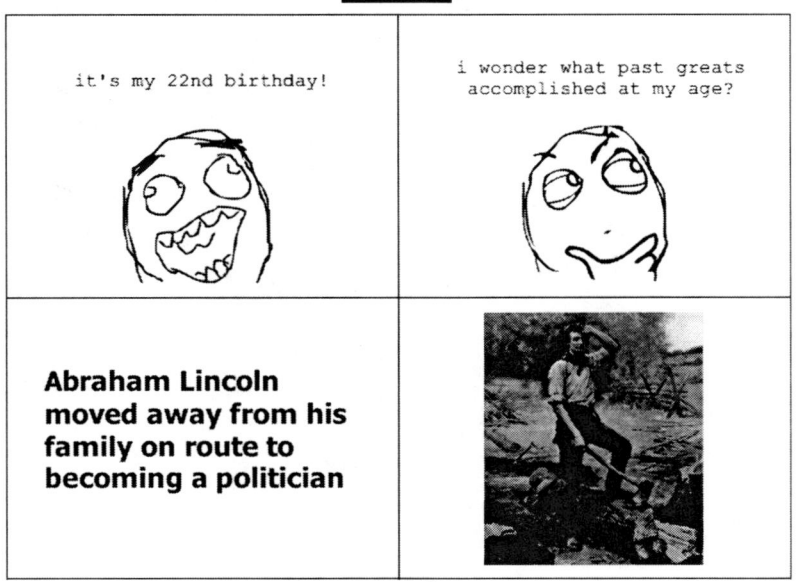

Oh man, if I had a $100,000, I would be a millionaire!

Huh? You have $990,000 in the bank, I guess?

---

it's my 22nd birthday!

i wonder what past greats accomplished at my age?

Abraham Lincoln moved away from his family on route to becoming a politician

Jackie Robinson played baseball, basketball, track and field, and football at UCLA (school's first)	
Slash was part of Guns N' Roses as they just released Appetite for Destruction	
Charles Darwin set sail for the Galapagos Islands	

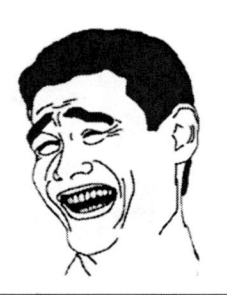

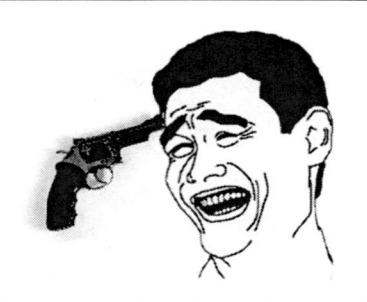

242.

*me, a med student, talking to a woman who has been trying to get pregnant
"So Ms. Herp, I see you've been prescribed Fertiliderp. Are you still taking it?"
"Of course!"
"And you've been trying to get pregnant for over 6 months now?"
"Yes, and I really want to have a baby!
"If you don't mind me asking Ms. Derp, how often do you have le sexytime?"
"I haven't been having le sexytime"
"Ms Derp, you can't get pregnant without le sexytime"
"I thought that's what Fertiliderp is for"

* me, browsing the internet
* a wild brother wanders in.
"hey, can i borrow your laptop to look up something for class?"
i am a nice sister.
TWENTY MINUTES LATER

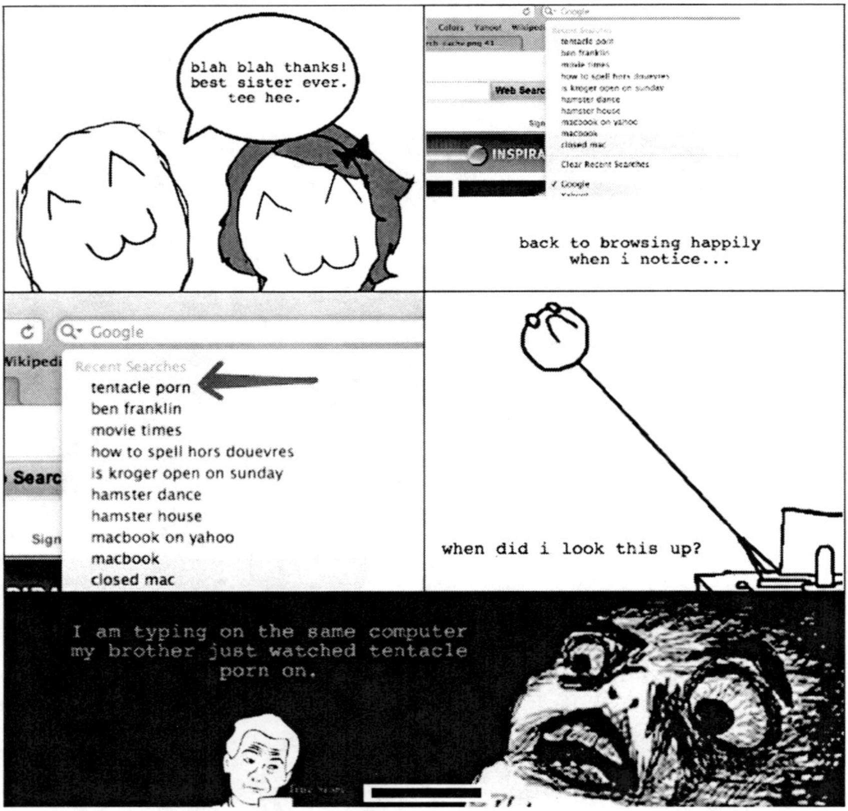

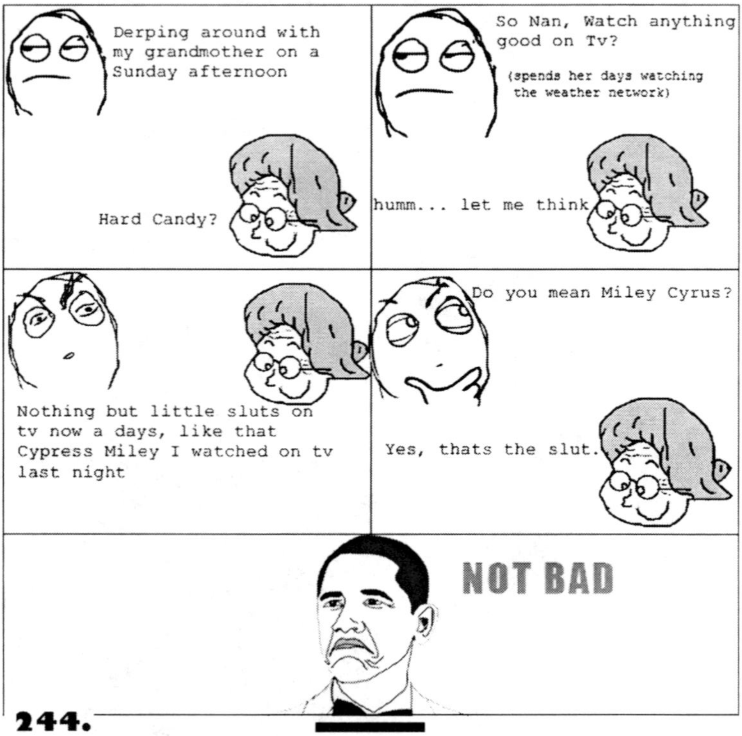

"Hi, I'm Wendy..."

Wait... YOU'RE Wendy?

"Yep, that one!"

Okay

Ride the tallest rollercoaster in the state? No problem!

Stand at the edge of a canyon? Sure!

Chill out next to tornado? With me!

Kill a cockroach? JESUS CHRIST WHAT DO I DO?!

245.

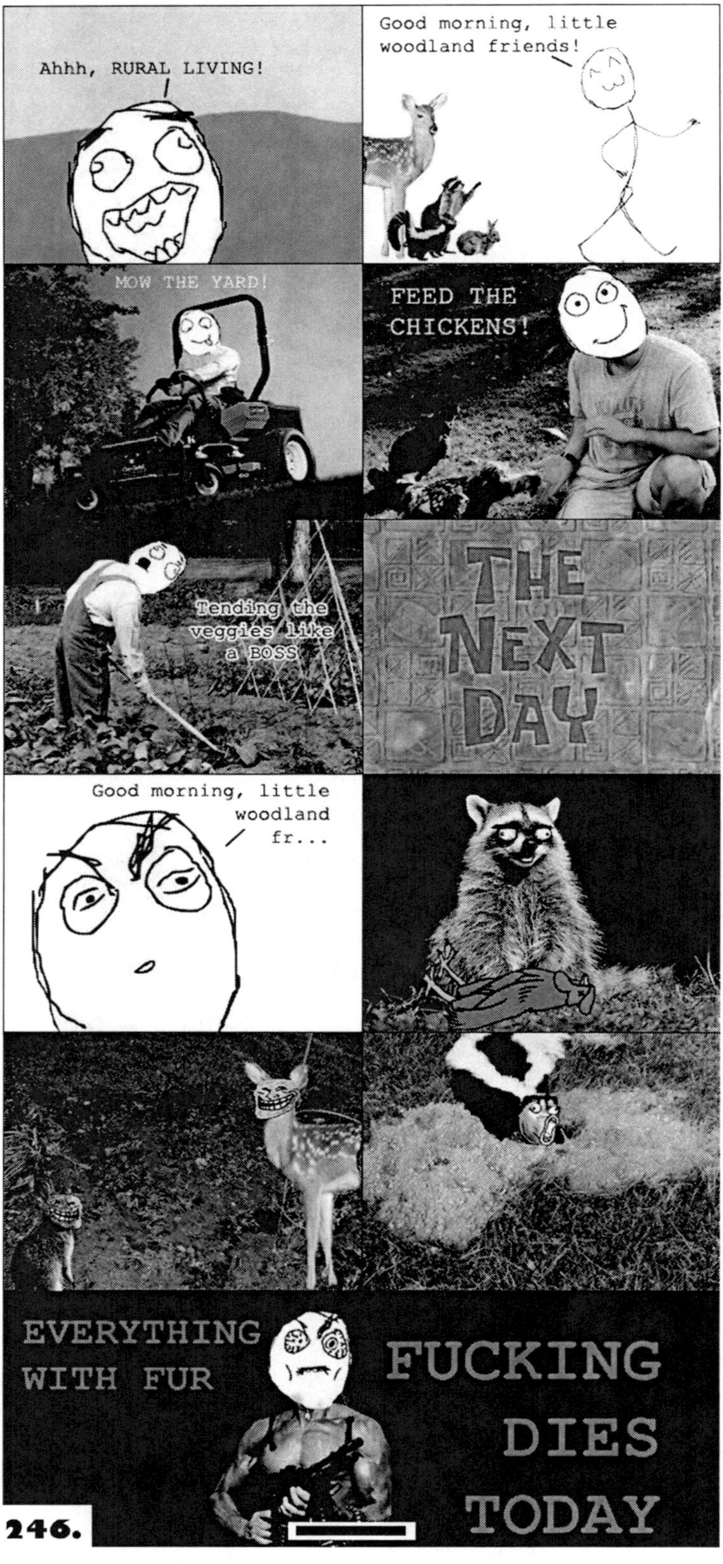

Ahhh, RURAL LIVING!
Good morning, little woodland friends!
MOW THE YARD!
FEED THE CHICKENS!
Tending the veggies like a BOSS
THE NEXT DAY
Good morning, little woodland fr...
EVERYTHING WITH FUR
FUCKING DIES TODAY

Derpito, I think you should take it easy on that tequila.
I didn't know my name was Ishmael.
What?
I said I didn't know my name was Ishmael.
I never said it was.
Well, call me Ishmael because you're being a Moby Dick.
Ahoy there, tequila!
I'm leaving.

BREAD
Twist left
BREAD
Twist right
BREAD
Twist left
BREAD

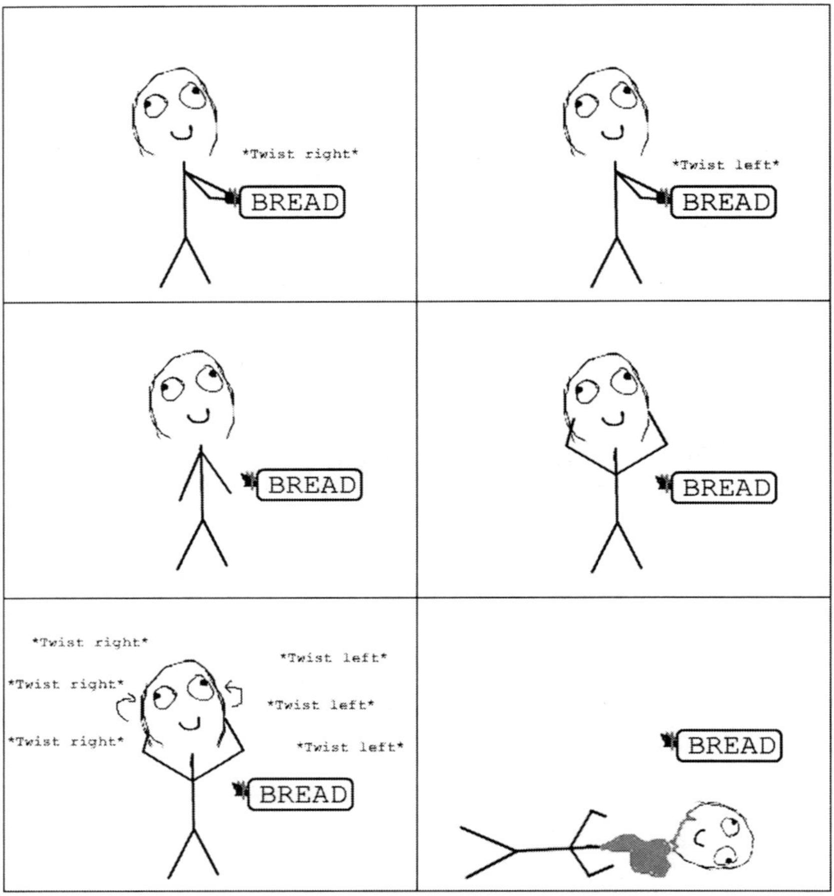
Twist right
BREAD
Twist left
BREAD
BREAD
BREAD
Twist right
Twist left
Twist right
Twist left
Twist right
Twist left
BREAD
BREAD

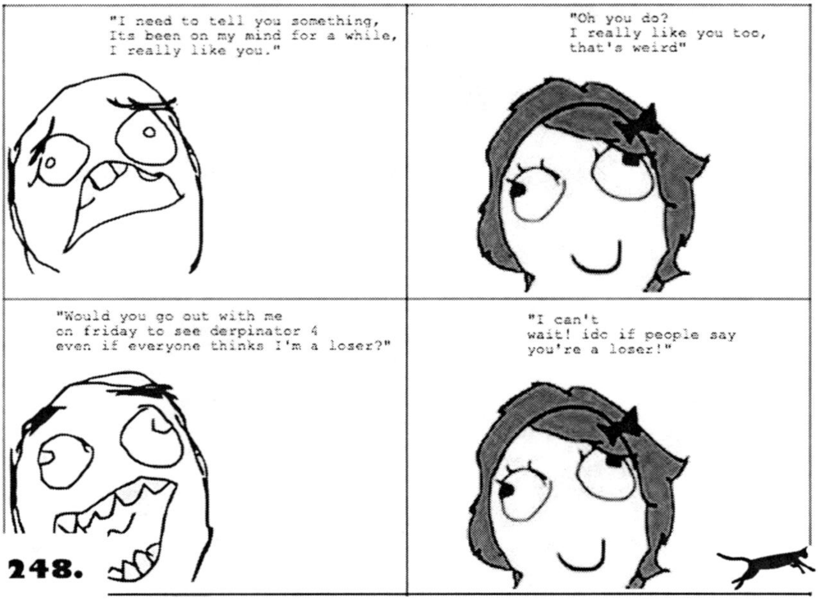
"I need to tell you something,
Its been on my mind for a while,
I really like you."
"Oh you do?
I really like you too,
that's weird"
"Would you go out with me
on friday to see derpinator 4
even if everyone thinks I'm a loser?"
"I can't
wait! idc if people say
you're a loser!"

Okay

forever alone

Confused by the ending?

twist: read only the first and third lines in each panel for what really happened.

Me, mildly surprised because dumb jock is reading.

John Grisham's written some good stuff, what do you think of it so far?

I only got it because it said "sports" on the cover

finally! a new car!	hmm need le auto insurance lets see...
creepy military midget...	psychotic battle-axe...
wannabe encino man...	smug doucebag...
reasonable black guy...	reminds me of coworkers...
magical lizard...	cant trust any any of them...

250.

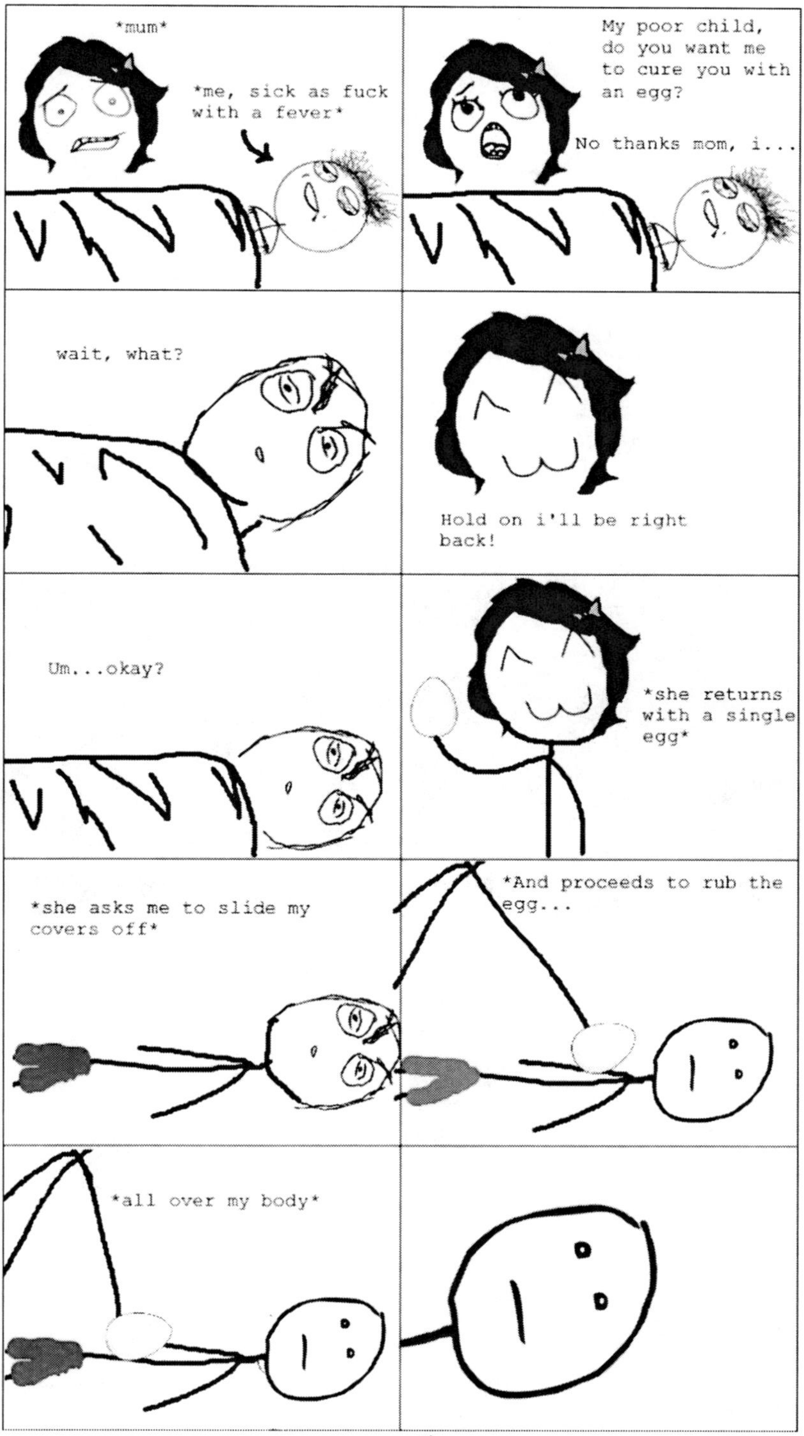
mum
me, sick as fuck with a fever
My poor child, do you want me to cure you with an egg?
No thanks mom, i...
wait, what?
Hold on i'll be right back!
Um...okay?
she returns with a single egg
she asks me to slide my covers off
*And proceeds to rub the egg...
all over my body

*she then stops..

*and cracks it inside a cup..

...the yolk is filled with little black marks*

and my headache is gone

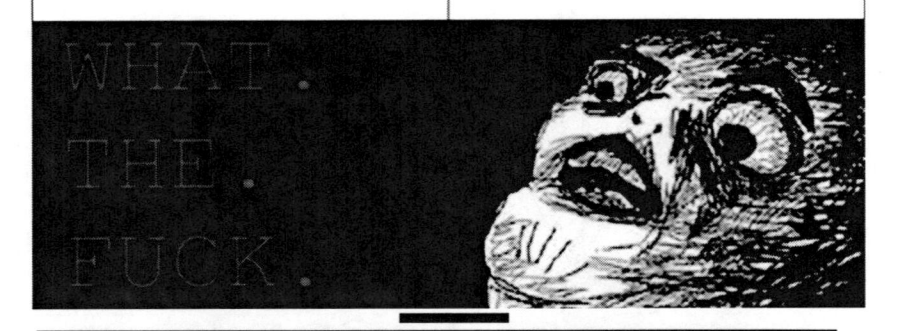

WHAT. THE. FUCK.

3 AM in the morning, sister finishing her school project.

Hey bro, my teacher wants my PowerPoint burned onto a DVD. Can you help me?

Sure, sis. I'll go grab a DVD. Dad should have some in the cabinet.

yawn

Hmmm, this top DVD is scratched to hell. I'll just grab the one below it... it looks fine.

Here. Put this in.

K.

3 AM in the morning, sister finishing her school project.
Hey bro, my teacher wants my PowerPoint burned onto a DVD. Can you help me?
yawn
Sure, sis. I'll go grab a DVD. Dad should have some in the cabinet.
Hmmm, this top DVD is scratched to hell. I'll just grab the one below it... it looks fine.
Here. Put this in.
K.
Wow, this sure is taking a long time to load.
Yeah, this computer is really old but this is ridiculous...
Wait a minute. There's only one reason why the computer would take an entire minute to load a CD. There must be something on the disc.
Eject the disc. Now.
What? Why? It's frozen, it won't even respond. Wait, look! Windows Media Player is loading!
Father...
why have you forsaken me?
POKER FACE
POKER FACE
OOOH! OHH YEAH!
FUCK ME HARDER! Fuck! FUCK!
unnnnuhnununhunugn...yeah, suck that dick dry.
(sister clicks close)

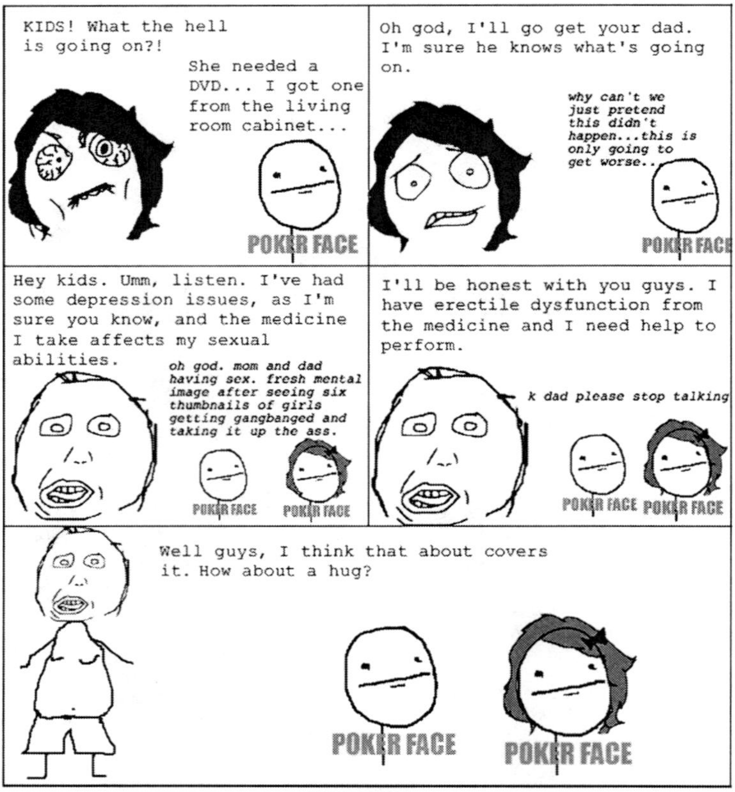
KIDS! What the hell is going on?!
She needed a DVD... I got one from the living room cabinet...
POKER FACE
Oh god, I'll go get your dad. I'm sure he knows what's going on.
why can't we just pretend this didn't happen...this is only going to get worse..
POKER FACE
Hey kids. Umm, listen. I've had some depression issues, as I'm sure you know, and the medicine I take affects my sexual abilities.
oh god. mom and dad having sex. fresh mental image after seeing six thumbnails of girls getting gangbanged and taking it up the ass.
POKER FACE
POKER FACE
I'll be honest with you guys. I have erectile dysfunction from the medicine and I need help to perform.
k dad please stop talking
POKER FACE
POKER FACE
Well guys, I think that about covers it. How about a hug?
POKER FACE
POKER FACE

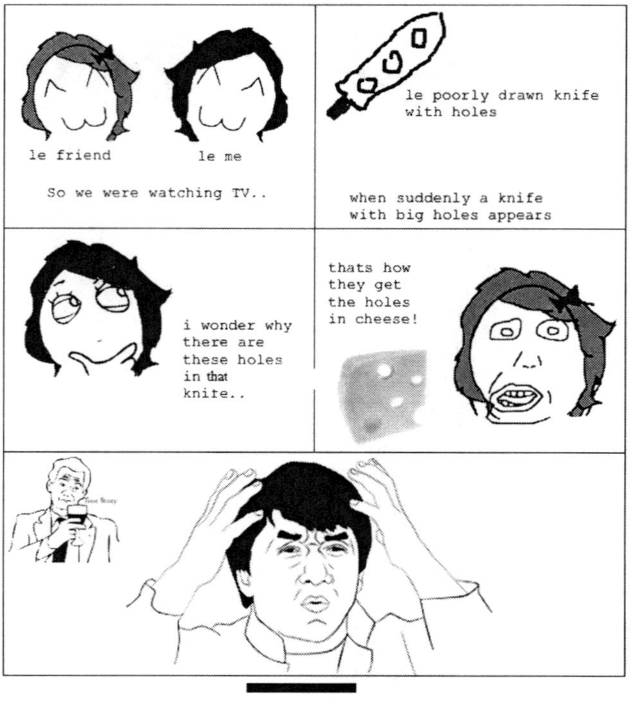
le friend
le me
So we were watching TV..
le poorly drawn knife with holes
when suddenly a knife with big holes appears
i wonder why there are these holes in that knife..
thats how they get the holes in cheese!

Me getting my hair cut...
Like a boss.
"Okay! You're all set! Now to keep that look, you'll have to come back to get a touch-up in a couple of weeks."
le Bill
haircut...$40

So I was browsing the news during a typical, boring day...
When, suddenly...

Chocolate may protect the brain and heart

Eating high levels of chocolate could reduce the risk of coronary heart disease and stroke, according to a review of previous research.

Data from 114,009 patients suggested risk was cut by about a third, according to a study published on the BMJ website.

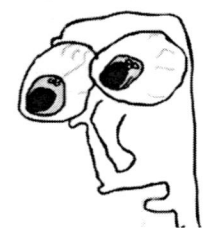

*montage!

AAAAAAAAAAWWWWWW

YYYYYYEEEEEEEEAAAAAAAAAA

"We can't start advising people to eat lots of chocolate based on this research"

Finally home after a long day at work!

Hey, babe! I'm home!

256.

I've been thinking about popping you in, all day today, if you know what I mean...
So let's do it...
BABE
I love you, babe.

Sitting in US History class learning about pre civil war events.
Class, does anyone know where plantation owners went to buy a slave?
The black market?

Cmon dad, we're gonna be late if we don't leave now.
"Fine but do you mind if I grab a bowl of cereal first?"
No dad! I've gotta be there as soon as possible!
"Alright, fine."
*Walking towards car
"Hold on son, I forgot something inside."
15 MiNUTeS LATER...
WHAT IS TAKING HIM SO LONG
*Le peek through window
FFFFFFF
FFFFFFF
FFFFFF
FFFUU
UUUU
UUUU
UUUU
UUUU
UUUU-

(Me working at Walgreens)
(Customer I'm helping)
Can I help you find anything today?
My son needs a flash drive for school and I was hoping to find one here.
We sure do, m'am. Right now we have one kind in stock. It even swivels.
Okay...well, how many "gee bees" is it? My son said he wants a decent amount of "gee bees."
Well, this one can hold 4 gigs of memory.
You're obviously lying to me, something that small can't hold 4 gee bees of anything!!

*le me, being a security guard like a baus hmm okay, time to check to cameras...	nothing on camera 1
nothing on camera 2	nothing on camer--
the fu...?	*i look closer at the screen
	I see two guys with their trousers around their ankles, one of which was stomping on a newspaper, whilst a third bystander watched...

NOTHING CAN EXPLAIN THE SITUATION WHICH I AM CURRENTLY WITNESSING...

Hi son!
hey dad!
you know son, i saw something pretty cool today.
what dad?
ice!
FFFFFFF
FFFFFFF
FFFFFF
FFFUU
UUUU
UUUU
UUUU
UUUU
UUUU-

*Me, Derpantha
Looking for a DVD to watch from my Dad's movie collection
FLESH GORDON
A wild copy of "FLESH GORDON" appears!
I decide to make Dad really uncomfortable and approach him about it...
"Hey Dad, nice porn you got there. I wonder what Mom would think..."

"Well Derpantha, maybe you should guess again before assuming she doesn't know about it."

*Le Mom

"Yeah, why are you so sure it isn't mine?"

"It's okay dear, why don't we watch it as a family?"

And that is when I decided never to troll my parents again.

*le me, entering my house high as fuck, preparing to act normal

*a wild trolldad appears

derpina, you high again?

no dad, what makes you think that?

ok so tell me who wrote the diary of anne frank?

what? how the fuck am I supposed to know that, leave me alone dad

*my dad laughing on his way back to the living room

LOL

*me, going full retard, wondering what just happened

LATER THAT SAME EVENING

FFFFFFF
FFFFFF
FFFF
FUU
UUU
UUU
UUU
UUU
UUUU
UUUU-

262.

Le me sitting on a chair
Oh wow, I should Probably trim my nails.
Aaaah, that looks so much better, why didn't I do this earlier?
TWELVE SECONDS LATER
YOU... WHAT HAVE YOU DONE?

*Me, just a standard pizza dude, finishing up a delivery at some shitty apt complex on a nice sunny day.
<-Empty Pizza Bag
All the sudden, water starts falling from above me, so I stop and check out the situation...

*No big deal, just a woman on her balcony watering her plants.
But on closer inspection..
*A 300 pounder in her bathrobe, hair still wet from a shower.
*Knowing whats coming, I try to look away, but I cant seem to tear my eyes from the scene.
*Finally, the piece de resistance
SUPREME ROAST BEEF IS CENSORED FOR YOUR SANITY
"Holy Shit..."
A puss is a puss
NOT BAD

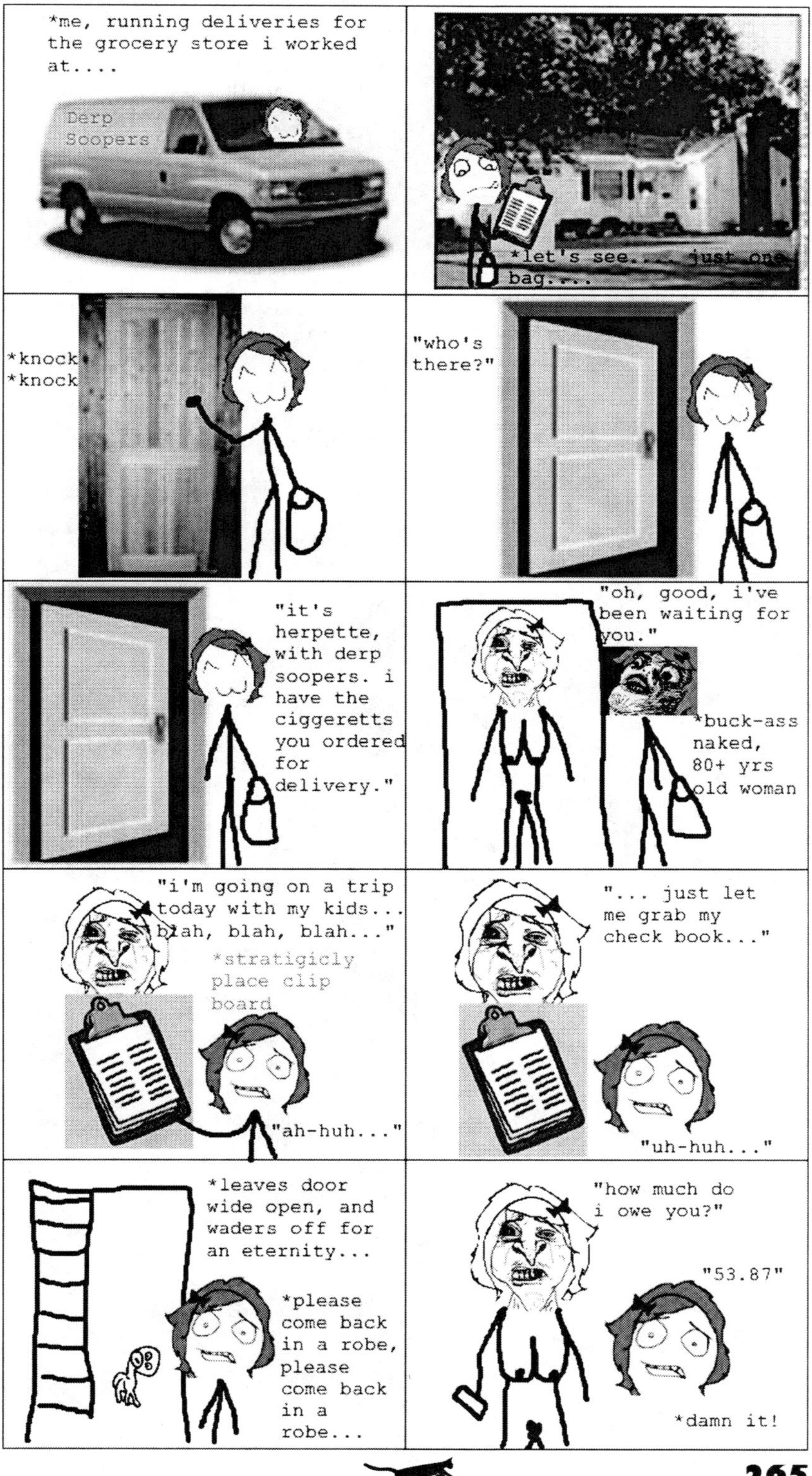
*me, running deliveries for the grocery store i worked at....
Derp Soopers
*let's see.... just one bag....
*knock
*knock
"who's there?"
"it's herpette, with derp soopers. i have the ciggeretts you ordered for delivery."
"oh, good, i've been waiting for you."
*buck-ass naked, 80+ yrs old woman
"i'm going on a trip today with my kids... blah, blah, blah..."
*stratigicly place clip board
"ah-huh..."
"... just let me grab my check book..."
"uh-huh..."
*leaves door wide open, and waders off for an eternity...
*please come back in a robe, please come back in a robe...
"how much do i owe you?"
"53.87"
*damn it!

"just let me write it out..."

One Eternity Later

"here you go."

"thanks... have a good day..."

it's been 7 years, and i still can't unsee that shit!

I'll start washing my own clothes, can't be too hard...

CENSORED

266.

le BF and me playing Mario Party for the Wii
(Hasn't played Mario Party since N64)
"This minigame is new, how does this one work?"
"Whoever shakes the soda the hardest wins"
"Alright, lets go."
"Bring it on."
Commence rapid Wiimote shake
FAP
FAP
FAP
akaLokii WINS!
BF's roommates (all male)
"LOL! What a lucky guy."
...
I FAP BETTER THAN A DUDE.

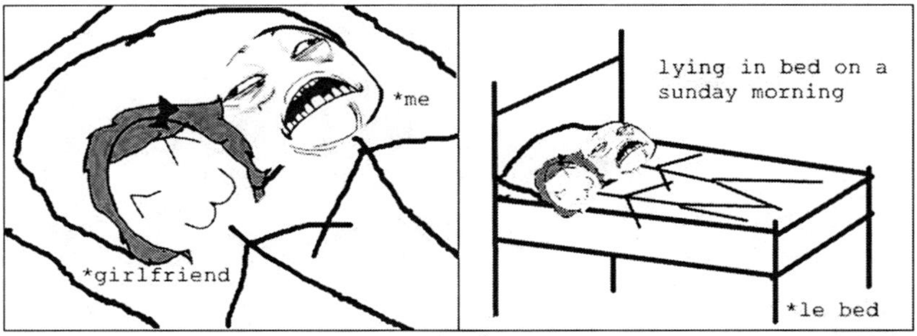
*me
*girlfriend
lying in bed on a sunday morning
*le bed

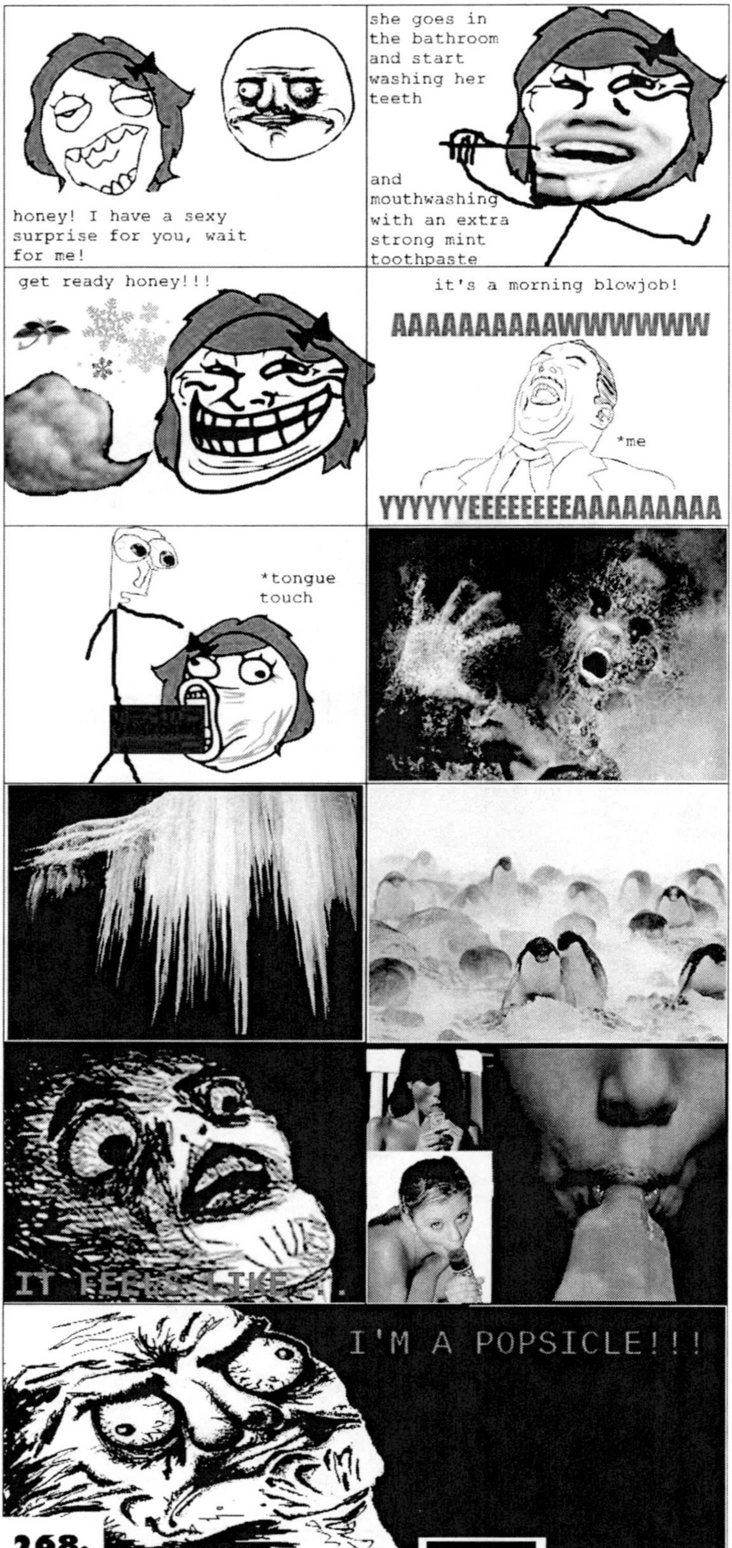
honey! I have a sexy surprise for you, wait for me!
she goes in the bathroom and start washing her teeth
and mouthwashing with an extra strong mint toothpaste
get ready honey!!!
it's a morning blowjob!
AAAAAAAAAAWWWWWW
*me
YYYYYYEEEEEEEEAAAAAAAAA
*tongue touch
IT FEELS LIKE . . .
I'M A POPSICLE!!!

Running at night like a boss

*le trip over sidewalk

Act cool, pretend nothing happened...continue running

WHY DID I ACT COOL NO ONE EVEN SAW THAT

I SAW EVERYTHING THAT SHIT WAS HILARIOUS

*little me - age 6, at the supermarket with my grandmother

"Nana! Nana! My Doodle just went pointy!"

"okay dear, shhh be quiet"

269.

Panel 1:
(Yelling now)
"NANA! MY DOODLE'S STICKING OUT LIKE PINNOCHIO'S NOSE!!!!"

"Shhh! Shhh! be quiet!"

Panel 2:
LOL

"WHY IS IT SO HARD AND POINTY!! NANA! NANA! WHY?"

Panel 3:
22 years later...

I'M SO SORRY NANA

Panel 4:
me, a poor, starving grad student TA

Herp, can you help me outside of office hours? I can pay you

Panel 5:
Sorry Herpina, I can't accept money from students to tutor them

Panel 6:
Well, maybe I can pay you back in another way...?

Panel 7:
(no text)

Panel 8:
CAFETERIA

For him as well, please

270.

Without light blocking curtains: **With light blocking curtains.**
My Room

Me cavesta.

How I Sleep

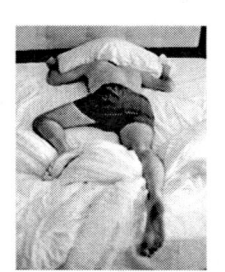

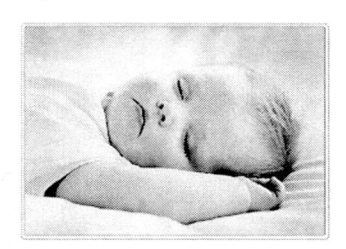

When I Wake Up

7am 1pm

What YEAR is it!?

Hi! I work in a rug store, we're having a CLOSING DOWN SALE ! all rugs must go. One day only"

WE NEVER CLOSE DOWN!!!!!!

271.

*le me walking back home on campus after a particularly hard midterm
*notices butt of girl walking in front of me
NOT BAD
hey isn't that girl in my morning class?
blink
did i just identify a girl by her butt??
i'm a terrible person

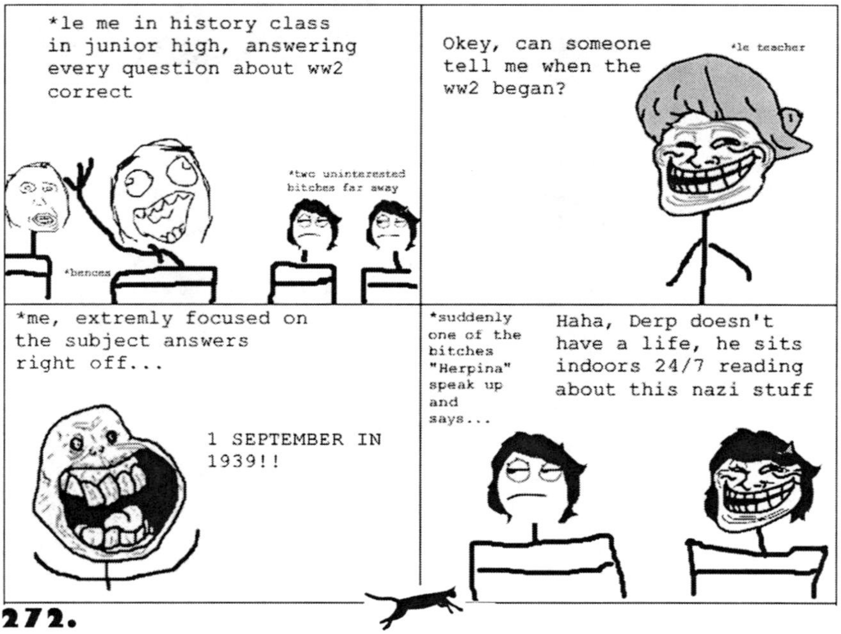
*le me in history class in junior high, answering every question about ww2 correct
*two uninterested bitches far away
*benches
Okey, can someone tell me when the ww2 began?
*le teacher
*me, extremly focused on the subject answers right off...
1 SEPTEMBER IN 1939!!
*suddenly one of the bitches "Herpina" speak up and says...
Haha, Derp doesn't have a life, he sits indoors 24/7 reading about this nazi stuff

HAHA YEAH TOTALLY!!
HAHAHA
*le entire class
HAHAHA!!
LOLOLOLOL
HAHA
LOL
That wasn't nice of you Herpina, it's only because my grandpa spoke a lot of the world war with me before he passed away that I find this subject interesting, and it hurts my feelings when you say that... a lot...
Okay
Derp, Herpina says so because she is jealous of your grades and your performance, because it is absolutely perfect compared to Herpina's work
Wait, what?
I have spoken to the other teachers of the school. And Herpina, you don't have a single chance of a good future! At all! Due to all your F-grades!
Please be quiet!
Derp has the best possible future availible, unlike you.
What?
Haha what a fucking loser
HAHAHA
Pwn'd
Fuck that bitch
HOW CAN YOU TALK TO MY FRIEND LIKE THAT? FUCK YOU, YOU ARE THE WORST TEACHER EVER
Well, apparently I am. She still knows about history as much as a kindergarten child
*le class
LOL
LOL
LOL
Way too many cursewords
*le me

oh i hear a buzzing sound, must be my phone!

*check my phone

no new messages

Oh its just a fly

*bzzz bzzz

maybe next time

Entering car in 110 degree heat

Metal part of seatbelt touches your skin

FFFFFFF
FFFFFF
FFFFFF
FFFUU
UUUU
UUUU
UUUU
UUUU
UUUU-

274.

*me taking massive shit at mcdonalds.
*random hand appears
*reaches up and grabs the rest of my toilet paper
what the fuck?

German Class
basically learning sex education in German, as a learning exercise.
le Bad ass teacher.
Annoyingly immature kid, trying to make people laugh by asking the word for condom.
"Miss, What's "Condom"?"
"What your parents should've used!"
That little bastard's gonna get her fired!

Eye specialist
I'm afraid you'll need glasses
Me, age 15
First week of glasses...
My POV.
Super Clean glasses
Super tiny dirt spot
A few milliseconds later....
Must clean thoroughly
Me, age 25
My POV.
Possibly the dirtiest glasses ever

At le restaurant on my birthday
Man, I hate when they sing for you. It's so embarrassing... and everyone looks over at you.
Happy happy birthday, from all of us to you. we wish it was our birthday, so we could party too.
Le waiters and waitresses
I lied.
I requested it for myself!

cant travel to the sun

it is too hot

wait until night

If you wish to make an apple pie from scratch...

You must first invent the universe.

FLOUR

FFFFFFF
FFFFFFF
FFFFFF
FFFUU
UUUU
UUUU
UUUU
UUUU
UUUU-

277.

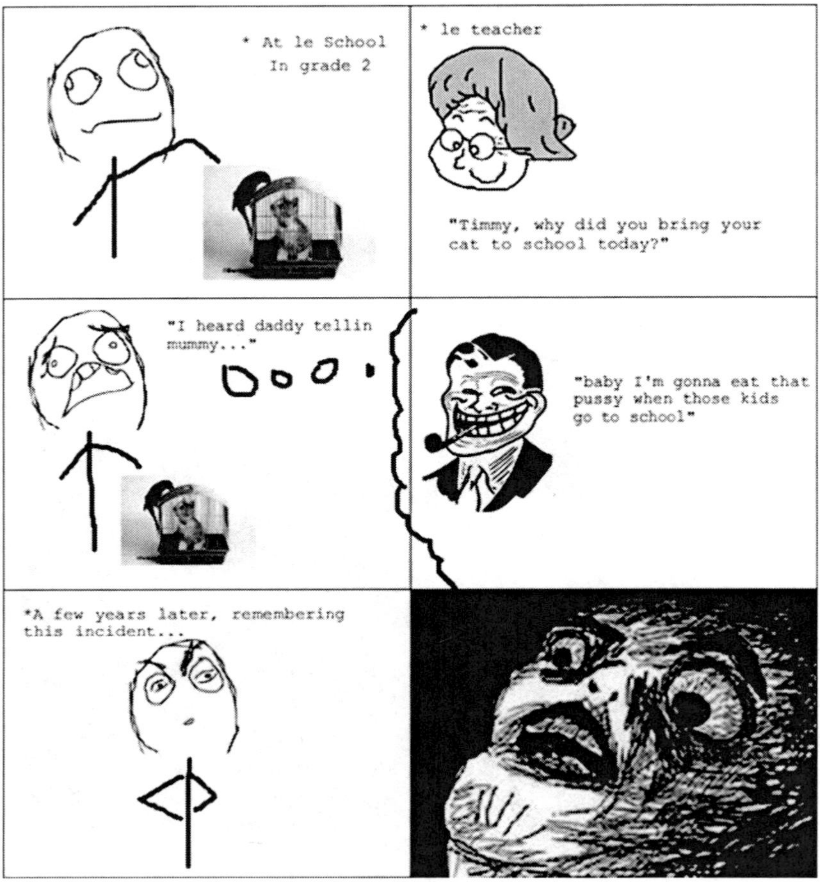
* At le School
In grade 2
* le teacher
"Timmy, why did you bring your cat to school today?"
"I heard daddy tellin mummy..."
"baby I'm gonna eat that pussy when those kids go to school"
*A few years later, remembering this incident...

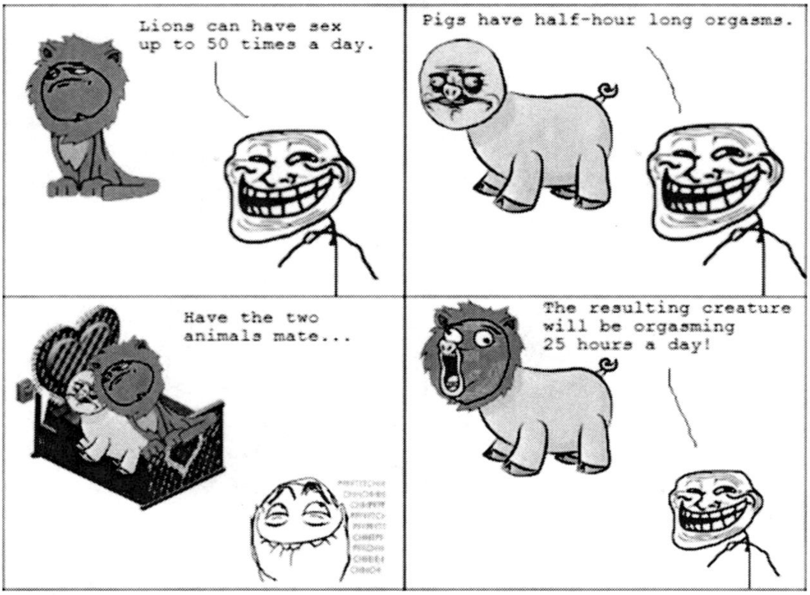
Lions can have sex up to 50 times a day.
Pigs have half-hour long orgasms.
Have the two animals mate...
The resulting creature will be orgasming 25 hours a day!

*driving with le gf listening to NPR

Radio: "Greece may go bankrupt blah blah blah"

Gee...Greece is going bankrupt...

I thought they were still making money off that movie.

OMG You can't be serious. I'm telling the whole world what you just said.

LOLOLOLOL

Oh! Haha blonde moment! They mean cooking grease. Though still weird that stuff's goin bankrupt.

279.

They say you are what you eat...

Well...

I AM PIZZA

According to some SCIENTIFIC tests, 3 orgasms a week extend the expectancy of life
Babe, check that out! We are gonna live much longer
Really? How's that? Let me see!
You, maybe

This is my favorite movie! You'll love it!
So excited!
intro
super important part that sets up the whole story
plays with the cat
main character reveals who he really is
messes with hair

main character's best friend dies

looks out the window

Wait, who is that guy? Where are they at? What's going on? I don't know what's happening. This movie is weird.

Me skipping past shows intro.

Partrick!

What did i miss??? Gotta Rewind

Hi Patrick!

Worth It

282.

An Apple A Day Keeps The Doctor Away!!

Parents read article about how GTA is a disgusting, violent game that will turn their son into a murderer

Son, I want to watch you play this game

Okay

*driving around obeying the law and eating food, buying clothes...

A FEW MINUTES LATER...

283.

Son, aren't you going to go kill people?
W..what? Why?
Ok son I guess we were wrong

Now that the Republican primary race is underway, I should get my campaign for President started.
President Obama
I know! I'll call Shepard Fairey, the guy who made the "HOPE" poster.
Hello Shepard, can you make me a poster for my 2012 campaign?
Sure, Mr. President. How do you want it to be different from the previous one?
Shepard Fairey
I want to capture the positive spirit of the '08 campaign, while acknowledging that things are not as good as we hoped.
I'll get started right away. Come take a look in a week.

ONE WEEK LATER...

Here it is, Barack. Tell me what you think.

NOT BAD

*le crazy gf
*me
I CANT TAKE IT ANYMORE YOU MAKE A RAGE COMIG ABOUT OUR RELATIONSHIP EVERY CHANCE YOU GET
-that's not true
IT'S TRUE AS HELL LOOK YOU'RE DOING ONE RIGHT NOW ABOUT OUR CURRENT CONVERSATION
Oh... Right.

"I had sex with 5 guys this weekend!"
"Lol, you slut."
Why is it that when a guy humps alot of hot girls he's the greatest, but when a girl does the same with guys, she's a whore?"

"Imagine a key that can open every lock in the whole world - that's a pretty good key, right?"

"Well, yeah! get to your point"

"Now imagine a lock that can be opened by every key in the whole world, that's a pretty shitty one, isn't it?"

FFFFFFF
FFFFFF
FFFFF
FFUU
UUU
UUU
UU
UUUU
UUUU

287.

me, an italian 20 years old exchange student in the USA
IN FEBRUARY
damn, i can't believe i still can't purchase alcohol in this country.
wait a sec. i was born on december 1st, that means that on my italian ID, the date is 1/12
american people might actually believe that i was born in january 12th here, therefore being 21.
hi, may i see your ID please?
yes, it's an european ID, I hope it is ok
sure just show me the birthdate
BAD POKER FACE
LIQUOR STORE

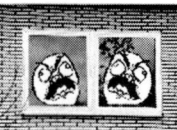

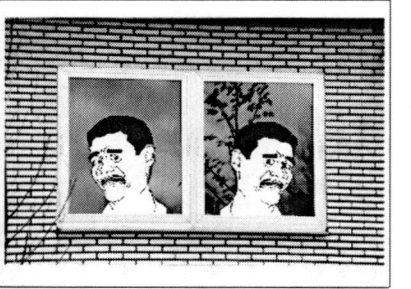

Me derpin around at 8 years old...	My mom wasn't that harsh in my childhood however... "Derp stop doing that!!"
If she would get REALLY pissed she had "The Look"	
I was always scared shitless after "The Look" and was afraid she was going to eat my soul...	20 years later and recently living in my new apartment I have these annoying neighbourkids screaming all the time over nothing.
One day, going to le grocerystore, I pass by their window. The kids were - as usual - screaming over nothing..	"Screw this, I'm fed up with this constant screaming". So I decided to use.... "The Look"

289.

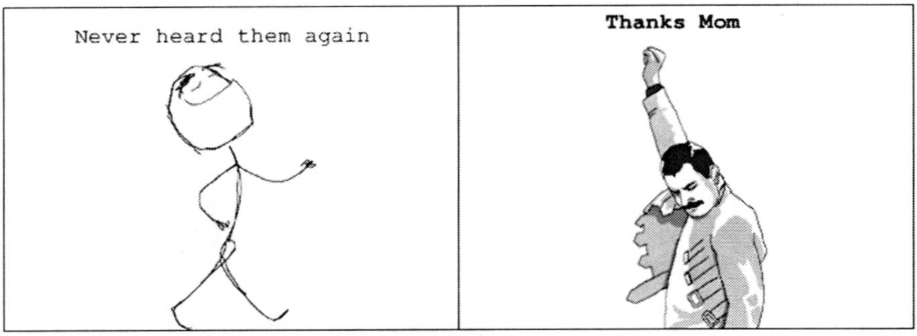
Never heard them again
Thanks Mom

le me, baking awsomely drawn cookies
oven
sets time, 10:00 min
15 min later...
burnt cookie smell
Y U No watch time?!
Freezer
BEER
putting beer in freezer to get cold...
MUCH, MUCH LATER...
Frozen beer

le sexytimes...
I'm pregnant!!
I can't pull ANYTHING out in time!!!!

*Me working at prize redemption in arcade
*Mother and son walk up and hand me their tickets
We musta got a million tickets, mommy!
Wow, you got 500 tickets. Good job! What kind of prizes do you want?
Hey, Derp. Why don't you get that heliciptor? That is 500 tickets!
That looks so fun!
Yeah, or you could even get a hundred bouncy balls with that many tickets!
MOMMY! I WANT THAT! I WANT ALL THE BOUNCY BALLS!

Derp, wouldn't you rather have the fun helicoptor?
BOUNCY BALLS! BOUNCY BALLS!
Have a nice day, Ma'am!
I love this job

Im hungry, let's order some pizza.
PIZZA!
Dominoes? Cheese Pizza? Half Hour? No problem, see you then.
What are we going to do? Such a long time to wait.
LETS SMOKE. SO WHEN THE PIZZA GETS HERE IT WILL TASTE AWESOME!
Oh man I am so baked
LOL

DING DING
KNOCK KNOCK
KNOCK KNOCK
OH GOD OH GOD
WHO COULD BE AT
THE DOOR AT THIS HOUR
IT MUST BE THE KILLER!
A PROBLEMO?
PIZZA
PIZZA PIZZA PIZZA PIZZA
PIZZA PIPZZA
PIZZAPIZZIPPPIZIP
IZZZZZ
AAAAAAAAA
PIZZA
I can't believe this guy knew we
wanted a pizza. He must be a wizard.

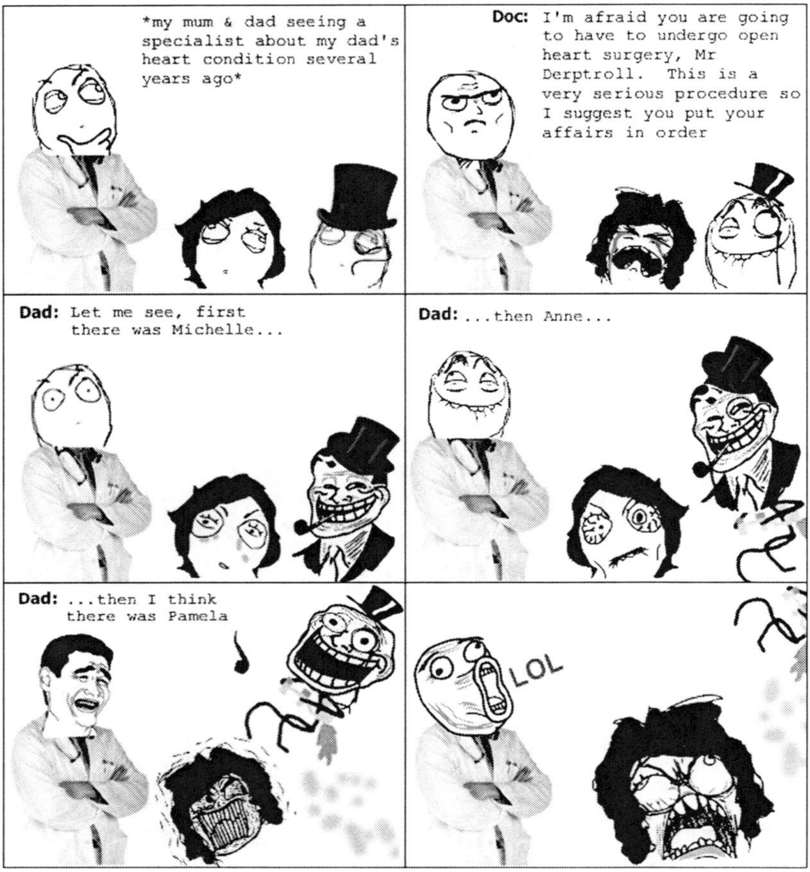
my mum & dad seeing a specialist about my dad's heart condition several years ago
Doc: I'm afraid you are going to have to undergo open heart surgery, Mr Derptroll. This is a very serious procedure so I suggest you put your affairs in order
Dad: Let me see, first there was Michelle...
Dad: ...then Anne...
Dad: ...then I think there was Pamela
LOL

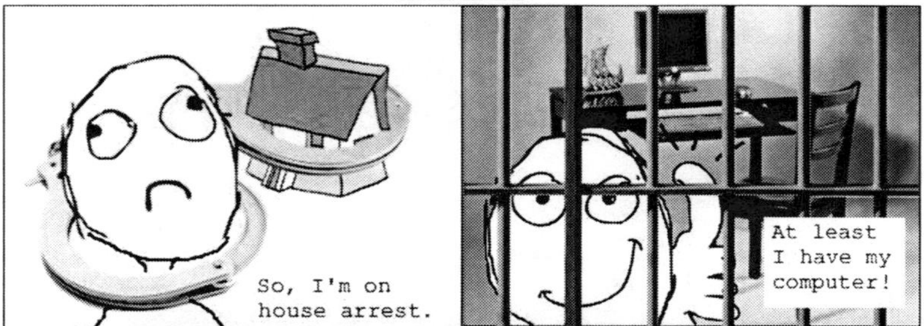
So, I'm on house arrest.
At least I have my computer!
4 TO 6 WEEKS LATER
All I have is my computer..

*le wild phone call appears..
RING
RING
RING
HI MOM!
Hello son! How are you?
I'm good! Just hanging out with my computer...
You're hanging out with Mike and Peter? That's nice, stay out of trouble!
Yes.
Mike and Peter.

le me, reading intently on the bus, when someone gets on and sits next to me.
I don't look up, but I begin to notice a pleasant bodily odor wafting my way.
sniff
sniff

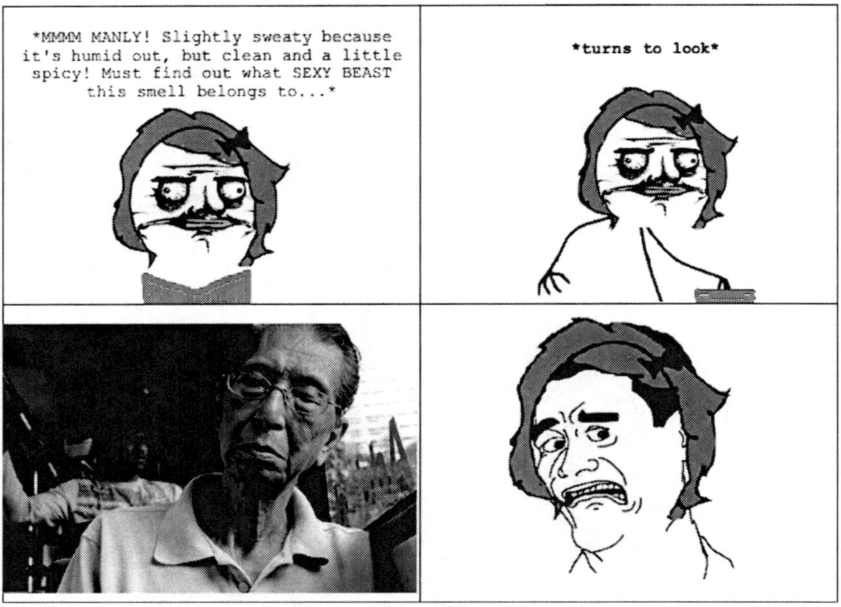
MMMM MANLY! Slightly sweaty because it's humid out, but clean and a little spicy! Must find out what SEXY BEAST this smell belongs to...
turns to look

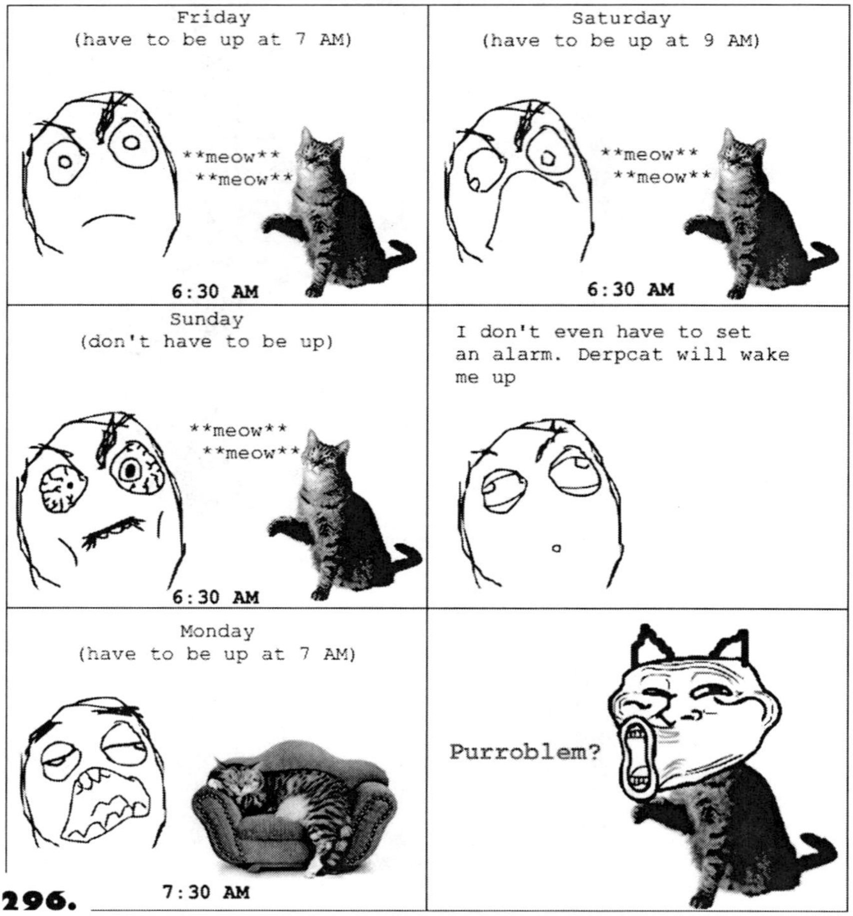
Friday
(have to be up at 7 AM)
meow
meow
6:30 AM
Saturday
(have to be up at 9 AM)
meow
meow
6:30 AM
Sunday
(don't have to be up)
meow
meow
6:30 AM
I don't even have to set an alarm. Derpcat will wake me up
Monday
(have to be up at 7 AM)
7:30 AM
Purroblem?

Every minute of walking can extend your life by 1.5 to 2 minutes, on average

Walk for 13 hours each day resulting in extending your life by 26 hours each day

Repeat infinite times for immortality

Problem, death?

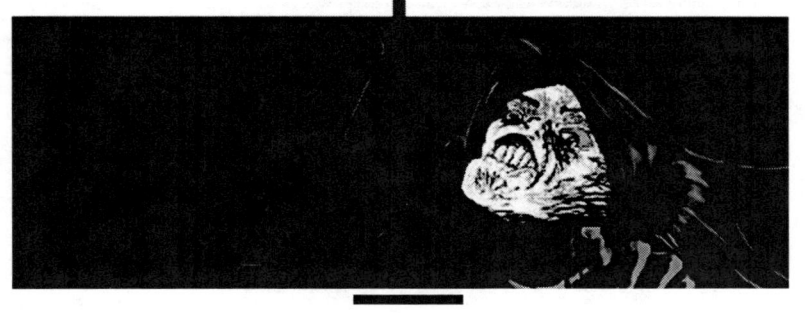

me chopping some shit food for dinner.... boring!!

notices japanese writing on kitchen knife....

297.

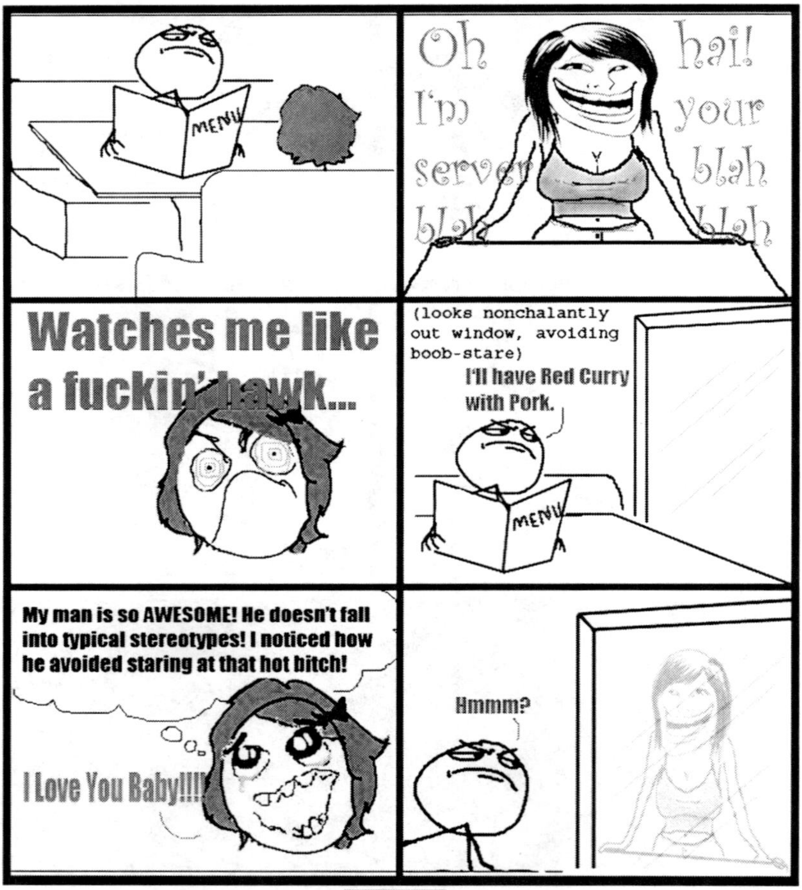

MENU
Oh hai!
I'm your
server blah
blah
Watches me like a fuckin' hawk...
(looks nonchalantly out window, avoiding boob-stare)
I'll have Red Curry with Pork.
MENU
My man is so AWESOME! He doesn't fall into typical stereotypes! I noticed how he avoided staring at that hot bitch!
I Love You Baby!!!!
Hmmm?

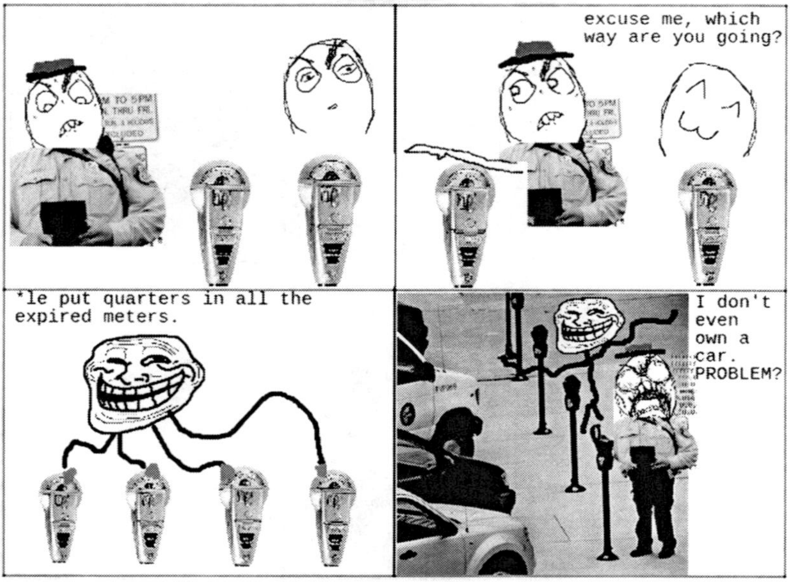

excuse me, which way are you going?
*le put quarters in all the expired meters.
I don't even own a car. PROBLEM?

me workin' drive through at Derpo Bell
Hi, what can I get you?
Hi uh, can i get, 20 chicken burritos, you want what? okay, 2 more burritos, uhhh- what? dude that's McDonald's!
Sir?
haha my bad, uh yah I'll also get one lemonade an- what that's so gay...nevermind a Fruitista...
what flavor
Fruitista...wait. hahahah no Pina Colada.
Okay..that'll be 24.25, second window.
yo, here's a giftcard
this is for wal-mart sir
oh. shit.

VVRRR

Thanks for the giftcard motherfucker.

*le me, spanish exchange student in le states

everybody say hi to our new student from spain, el derpo. since he is from abroad this is a splendid opportunity to ask him questions about life in spain.

so please, does anyone here have a question?

*le teacher in class

yeah, uhm. i have a question... do spanish people think in spanish?

*le classmate

300.

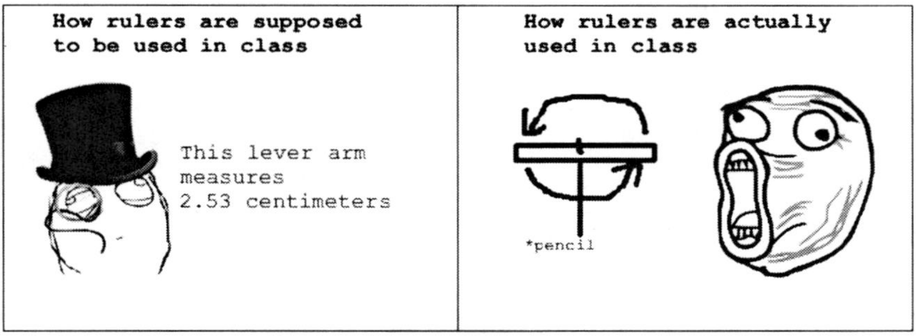

How rulers are supposed to be used in class	How rulers are actually used in class
This lever arm measures 2.53 centimeters	*pencil

le sextime with gf when she asks...	GF: Do you think anal would hurt?
ME: Welp...	There's only one way to find out...

GOOGLE

301.

"Hey, Mesonoxian. Have you heard of Cha cha?"
"Nah..."
"it's a question answering service. You can ask it whatever you want."
later that day on my un-smart phone
when did Ghandi die?
How old is Jackie Chan?
How many calories are in a hard-boiled egg?
when is Jim Carrey's birthday?
*tap tappety tap *
the following day.
"How much semen do you you suppose a man ejaculates in his life time?"
I got this...."
how much...
does a man...
in his life time...
*tap tappety tap *
five minutes later.
"still nothing?"
"Nah, not- oh, here we go."
vbbbbvv vbbbvbv
Facebook notification
Ashley So-N-So commented on your status: "WTF??"
vbbbbvv vbbbvbv
Facebook notification
YOUR MOTHER commented on your status: "WHAT!?"
vbbbbvv vbbbvbv
Facebook notification
THE GIRL YOU LIKE commented on your status: "Seriously??

*vbbbbvv
vbbbvbv*
Facebook notification
YOUR GREAT AUNT
commented on your
status: "That's gross."
I sent it to facebook.
fuck me.

After 2 years of a shitty flip phone i get an iphone with my upgrade discount.
Leaving store feeling like a boss... when suddenly..
Troll kid trips me for no reason!
Phone falls into a puddle just outside the door of the store.
Kid's mother says the kid didn't trip me and she shouldn't have to pay to replace my phone because I'm a clumsy bitch.
About to unleash the fury on this epic asshole but then the kids father steps in...

I know he did it. He's a little bastard. We'll replace the phone and punish him for tripping you. Instead of buying him the ipad like we came here to do we will give it to you.

no fucking way....

AAAAAAAAAWWWWWW
YYYYYYEEEEEEEAAAAAAAA

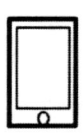

* Room mate and I at a populated bus stop

* me   * room mate

*room mate pulls out a can of corn

Are you really going to eat that here?

Yeah

Mmm corn water

304.

Working at walderp on the remodling crew.

(Not as horrible as you'd expect)

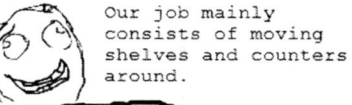

Our job mainly consists of moving shelves and counters around.

In the pharmacy today...

Hey derp, help me move this shelf.

this shelf?

PFFFTTTCHH CHHCHHH CHHPFFF PFFFFTCH PFFFFFTT CHHTPF PFFCHH CHHHH CHHCH

yes.

305.

NOT BAD

picking up daughter at day care

kids playing outside

ball rolls over

le kick

waaaaaaaaaaaaaaaaaaaaaaaaaaaaaa aaaaaaaaaaaaaaaaaaaaaaaaaaaaaa...

it was their hamster ball

306.

Waiting to cross the street with a bunch of people.
University of Herpderp
me
The traffic light turns yellow, so I start walking across the street before the walk sign appears.
They're following me across the street even though the walk signal hasn't appeared.
THESE ARE MY PEOPLE.
I AM THEIR LEADER.

You there, peasant!
Yes me lord?
Destroy The Enemy Fortress
Okay

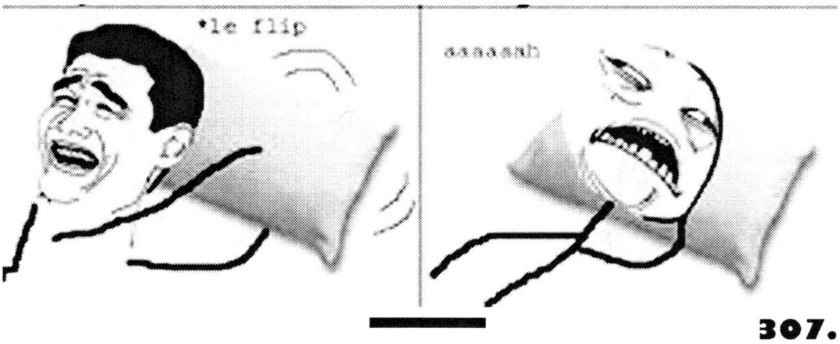
*le flip
aaaaaah

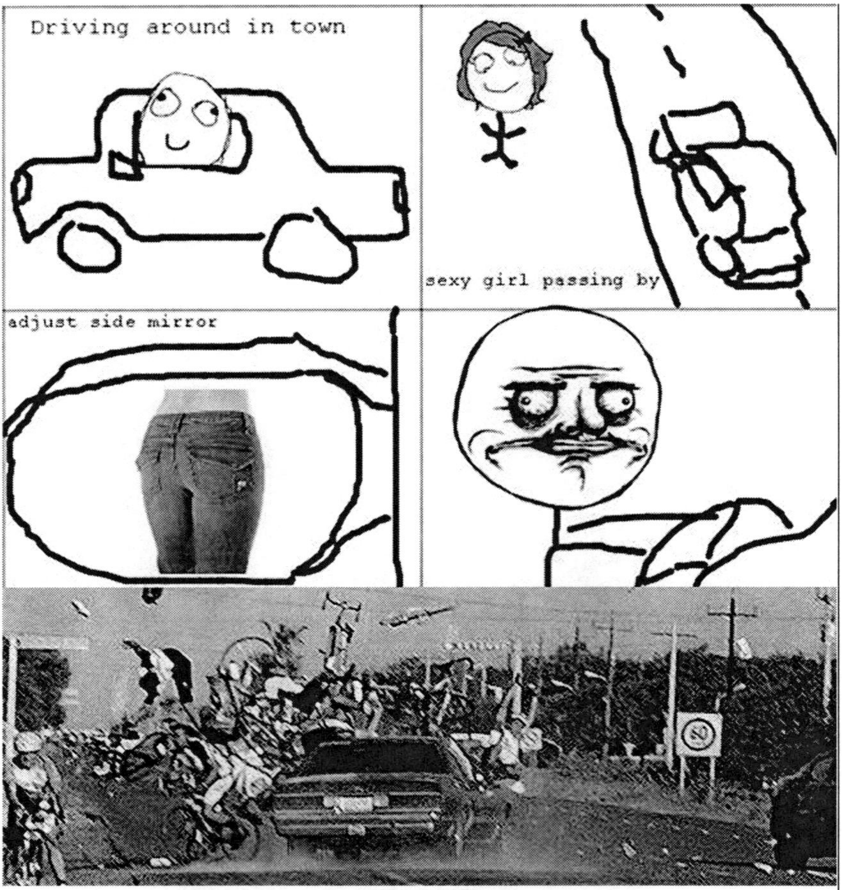

Driving around in town
sexy girl passing by
adjust side mirror

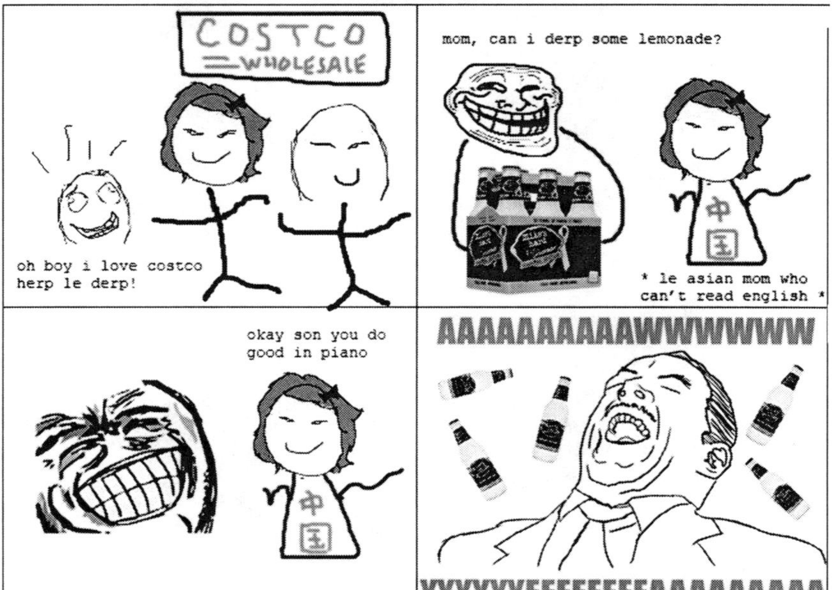

COSTCO
WHOLESALE
oh boy i love costco
herp le derp!
mom, can i derp some lemonade?
* le asian mom who
can't read english *
okay son you do
good in piano
AAAAAAAAAWWWWWWW
YYYYYEEEEEEEEEAAAAAAAAA

*In the living room giving girlfriend a head massage
*Girlfriends mom walks in. Akward stares ensue
"What are you guys doing?"
"Head.. massage.."
"Looks good, can I have one?"
What
I Uhh....
Fuck...

honey, I got an idea, tie me on bed and then do whatever you want

Sir you are drunk

Madam, you are ugly. In the morning I shall be sober

LOL Churchill has the best quotes

BLACK BOOK of Quotes

Sir, if you were my husband, I would give you poison

If I were your husband I would take it.

310.

LOL
LOL
LOL
BLACK BOOK
of
Quotes
"It is a good thing for an uneducated man to read books of quotations"
BASTARD

Today we are doing a group assginment
Looks like I'm gonna have to work by myself again
I'm choosing the groups

7AM, pulling an all nighter
need a new pencil... get up to get one in other room
LATER
back!
OMG! MY VA-JAY-JAY HURRRRTS!!!
Ok, Ma'am. Please sit in this room, we're going to get an x-ray first.
after le x-ray
Uh... do you want to take a look at this?
le doctor
Sure?
Wait is that a... FORK???
A FORK IN HER VAGINA

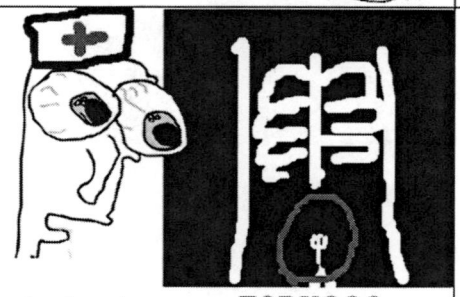

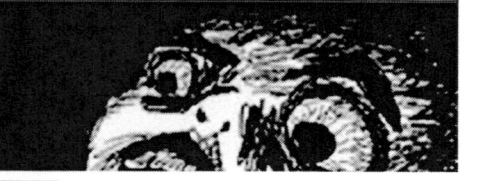

Panel 1:
young me choo-choo'n the fuck outta this train

Gramps lookin after me at his cottage

Panel 2:
cute bunny shows up

"fuck trains i love bunnies!"

Panel 3:
"did you know that putting salt on a rabbits tail will make it slow, then you can keep it as a pet"

"im gunna name him murphy"

Panel 4:
GET BACK HERE BUNNY!

Panel 5:
TWO HOURS LATER

Panel 6:
ZZZzzzZZZzz

Panel 7:
"That's how you babysit"

"That lady on the tv, I heard she is a lesbian, which means she has sex with other women."
(My 6-year-old self)
(6-year-old cousin)
"How does that even work, how can two *women* have sex?"
(Dad starts listening in)
"LOL, don't you know anything!? Lemme explain how it works:"
(Trying to sound like a know-it-all)
"First, one woman takes her boob and puts it in the other woman's vagina."
"Then the second woman takes *her* boob and puts it in the first lady's vagina."
"Then they keep pushing their boobs in and out of eachother's vagina until, finally, milk shoots out!"
"...and that's called an '*orgasm*'"
"Wow cousin Derp, you're so smart!"
WTF is wrong with this kid...

Honey, WE should take the garbage out, it's starting to smell bad.
Me
The gf
We live together...

Babe, I'm running out of clean underwear, WE should do some laundry.

Sweetie, it's about time to go, WE should pack our lunches.

Hey hun, WE...

YOU KEEP USING THAT WORD
I DON'T THINK IT MEANS WHAT YOU THINK IT MEANS

Playing Call of Duty with le gaming headphones on.

talking le talk of shit

"well at least I don't live in a trailer and have to steal my internet from Kmart."

A wild mom sneaks into my room

"BITCH MAKE ME A SANDWICH NOW!!!!!!!!!!!"

A FEW MINUTES LATER...
"Here is your sandwich Derp, You didn't say what you wanted, so it is just turkey."
"Next time, can you ask a little more nicely. "
Mom, I am so sorry. I was telling someone online to make me a sandwich. I have failed you as a son.
ps the sandwich tasted like shame and dishonor

friend at my house for the first time
sweet house bro
thanks bro
is this where the magic happens?
friend points to my bed
ya, you know it lol
LOL
later that night
MAGIC
DECKMASTER

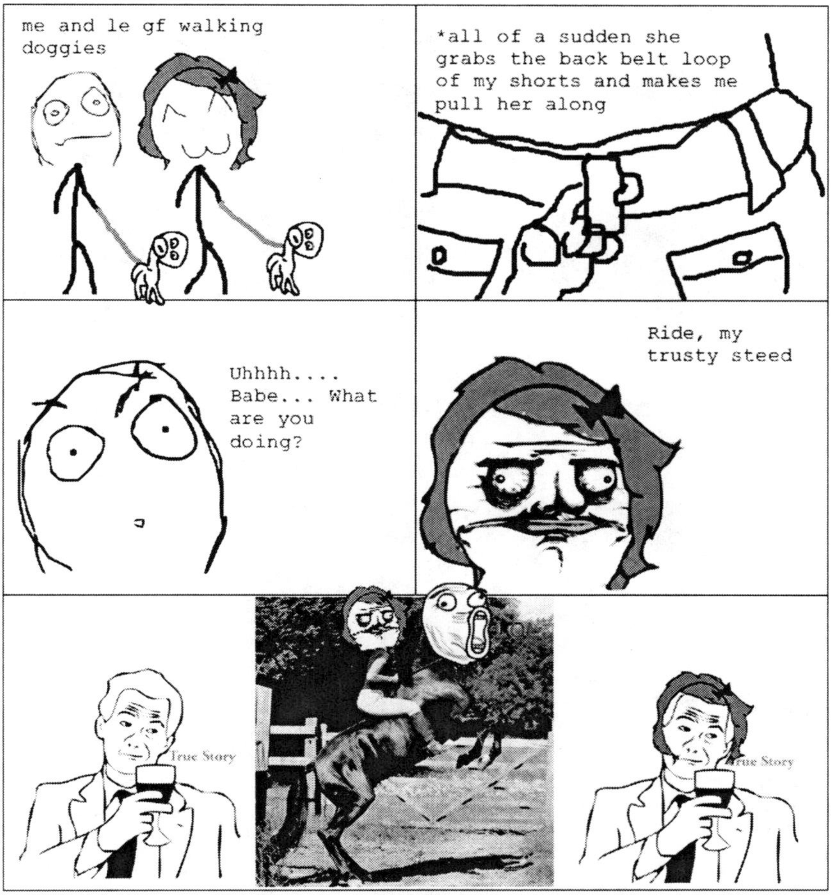
me and le gf walking doggies
*all of a sudden she grabs the back belt loop of my shorts and makes me pull her along
Uhhhh.... Babe... What are you doing?
Ride, my trusty steed
True Story
True Story

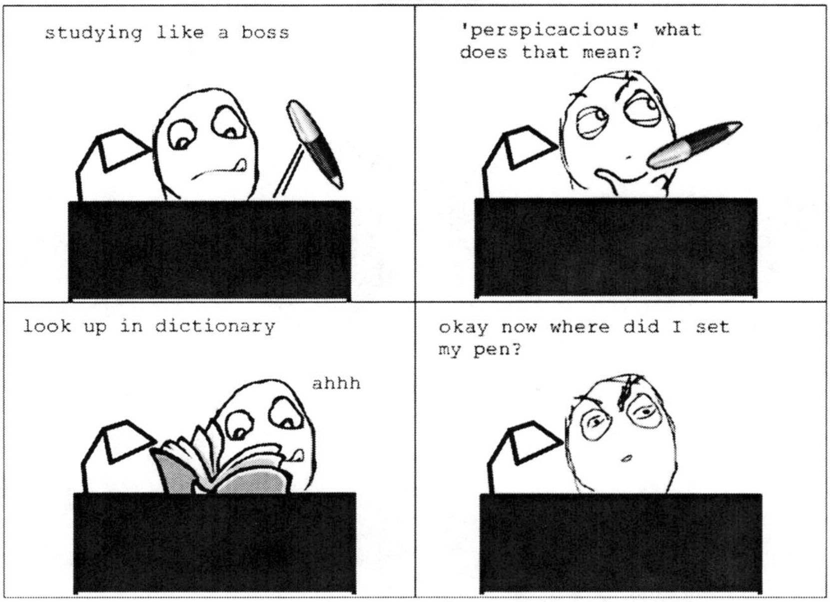
studying like a boss
'perspicacious' what does that mean?
look up in dictionary
ahhh
okay now where did I set my pen?

can't find it anywhere	WHERE IS MY FUCKING PEN!!!!!

Bermuda
Miami
Gulf of
Bermuda Triangle
San Juan Puerto Rico

le Father

Son, have you brought weed into our home?!

No, I havn't got any with me, and i havn't had any in ages.
Me

Good, becasue i don't EVER! ... EVER want you bringing any thing like that into my house ....

... Without offering me some first!

318.

book and design © 2011

CPSIA information can be obtained at www.ICGtesting.com
Printed in the USA
BVOW032303300112

281766BV00007B/88/P

9 781466 481725